Pentecostal Unity

Pentecostal Unity
Recurring Frustration and Enduring Hopes

by Terrence Robert Crowe

A Campion Book

Loyola University Press
Chicago

Loyola University Press
3441 North Ashland Avenue
Chicago, Illinois 60657

Cover design by Nancy Gruenke. Cover art by Robert Voigts.

Library of Congress Cataloging-in-Publication Data

Crowe, Terrence Robert.
    Pentecostal unity: recurring frustration and enduring hopes / by Terrence
Robert Crowe.
        p. cm.
    Includes bibliographical references and index.
    ISBN 0-8294-0746-4 (pbk.)
    1. Baptism in the Holy Spirit and Christian union. 2. Assemblies of
God—Relations—Catholic Church. 3. Catholic Church—Relations—
Assemblies of God. 4. Pentecostalism—Catholic Church. 5. Catholic
Church—Doctrines. 6. Assemblies of God—Doctrines. 7. Pentecostal
churches—Doctrines. I. Title.
BX9.5.B34C76 1993
280'.042—dc20.   93-20683
                                                                        CIP

Contents

Foreword

The twentieth century has been a rich and surprising moment in the history of the Christian community. Among the fresh developments that have emerged can be counted the modern ecumenical movement; the pentecostal phenomenon and the rise of the classical pentecostal churches; the Roman Catholic renewal following the Second Vatican Council, including its own entry into the ecumenical mainstream; the charismatic awakening among the Roman Catholic and mainline Protestant churches; and, naturally, all the tensions inherent in these events.

Thus, in the first decade the Asuza Street revival in Los Angeles marked the entry of the Holy Spirit's reconciling presence among Christians from a variety of churches and races in and around a new phenomenon: the baptism of the Holy Spirit. Branching out in the second decade, the Spirit's call to reconciliation found Christians gathering from around the world to proclaim Christ together for the sake of the Kingdom. Throughout the 1920s, the developing sense of unity found institutional expression, and newly connected Protestant assemblies saw themselves embarking on a common mission. Meanwhile, the Roman Catholic Church was consolidating its image and resources after the traumatic institutional experiences of the 1800s. But both the Catholic Church and the pentecostal churches remained outside the ecumenical movement that began to take shape among those Orthodox, Anglican, and mainline Protestant Christians for whom a unity in mission, faith, and sacrament was proving to be central to the evangelical nature of the church. For Catholic and pentecostal communities, conversion in this respect would have to wait to the midcentury.

Regarding the twentieth century as a whole, more reconciliation and renewal have taken place than the pentecostal, ecumenical, and Catholic leaders could have projected. This must undoubtedly be attributed to God's grace and the Holy Spirit's power over human sinfulness. At the same time, the array of internal tensions studied in these pages makes it clear that the story is unfinished. God is not yet done with the church, nor is the Holy Spirit satisfied with the forward progress of the renewal movement characterized by the Spirit-baptism experience. Still, on balance, the ecumenical and spiritual advances here documented far outweigh the tensions, disappointments, and delays.

Manifestly, a cross must be carried on the road to reconciliation and resurrection. Likewise, the several tensions experienced by the Assemblies of God and Roman Catholic charismatics reflect the normal growing pains evidenced in all renewal movements. Undoubtedly, the spirited debates, some divisiveness, and the fact that decisions here and there were off the mark represent more the inexperience and first enthusiasm of a romantic movement than a falling off in faithfulness to the Gospel impulse to reconcile. God has not revealed, in detail, the route our reconciling mission is to follow. Differences must be surfaced clearly and significant blocking will necessarily arise before we can discern the Holy Spirit's will for the church.

In view of the careful scholarship, the historical reflections, and the theological understanding displayed by the author, this book promises to be an important gift to the several movements that figure in these pages. To date, such seasoned input has not necessarily been prominent in the ongoing experience of the pentecostal communities. But the need for it has come to a head, now that pioneers like David du Plessis, Kilian McDonnell, and Jerry Sandidge, among others, have laid the foundations for the critical work here brought together.

As might be expected, a healing of mind, hearts, and memories, including recollections of some bitter anti-Catholicism, is called for as the process of reconciliation goes forward. In this area, we can be grateful for the work of the Society for Pentecostal Studies in bringing together Catholic and Protestant scholars to explore the theology and history of the pentecostal movement. This contribution by Dr. Crowe is a further instance of the ongoing healing process. In particular, the author recommends that Catholic and classical pentecostal relationships allow for unity with diversity. Already, the Assemblies of God and other classical pentecostal churches are working toward this aim, alongside the National Association of Evangelicals and the Pentecostal Fellowship of North America.

A further use of the conclusions reached in this book will affect the Latin American and Latino North American communities where, unfortunately, the tensions between pentecostals and Roman Catholics are particularly acute. As things stand, some time and care on the part of the Assemblies of God and other pentecostals will be needed if they are to discern the fully Christian character of the Catholic understanding of the church and, equally, to respect the faith and culture of Catholic Ibero-Americans. Reciprocally, the Catholic leadership in the Ibero-American community has its own problems in discerning whether the charismatic and Pentecostal experiences can really serve the needs of its people. In any case, defensive stances and accusations of "sheep-stealing" among these communities are bound to be a waste of time and counterproductive. A renewed sensitivity and improved mutual understanding will be increasing priorities among U.S. Latinos, Latin Americans, and indeed all Christians in the time ahead.

Jeffrey Gros, F.S.C.
Associate Director, Ecumenical Affairs
National Conference of Catholic Bishops

Introduction

In the tradition of many pentecostals and charismatics, I open with a narrative of personal experience. On Easter morning 1976, I stood waist-deep in the waters of northern Wisconsin's Chippewa River. A small group of people—including my parents—were onlookers. Although I had been baptized as an infant, I was undergoing total immersion as my sign of adult commitment to Jesus Christ.

A friend from the local Bible study recited some verses and plunged me into the water. As I was pulled up and onto my feet, something like a bolt of energy shot through me, entering at the crown of my head and penetrating into my innermost parts. Immediately, I experienced what I can best describe as an internal explosion of light and a feeling of pure intoxication. My lips began to quiver and I spoke in tongues, much to the amazement of those around me.

What I have just described was my experience of Spirit-baptism, and I come to pentecostalism, not as a disinterested observer, but as a long-time participant. I began this study by asking myself a question: Can historically conditioned, culturally diverse, and theologically distinct Catholic and classical pentecostal groups unite in a common witness? My question has a practical implication, since large-scale planning continues by ecumenical pentecostals hoping to launch an unprecedented campaign of world evangelism. Given their historic differences, can they reasonably hope to succeed?

I have come to believe that the Spirit-baptism experience provides a special grace to unite disparate pentecostals in a common witness. Errors have been made when the human element has interfered with this divine initiative. I also believe that Spirit-baptism is a source of hope to unite all Christians. As such, it merits serious and close investigation by all of the churches.

Pentecostal common witness, as the term is used in this book, is an expression of common belief intended to create a bond of fellowship among pentecostals of different backgrounds. This common witness is given first from one pentecostal to another. It then becomes a united witness to all the churches. Finally the witness is extended to the whole population, believers as well as nonbelievers.

This is a witness that pentecostals, even while denominationally separated, can bear together. Included are the many effects of Spirit-baptism upon Christian life and witness. The source of Spirit-baptism is Jesus Christ. The means through which common witness is achieved is a deep realization of the potential spiritual unity present to the Christian family. The result of common witness is shared empowerment and hope where before there may have been estrangement or aloofness resulting from denominational differences. Common witness is not to be confused with common evangelization, since that implies incorporation into a specific church. But it can be understood as a type of proto-evangelism.

Along the lines of St. Anselm's great dictum, mine is an exercise in faith seeking understanding. I have had an experience that I cannot deny. This experience, centered in my spiritual being, transformed my life and gave it a new cast. It formed in me an avid interest to search the Scriptures and, along with the eucharist, helped bring me back into full participation in the church. It brought me to the study of theology. A similar transformation through the power of Spirit-baptism can be testified to by millions. I am trying to better understand the implications of that experience.

Faith seeking understanding is not an uncritical process, nor is it divorced from the use of investigative tools. Thus, I examine the origin and development of two very different pentecostal groups, the Assemblies of God and the Catholic charismatic renewal. I chose the Assemblies of God and the Catholic charismatics because of the need to limit my study and because these groups represent extremely different Christian traditions that lay claim to a common spiritual experience. I used the historical method initially because I was trying to recover the original charisms of these two groups and then discover how they were changed and modified over time. I believe these charisms are still recoverable and therefore useful.

In doing this project, I am responding to a call that came out of the Second Vatican Council. The method of historical recovery was recommended for examining original charisms of the founders of religious orders in the *Decree on the Appropriate Renewal of Religious Life,* sec. 2:

> The appropriate renewal of religious life involves two simultaneous processes: (1) a continuous return to the sources of all Christian life and to the original inspiration behind a given community and (2) an adjustment of the community to the changed conditions of the times.
>
> It serves the best interests of the Church for communities to have their own special character and purpose. Therefore loyal recognition and safekeeping should be accorded to the spirit of founders, as also to all the particular goals and wholesome traditions which constitute the heritage of each community (Abbott 1989, 468).

I also compare the varied understandings of the meaning of Spirit-baptism that are found in Assemblies of God and Catholic charismatic theological studies and denominational statements. I interviewed ecumenically sensitive leaders from both groups to determine their current views on the possibilities for a common witness. On the basis of my investigation, I propose theoretical and practical reasons and a method for launching a common witness effort.

Since 1970 the Roman Catholic Church and the World Council of Churches have been making joint statements on the forms of common witness that are possible among Christians (see, for example, World Council of Churches 1971). My study is also an attempt to search out and encourage a pentecostal common witness in response to these statements. To my knowledge, there has been no comparable attempt to fully investigate the parameters of common witness among pentecostals.[1]

The Assemblies of God

The denomination known as the Assemblies of God has its roots in nineteenth-century revivalism, particularly that of the post–Civil War era. A principal element coming out of that surge was classical pentecostalism, the first wave of what has come to be known as the pentecostal-charismatic movement. The Assemblies of God is generally regarded as the primary representative of that classical pentecostal tradition.

Many would say that a move from a charismatic to an institutional identity has been the historic experience of the Assemblies of God (see, for example, Poloma 1989). I would argue that in progressively shifting its focus of identity from that of a Spirit-led movement to that of a religious organization the Assemblies lost touch with its original charism for pentecostal unity. This development moved the denomination away from the pentecostal common witness ideal and toward isolationism and a conservative evangelical stance.

To test whether this is the case, I have used sociologist David O. Moberg's typology for change in religious groups (1984, 119–23). Building upon the work of Ernst Troeltsch (1865–1923) and Max Weber (1864–1920), Moberg depicts religious groups as moving through a cycle of change that causes a gradual loss of vision and vitality. There is a certain arbitrariness in the use of models, since the groups being categorized usually do not exhibit neatly defined behaviors. Nonetheless, I find Moberg helpful in judging how far the Assemblies of God has changed in a continuum from movement to organization.

Remote Antecedents to the Assemblies of God

Martin Marty has correctly observed that nineteenth-century Protestant revivalism[1] promoted an aristocracy of the spirit (1975, 223). Conservative evangelicals believed they were witnessing the vitality of pre–Civil War revivalism being sapped away by a this-worldly spirit. Their emphasis upon elevated personal holiness represented an escape from the secularizing pressures of an expanding culture through the ardent pursuit of personal sanctity.

For many, the years that followed the Civil War were disconcerting and characterized by a spiritual malaise. The ruthless battlefield ethics of the Civil War were seen to have invaded business, government, and even many of the churches. In addition to the problems of social transition brought on by the war, American society was confronted by the near exponential growth of its cities. This growth produced the challenge of a large urban underclass who were strongly influenced by ongoing financial crises and labor strife. They existed alongside a visibly affluent private and institutional sector. Wealth became prominently displayed in many of the mainline Protestant churches, which quietly began to retire the trappings of "old-time religion," especially public calls to conversion (Nichol 1966, 25–26).

Many traditional evangelicals also were exacerbated by the training of Protestant ministers. The teachings of speculative German theologians such as Albrecht Ritschl (1822–1889) and Adolf Von Harnack (1851–1930) were being introduced into denominational colleges and seminaries. There was the perception that a professional clergy, distanced from the basic spiritual needs of the congregations, was using the pulpit to expound views of questionable orthodoxy.

The emerging social gospel movement was also perceived as a threat. The idealized setting for revivalism had been rural and small town America. Progressive urban churches, with their large budgets and complex public agendas, were seen as subverting a simpler ideal. The perceived result was, again, a deliberate ignoring of holiness living with its personalized understanding that salvation could be achieved through sanctified behavior.[2]

Liberalizing trends in the mainline Protestant churches caused many evangelicals to fear that the crisis-conversion emphases of revivalism would soon be considered too crude for a new urban generation. Many of these evangelicals particularly refused to embrace the theological emphases that were becoming prominent in many Protestant churches (Kendrick 1961, 29). Conservative evangelicals perceived a loss of respect for social traditions and the received doctrines of their churches (Synan 1971, 34). As liberals attempted to construct new and more socially relevant theologies, many conservative evangelicals turned elsewhere, desiring a return to traditional, revival-oriented values. The perception that evangelical values were under attack produced several powerful responses.

Fundamentalism

One of these responses was fundamentalism,[3] which insisted that the Scriptures be understood as a system of propositional truths. The most sophisticated representations of this view were developed at the Presbyterian seminary at Princeton University and became known as the Princeton theology.[4] Biblical literalism under Charles Hodge (1822–1889) and his associates took on an aggressive tone. This group was generally known to be more interested in refuting supposed enemies of evangelical orthodoxy than engaging them in dialogue.

Another very influential fundamentalist position became known as dispensationalism (see Weber 1983). Dispensationalists maintained that there were several discernible stages to salvation history. They had a special understanding of the direction of history based on their reading of the Scriptures. This view was in opposition to a purely scientific history or to historicism and was centered on an eschatological distinction between the nation of Israel and the church. The end of the church's dispensation would be marked by its rapture from the earth and would initiate the final stage of salvation history. Those events would be inextricably tied to the destiny of the restored nation of Israel. Dispensationalists used the strategically footnoted Scofield Reference Bible as a tool to propagate their views. They argued that the rapture of the church, the physical restoration of the nation of Israel, and the premillennial return of Jesus Christ were all imminent events.

Fundamentalist thinking had a profound influence upon the early pentecostals. Although fundamentalists never embraced the pentecostals' radical experiential claims, dispensationalism and other fundamentalist views were embraced by many pentecostals. Throughout its history, the Assemblies of God has generally defined itself in fundamentalist terms (Brumback 1961, 131).

The Holiness Movement

Another major factor in the rise of the Assemblies of God was the National Holiness Movement (see Ahlstrom 1972, 816–18). Many Assemblies leaders came out of this movement and the new church groups that arose from it. The holiness movement was an urban-based phenomenon that grew out of a desire to return to the basics of camp revivalism. The first of many week-long holiness camp meetings took place at Vineland, New Jersey, in July 1867. The purpose of the nondenominational, though principally Methodist, gathering was simple in design:

> To offer united and continual prayer for the revival of the work of holiness in the churches . . . to strengthen the hand of those who feel themselves comparatively isolated in their profession of holiness . . . to realize together a Pentecostal baptism of the Holy Ghost—and all with a view to increased usefulness in the churches of which we are members (McDonald and Searles 1885, 190).

The resulting celebration of "old-time religion" was viewed as a great success. By 1869, attendance at the Round Lake, New York, camp meeting approached twenty thousand (see T. Smith 1962, 16–21).

The primary concern of most in the holiness movement was right practice. Their emphasis upon the open evidence of a sanctified life demonstrated the movement's origins in the perfectionist theology of John Wesley (1703–1791), the founder of Methodism, who held that one could be purged of sinful tendencies through prayer, right conduct, and the grace of the Holy Spirit. The stress upon transformation of heart and deportment, described as the second blessing, also had Wesleyan antecedents. The strongest proponents of holiness found a unifying bond in the pursuit of entire sanctification, which they believed would root out the very effects of Adam's sin. The term *baptism of the Holy Spirit* came into use to designate this subsequent spiritual experience.[5] Pentecostals later were to use the same term to describe their experience of empowerment as evidenced by speaking in tongues.

The holiness movement quickly became involved in internal disputes over the meaning of this second blessing. A focus of the issue became the introduction of British Keswickian theology, an interpretation of the second blessing that emphasized its potential to empower Christian commitment and dedication. The Keswickian view particularly challenged certain Wesleyan motifs, such as the possibility for absolute sanctification and the full eradication of sin.

Keswickian theology taught that "fullness of the Spirit" was possible in the Christian life. But this "fullness" was not to be confused with Wesleyan perfectionism. Believers would always fall short of perfection and thus need to be filled and refilled by the Holy Spirit throughout their lives. In contrast, the Wesleyans in the holiness movement understood the second blessing to be a perfection in love, a culminating event of holiness hard to define but nonetheless real. The conflict between these two views carried over into pentecostalism, with the Assemblies of God eventually embracing the Keswickian position.

The holiness movement became nationwide within its first twenty years. This rapid expansion caused tensions within the established churches, especially among the Methodists. Charles Edwin Jones noted that

> [holiness] leaders encouraged the development of regional and local associations modeled after the national

one, which easily became instruments for pooling local holiness grievances. . . . Thus, thoroughly conventional Methodist ministers in search of radically conservative reform within their own church had unwittingly become agents of controversy and disunion both within and outside their own communion (1968, 191).

The tendency on the part of the Methodist leadership was to resist the call to change.[6] In reaction, many disillusioned holiness people questioned the continuing salvific relevance of their established churches. Between 1893 and 1907, twenty-five holiness associations moved out to become separate denominations (see E. Clark 1949, 76–81).

The Fire-Baptized Movement

The search for the validation of baptism in the Holy Spirit "filled the pulpits, the schools, and the minds of sincere individuals among the great group of holiness folk as the twentieth century dawned upon the world" (Harrison 1954, 59). The reasons for this great interest in Spirit-baptism were atmospheric and are hard to recapture. Perhaps the major factor was the desire to have a powerful spiritual experience as proof positive against the sophisticated skepticism that had come to dominate much of mainstream religion.

Representing this quest for religious certitude was the Fire-Baptized Holiness Church, which was a direct precursor to the pentecostal movement (see Campbell 1951, 193–215). By teaching that Spirit-baptism was an experience separate from and subsequent to sanctification, this group laid down the key doctrinal premise for early pentecostals (Synan 1971, 68).

The Fire-Baptized movement began in Lincoln, Nebraska, in 1895 when a "come-outer" group (a group that had separated from the Methodist Church) separated from the Iowa Holiness Association. Benjamin H. Irwin (1854–n.d.), the founder, proclaimed a third blessing of the Holy Spirit. This was an experience beyond either water baptism or Spirit-baptism. Irwin's view was influenced by the writings of John Fletcher (1729–1785), a colleague of John Wesley (see Knight 1966). Fletcher described a "baptism of burning love," which

Irwin recast as a "baptism of fire." He promulgated his view in holiness movement circles, but with limited success.

Irwin's "come-outer" extremists described themselves as those who had "received the fire." They became known for enthusiastic shouting, screaming, and "speaking in other tongues." Irwin himself did not promote tongues, but it became common for the practice to accompany the baptism of fire among his followers (Synan 1971, 62).

Over time, Irwin became more extreme. He named further necessary baptisms of dynamite, lyddite, and oxidite, although he did not elaborate on how these baptisms would be received. Women were forbidden to wear jewelry, and men could not wear neckties. All were commanded to adhere to Old Testament dietary restrictions. Fire-Baptized devotees became known as "the no-necktie, no hogmeat people" (Taylor 1921, 9). In the spring of 1900, Irwin confessed to an unspecified "open and gross sin" and abruptly quit the movement. Following this, "it looked as though the little church would evanesce completely" (Campbell 1951, 205). In many places Fire-Baptized meetings disappeared, but elements of the group did survive. In April 1908, the church leadership endorsed tongues as the initial evidence of having been baptized in the Holy Spirit. This made the Fire-Baptized Holiness Church the first denomination to identify fully with the nascent pentecostal movement.

The Christian and Missionary Alliance

Many future Assemblies of God leaders received their early training in the Christian and Missionary Alliance (Nienkirchen 1988, 163). This group was incorporated in 1897 through a merger of the Christian Alliance and the Evangelical Missionary Alliance. Its inspirational leader was a Presbyterian minister, Albert Benjamin Simpson (1843–1919), who had founded the Christian Alliance in 1887 at Old Orchard, Maine. He described his motive in this way:

> The Christian Alliance is not an ecclesiastical body in any sense, but simply a fraternal union of consecrated believers in connection with various evangelical churches. It

does not organize distinct churches or require its members to leave their present church connections. There is no antagonism whatever in the Alliance to any of the evangelical churches, but a desire to help them in every proper way and to promote the interests of Christ's Kingdom in connection with every proper organizational work (J. H. Hunter 1964, 17).

The heart of Simpson's message was a simple, fourfold gospel proclamation: Christ as Savior, Christ as Healer, Christ as Baptizer in the Holy Ghost, and Christ as Coming Lord. This message incorporated elements from both the holiness and premillennialist movements, and it was later fully adopted by the Assemblies of God (Dayton 1987, 21).

The Alliance's influence on early pentecostals was pervasive. The commitment to the imminent return of Christ was foundational to an aggressive social reform and missions emphasis (Weber 1983, 79). Their insistence upon a premillennial, physical return of Christ was a doctrine that would be enthusiastically embraced by the Assemblies of God. Since the Christian and Missionary Alliance represented an influential segment of the Keswickian wing of the holiness movement, its progressive sanctification emphases had a special impact (Menzies 1971, 28). Finally, Simpson's stress upon divine healing helped condition many in the evangelical population to the possibility of such direct divine interventions (Nichol 1966, 54).

The Zion City Experiment

The Zion City commune in northern Illinois proved to be another important nurturing ground for Assemblies leaders. Its founder was John Alexander Dowie (1847–1907),[7] an itinerant minister from Australia who had immigrated to the United States in 1888. His passion was to proclaim the present reality of divine healing. After two years of circuit preaching, Dowie settled in Evanston, Illinois, where he promoted Simpson's fourfold, full gospel message with a special emphasis on healing.

In 1893, Dowie set up a revival tent next to the Chicago World's Fair. He preached daily, stressing holy living and divine healing as a substitute for doctors and medicine. Many were attracted to his eccentric views, and some of those attending his meetings testified to miraculous healings. Following this successful campaign, Dowie opened a evangelism center in Chicago and began to circulate a publication, *Leaves of Healing.*

In 1895, Dowie founded his own denomination, the Christian Catholic Church. By 1900 he had decided to pursue his utopian vision in Zion City, Illinois. Zion City was built on the shores of Lake Michigan, fifty miles north of Chicago. There he developed a model for a self-sufficient society, separated from industrialized America.

Zion City was a highly structured community of about six thousand people. Its centerpiece was a temple that could hold up to eight thousand worshipers. Religious services were compulsory, and doctors, drugs, tobacco, liquor, theaters, and pork products were forbidden. The commune's refusal of conveniences and entertainments showed a wariness toward the modern world as a place of potential spiritual entrapment. Dowie's success in drawing thousands of followers to his experiment suggested the yearning in the hearts of many evangelical Christians for a depth of commitment coupled with a desire to experience the miraculous in their lives.

Dowie grew increasingly megalomaniacal. He believed that the revival of the "latter rain"—the prophesied outpouring of the Holy Spirit meant to prepare humans for Judgment Day (Joel 2:28–32)—had begun with his ministry. Because he saw himself as the herald of Christ's Second Coming, Dowie announced that he had become essential to the return. In 1901 he gave public notice that he was actually Elijah the Restorer. Dowie's claims grew even more extravagant over the next few years, and he began to wear elaborate, high priestly robes to Sunday services. In 1904, he declared himself Christ's chief restored apostle and predicted that eleven brother apostles would soon make their appearance to support his claims.

In September 1905, Dowie had a stroke. While sent away to recuperate he was deposed as leader of Zion City, "the victim of his own financial mismanagement and novel interpretation of Scripture" (Blumhofer 1985, 18). John Alexander Dowie died in 1907, universally ignored by those who had once been his followers.

Disillusioned supporters were left to look elsewhere for their restorationist hope. For most, the promise of a latter rain revival of apostolic power had not been discredited by Dowie's antics. In their minds, commitment to vital Christian living, based in a united witness to restored apostolic power, heralded the imminent return of Christ. This restorationist theme, along with divine healing, was a Zion City theme that was carried forward. Many began to see the pentecostal movement as God's confirmation of the rightness of a dream gone wrong at Zion City.

Pentecostalism: The Incipient Stage

Charles Parham and the Apostolic Faith Movement

Charles Fox Parham (1873–1929) is regarded by many as the founder of the pentecostal movement.[8] He brought many of the influences just described into some cohesion. Parham's efforts also represented the incipient organizational phase of pentecostalism. This early stage was characterized by fervent reaction against existing church structures and involved strong support and high levels of personal commitment from the lower socioeconomic classes (see Moberg 1984, 119).

Parham enrolled at the Methodist ministry school in Winfield, Kansas, in 1892. After three years of undistinguished study, he viewed further education as a hindrance to his true calling and launched out on a preaching and healing campaign throughout eastern Kansas. He proposed what many Methodists deemed to be unorthodox opinions, especially by questioning the doctrine of eternal damnation. This brought him into open conflict with church authorities. Since he viewed official church membership as fundamentally irrelevant and ecclesial discipline as too constraining, he went his own way.

Parham began to espouse a form of nondenominational Christianity that he called the Apostolic Faith. His teaching had a fairly typical mixture of theological emphases, including a traditional revivalist belief in radical conversion to Christianity; a Wesleyan understanding of sanctification as a second and subsequent work of grace; a Fire-Baptized understanding of "baptism with the Holy Ghost and with fire"; a belief in faith healing; and a dispensational eschatology structured on a time frame that would include a final, worldwide Christian revival and the physical rapture of the church followed by Christ's return (see Kendrick 1961, 38–45).

A continual examination of the Bible kept changing the course of Parham's ministry. In 1898, he and his wife, Sarah, opened Beth-el Healing Home in Topeka, Kansas. This was a combination rest home and faith-training center. At this point, the Parhams also began publishing a bimonthly journal, *Apostolic Faith*.

During the summer of 1900, Charles Parham felt compelled to visit other holiness centers throughout the country. He left Beth-el in the care of his wife and began a twelve-week tour that included visits to Dowie's headquarters in Chicago, Simpson's Missionary Training Institute in Nyack, New York, and Frank W. Sandford's (1862–1948) Holy Ghost and Us school-commune in Shiloah, Maine.

Sandford's school made a particular impression upon Parham because of the sincerity of the students and the single-mindedness of their efforts. There was no tuition at the commune; both students and faculty depended upon voluntary contributions. There was little ostensible structure, and the only textbook was the Bible. A special revelation concerning any scriptural text was considered sufficient reason to stop all other activities. Parham came back to Topeka determined to start his own school based upon what he had seen.

The Bethel Bible Institute opened in an unfinished Topeka mansion called Stone's Folly in September 1900. Parham described the spirit of the project in this way:

> No one paid board or tuition, the poor were fed, the sick were entertained and healed, and from day to day, week to week, and month to month, with no sect or mission or known source of income back of us, God supplied our every need, and He was our all sufficiency in all things (Nichol 1966, 28).

Following the Sandford school model, the Bible was made the sole text and Parham its prime expositor. Students were given topics to research and would explore all relevant passages concerning the issue at hand. After Parham directed an inquiry into the text's meaning, the group would move on to another issue. Biblical study was supplemented by long hours, even entire nights, spent in prayer.

By December 1900, Parham had given his interpretation of standard holiness topics such as repentance, conversion, sanctification, divine healing, and the premillennial return of Christ. Since he was scheduled to attend a meeting in Kansas City, he assigned his pupils the task of searching the Bible for consistent evidences concerning baptism in the Holy Spirit.

Parham claimed to be ignorant of what those evidences might be (S. Parham 1930, 58).[9] But, through Sandford, he had heard reports of tongues speaking among foreign missionaries. Such stories of xenolalic tongues—that is, the ability to speak and be understood in a language one had not learned—represented a sure signal of the imminent return of Christ and a coming worldwide revival.

Parham asked about the results of the study upon his return from Kansas City: "To my astonishment they all had the same story, that while there were different things occured [*sic*] when the Pentecastal [*sic*] blessing fell, the indisputable proof on each occasion was that they spake with other tongues" (ibid., 52). All agreed that they needed to investigate the matter further.

The Bethel Bible Institute group planned services to greet the new year and century on the evening of December 31, 1900. During the all-night vigil, a student named Agnes Ozman asked Parham to lay hands on her head. She prayed loudly that she might be baptized in the Holy Spirit and speak in tongues. Shortly after midnight, Ozman allegedly began "speaking in the Chinese language" and "a halo seemed to surround her face." Synan cites several reports concerning this incident (1971, 101), but it is unlikely that anyone at the school would have recognized the Chinese language.

Within hours, several other students also claimed to have received tongues and Parham owned to the experience a few days later. From this point onward, Parham and his followers insisted that Spirit-baptism was always evidenced by speaking in other tongues. Tongues was seen as a sure sign of the coming full restoration of apostolic power. More significantly, if the Holy Spirit was being poured out in such a dramatic fashion, then these indeed were the prophesied last days (Nichol 1966, 29).

The strange events at Bethel Bible Institute were soon proclaimed by the press. A headline from the *Topeka Capital* read: "A Queer Faith, Strange Acts . . . Believers Speak in Strange Languages." The *Kansas City World* wrote, "These people have a faith almost incomprehensible at this day." Reporters converged upon Bethel, and national wire services picked up the story. In late January 1901, Parham and his group traveled to Galena, Kansas, to begin a missionary journey during which they intended to spread their new revelation (Synan 1971, 102).

The Bethel group's enthusiasm was quickly tempered by an indifferent reception to their new message. They had planned a large-scale tour of East Coast cities, but within a few weeks they returned to Topeka because of a lack of funds. Another revival attempt was made at Lawrence, Kansas, in February 1901. The response was again lukewarm. Parham returned to Topeka, directed the closing of the Bethel Bible Institute, and moved his ministry to Kansas City. He saw the period immediately following this as the low point in his ministry:

> Both the pulpit and the press sought to utterly destroy our place and prestige, until my wife, her sister and myself stood alone. Hated, despised, counted as nought, for weeks and weeks never knowing where our next meal would come from, yet feeling that we must maintain the faith once for all delivered to the saints. When we had carfare we rode, when we didn't we walked. When buildings were closed to us we preached on the street (C. Parham 1926, 3).

In 1903, Parham was invited to conduct a series of revivals in Nevada, Missouri. The new message was better received there. Following this encouragement, Parham's small band conducted another series of meetings in El Dorado Springs, Missouri. This town was known for its medicinal waters, and Parham used this aspect to emphasize divine healing in his preaching. He interpreted the results of the El Dorado Springs meetings as an unqualified success: "People came by the hundreds to hear the message and were healed, bearing the message of God to all parts of the U.S. Our home was continuously besieged with sick and suffering for prayer" (ibid.).

The El Dorado Springs revival provoked greater interest in the new message, and tongues became associated with the power to heal. Parham's group conducted an extended revival in Galena, Kansas, in the fall of 1903. This proved to be the most powerful set of meetings to date. Parham wrote that at one session, on January 27, 1904, up to 500 people were "sanctified," meaning converted, and 250 spoke in tongues (Kendrick 1961, 60). By the end of 1904, Apostolic Faith congregations were springing up in Joplin, Missouri, as well as in Columbus, Melrose, Galena, and Baxter Springs, Kansas (Goss 1958, 29).

The new enthusiasm quickly spread to Texas. Converts from Parham's meetings convinced him to hold meetings in Orchard, Texas, during the spring of 1905. This revival started slowly but picked up momentum (see Frodsham 1946, 27–28). Among those attending was Mrs. John Calhoun, who reported the experience to her holiness church in the Houston suburb of Brunner. In July 1905, Parham was invited to preach there as well. The meetings were held at a large hall and reportedly featured unusually dramatic healings.

Interest in Parham's ministry continued to increase markedly, and his followers began to conduct simultaneous revivals in towns surrounding Houston. Pentecostal pioneer Howard Goss (1883–1964) described those meetings as being held at a fever pitch:

> The power of God was so great in the altar services here that seekers often fell as if they were dead, and would be immovable for hours, only their lips whispering softly to God. Early in the morning they would have to be piled like cord-wood into the back of a delivery wagon and taken home to continue their solitary soul's search after God. These usually came through to a glowing experience in their own homes. A thriving Pentecostal Church was the result of this revival (ibid., 30–31).

By the winter of 1905–6, twenty-five thousand persons had been converted to this new pentecostal experience. Many of these would later become leaders in the Assemblies of God (Menzies 1971, 48).

In December 1905, Parham opened another school in Houston to train workers to handle the burgeoning revivals. Like the Bethel Bible Institute, the new school emphasized a regimen of intensive prayer and a simple, Bible-based curriculum. One of the students enrolled was an African-American holiness preacher named William J. Seymour (1870–1922) (see D. Nelson 1981). Seymour had not had the tongues experience, but he was convinced of the truth of the pentecostal message. After a few months of studying at Parham's Houston school, Seymour was convinced by Neely Terry, a visitor to the school, to come to her church in Los Angeles and share the new revelation. Seymour left for the West Coast in the spring of 1906.

The Azusa Street Revival

Classical pentecostals point to the Azusa Street revival, led by William Seymour, as the formative event in their history.[10] It was primed by the Apostolic Faith surge as well as by hopes generated by the Welsh revival of 1904.[11] The Welsh revival began at a small church in New Quay, Wales. There, during a November evening testimony meeting, Florrie Evans stood up and cried out loudly: "If no one else will, I must say that I do love my Lord Jesus Christ with all my heart" (Hollenweger 1972, 177).

These words produced an inexplicably profound effect upon the hearers. Many were seized with intense religious excitement and began to weep and cry out. That night, the assembled group stood up and dedicated their lives to the wholehearted pursuit of the presence of God. Among those converted to this deeper faith commitment was a miner and blacksmith named Evan Roberts (1878–1951).

Roberts had a meteoric career as the high-profile evangelist of the Welsh revival (see Hollenweger 1972, 178–83). Roberts preached a type of repentance that led to intimate communion with God. His pulpit presence was legendary:

It was not the eloquence of Evan Roberts that broke men down, but his tears. He would break down, crying bitterly for God to bend them, in an agony of prayer, the tears coursing down his cheeks, with his whole frame writhing. Strong men would break down and cry like children. Women would shrink. A sound of weeping and wailing would fill the air. Evan Roberts in the intensity of his agony would fall in the pulpit, while many in the crowd often fainted (Bartleman 1980, 34–35).

The Welsh revival became famous for eruptions of hour-long songs and spontaneous half-sung, half-spoken prayers called *Hywl*. There was a general freedom to interrupt speakers at will and a moment-to-moment dependence upon the movements of the Holy Spirit.

The religious passions generating the Welsh revival had waned by 1905, but its intensity was romanticized by many American evangelical leaders, who saw it as a model for fervor. Marathon prayer meetings were begun in the United States in hopes of having a similar experience of the Holy Spirit. Rev. Joseph Smale (1867–1926), pastor of the First Baptist Church in Los Angeles, visited Wales in 1904. On the advice of Roberts, he returned to Los Angeles intent to begin a revival in his own church. Smale preached daily for fifteen weeks until his alienated board of deacons forced him to resign. He then recruited his own congregation to promote the revival message. Though he never formally embraced pentecostalism, Smale and another Baptist revivalist, Elmer K. Fisher (1866–1919), have been acknowledged as forerunners to the success of the Azusa Street revival.

William Seymour arrived at Los Angeles in April 1906 to preach the new message. The sermon he prepared for the small African-American holiness church where he was to speak was based upon Acts 2:4, "And they were all filled with the Holy Ghost, and began to speak with other tongues, as the Spirit gave them utterance." Seymour interpreted this verse to be proclaiming tongues as the definitive evidence for baptism in the Holy Spirit.

Sr. Hutchinson, pastor of the small Nazarene congregation to whom Seymour was to preach, believed that her people had already received the Holy Spirit's fullness. To her mind,

Seymour was asking them to disavow their traditional belief that tongues was but one evidence among many of the Holy Spirit's inner presence. She reacted to his proposed message forcefully by padlocking the doors to the church. Seymour could not preach at the afternoon service, and a chagrined Neely Terry, who had given the initial invitation, offered to let him stay with her relatives. He began to conduct daily services in their living room at 214 Bonnie Brae Street.

On April 9, 1906, during a prayer meeting, some of those attending experienced Spirit-baptism and fell to the floor, speaking in tongues. A crowd gathered outside the house, wondering what the shouting inside was all about (Brumback 1961, 26). Reports of these events circulated rapidly in the neighborhood, and Seymour began to preach to all comers, African-American and white, from the front porch. Seymour laid claim to the tongues experience himself several days later.

It became apparent within a few days that the front yard was inadequate to handle the burgeoning crowds. Seymour secured a large abandoned building at 312 Azusa Street in the industrial section of Los Angeles and there began conducting marathon revival meetings. Sessions ran almost continuously, from ten in the morning to midnight or two the next morning. The one-eyed Seymour was a far-from-polished messenger:

> He was meek and plain spoken and no orator. He spoke the common language of the uneducated class. He might preach for three-quarters of an hour with no more emotionalism than that of a post. He was no arm-waving thunderer, by any stretch of the imagination (Osterberg 1956, 1).

During the interminable meetings, Seymour would meditate by sitting with his head inside a shoe box. At other times, he would wander through the crowd, with five- and ten-dollar donations sticking out of his back pockets. From time to time, he would stop to harangue the assembled to repent of their sins, seek after Spirit-baptism, and accept the present reality of divine healing (Synan 1971, 108–9).

The Azusa Street revival grew both in numbers and intensity, in part as a result of the San Francisco earthquake of April 18, 1906. Tremors were felt as far south as Los Angeles.

Some interpreted the earthquake eschatologically, as a last heavenly bugle call before final judgment, and this increased an overall sense of urgency and expectation (Bartleman 1980, 49). This, coupled with the increasing scrutiny of the local press,[12] helped the revival thrive.

A visitor to Azusa Street would have encountered a bewildering spectacle. There were hundreds of people and was no discernible order:

> No subject or sermons were announced ahead of time, and no special speakers for such an hour. No one knew what might be coming, what God would do. All was spontaneous, ordered of the Spirit. We wanted to hear from God, through whoever [*sic*] he might speak. . . . The meetings started themselves, spontaneously, in testimony, praise, and worship. . . . The Lord was liable to burst through anyone. We prayed for this continually. Someone would finally get up, anointed for the message. All seemed to recognize this and give way. It might be a child, a woman, or a man. It might be from the back seat or from the front. . . . Someone might be speaking. Suddenly the Spirit would fall upon the congregation. God himself would give the altar call. Men would fall all over the house like the slain in battle, or rush for the altar en masse, to seek God. The scene often resembled a forest of fallen trees (Bartleman 1980, 58–60).

Extremism was the norm. Groups of men and women congregated to cry out to the Lord for hours on end. They would weep, laugh, fall to the floor, and then collect themselves to sing and pray in tongues. One peculiar feature of the revival was the so-called heavenly chorus, in which groups would break out and harmonize in unrehearsed tongues songs for hours.

By the end of the summer of 1906, the Azusa Street revival was a nationally known event, drawing thousands of visitors (see Ewart 1947, 40–49). A striking—for many, scandalous—feature of the meetings was the free mixing of racial, ethnic, and class groups. This was an almost unheard of phenomenon at the turn of the century. It probably reflected the revival's interracial origins as well as a rough egalitarianism in the burgeoning lower-class population of Los Angeles, where fixed group distinctions had not had full time to emerge. As a result, no one's views were dismissed because of race or lack of status or education (Frodsham 1946, 34).[13] At Azusa Street, the participants found a sense of community and dignity that had been denied them in the anonymous urban culture. Frank Bartleman (1871–1936), the main chronicler of the revival, pointedly remarked: "The color line was washed away in the blood" (1980, 54).

Social inclusion did not lead to a similar latitude in doctrine. Many participants might have been of questionable orthodoxy, but the central themes proclaimed by Seymour and the other recognized leaders were of a traditional holiness variety: forgiveness of sin through the blood of Jesus, divine healing through the atonement, and the expectation of a premillennial Second Coming. Christian unity, expressed through a rejection of denominational particularism, was another especially strong emphasis (Blumhofer 1985, 30).

Fearing the increased excesses he was witnessing at Azusa Street, Seymour counseled against putting too much stress on emotions (Frodsham 1946, 38). Attempts at moderation were successful for a time, reinforced by workers in the crowd who had been thoroughly trained in past holiness revivals. Still, Bartleman did acknowledge that serious problems of subjectivism existed at Azusa Street:

> In the embryotic stage of all new experience much allowance must be made for human frailty. There are always many coarse, impulsive, imperfectly balanced spirits among those first reached by a revival. . . . Our great battle from the beginning was with fleshly fanatics, purporting to be of the Spirit of God (Bartleman 1980, 62).

Renaming the Azusa Street Mission the Apostolic Faith Mission demonstrated Seymour's indebtedness to Charles Parham's ministry. In September 1906, Parham was invited to conduct a series of revival meetings. Despite Seymour's attempts to maintain order, Parham was openly shocked by what he saw happening at Azusa Street (see S. Parham 1930, 164–202). He preached two or three times but was "invited" to leave by some of Seymour's followers after he persistently denounced the hypnotists and spiritualists who were becoming increasingly more evident at the meetings.[14] Parham left to conduct a sedate and relatively unsuccessful revival in downtown Los Angeles.

Parham was only one of a growing number of critics of the Azusa Street revival. The most skeptical dismissed the whole thing as mass delusion. Casual mixing was a problem for some Christians, who were scandalized by open embracing and kissing between sexes and races. Such excesses were duly reported to Alma White (1862–1946), a nationally prominent Denver-based holiness preacher. White became a lifetime implacable foe of pentecostalism, concluding that it was a satanic ploy and "the climax of demon worship" (White 1949, 82).

Another prominent opponent of the early pentecostals was the holiness evangelist and teacher, W. B. Godbey (1839–1932). He was invited to visit Azusa Street in 1909, late in the revival's history. Upon his arrival, Godbey was asked if he had ever spoken in tongues. He responded with a phrase in Latin, and the group reacted by saying that Godbey had surely just been blessed with the heavenly gift. He left the meeting immediately and from that time onward excoriated pentecostals as a collection of "Satan's preachers, jugglers, necromancers, enchanters, magicians, and mendicants" (ibid., 120–27).

Indeed, by 1909, Seymour had largely lost control of the situation. Occult groups became a dominant factor in the meetings. Involuntary jerking and wild attempts to "tree the devil" by barking like a pack of dogs often supplanted legitimate pentecostal experiences.

But because early pentecostalism had no real structure, its focus of attention tended to shift rapidly. By 1908 the *Apostolic Faith,* the original Azusa revival newspaper, was being published in Portland, Oregon, and the Pacific Northwest had become an equally significant center for revival. It may well be that it was only in 1906 and 1907 that Azusa Street was the center of the new movement (Bloch-Hoell 1964, 47–49).

Still, Azusa Street has retained special significance for many pentecostals. The revival's dramatic nature brought pentecostalism to a more general public awareness. Its example served as a catalyst for revival efforts elsewhere. Many emerging leaders in the pentecostal movement either made the pilgrimage to Azusa Street or were influenced by reports. Often those who did travel to Los Angeles arrived as holiness preachers and left as pentecostal preachers. The pentecostal spark was struck by Parham's Topeka group in 1901 and had spread through that immediate area. Another spark traveled to the West Coast, and a mighty revival erupted in Los Angeles in 1906. By 1908, pentecostal fires were spreading from coast to coast.

The Spread of the Movement and Early Opposition

Early pentecostals were confident that they bore a special revelation to their time (Nichol 1966, 66).[15] Indeed, the hallmark of this Latter Rain movement, as the early pentecostals described their group, was its self-assurance. Its central proclamation was that God had dramatically intervened in current history, just as at the day of Pentecost. Evidences of divine healing, tongues, and prophecy were pointed to as support for this claim. Pentecostals interpreted this historic intervention to mean that a brief and intense new age had begun with their movement.

Typifying this overriding sense of urgency was a sermon given September 20, 1908, at the Stone Church in Chicago:

A new dispensation is dawning upon us, and like all dispensations, the present one will die and the coming dispensation will be born in the same crisis. . . . This conflict is already upon us. And it will grow harder, and thicker, and blacker; but God has promised that out of all our distresses we shall be delivered. . . . You must go to the wall and close your doors, or go into theatricals, oyster suppers, etc., or cut loose from the old moorings and launch out into the depths of the love of God and sail boldly into this Latter Rain Movement. . . . The Spirit has spoken in this church scores of times, urging the people that they go from house to house and tell the people that the time of Christ's coming draweth nigh. Oh, how few of you are doing it! My heart is sad, and if my heart is sad, what of the Master's? . . . Listen! You hold the lives of a certain number of people (God knows how many) in your hands, and they will be damned because of your neglect. Do you hear that? It is plain English. They will be damned because of your neglect (Piper 1908, 9–10).

Opposition to the Latter Rain movement grew, especially when the volatility of some of its adherents gave weight to charges of pentecostal extremism. Occasionally, early opponents to the new movement even resorted to physical violence (Synan 1971, 191–92), although verbal attacks were much more common. For example, the well-known fundamentalist teacher, Dr. G. Campbell Morgan (1863–1931), in the same castigating spirit as Alma White and W. B. Godbey, denounced pentecostalism as a demonic delusion, the "last vomit of Satan." Reuben A. Torrey (1856–1928), president of the prestigious Moody Bible Institute and a one-time proponent of Spirit-baptism as a special source of divine power, declared the new movement as "emphatically not of God, and founded by a Sodomite [Parham]" (ibid., 144).

By 1912, evangelical distancing from the pentecostal movement was nearly complete. The leaders of the Pentecostal Church of the Nazarene, the nation's largest holiness church, became concerned that traditional holiness emphases would be lost by a false identification with the controversial new movement. They changed their name to the Church of the Nazarene. Following this example, the Salvation Army, the Pilgrim Holiness Church, and the Free Methodists began to adamantly oppose pentecostalism and severed all ties (T. Smith 1962, 319–20).

In the South—where many of the early Assemblies of God leaders originated—the impact of Azusa Street and the other pentecostal revivals was very strong, perhaps because of the region's strong revivalist tradition. Several prominent holiness leaders were drawn into the new movement. One of these was Charles Harrison Mason (1866–1961), founder of the African-American Church of God in Christ. After visiting Azusa Street in March 1907, Mason came back professing tongues as the initial evidence of Spirit-baptism, a claim that split his denomination.

Mason decided to restructure the Church of God in Christ as an interracial pentecostal group. Because his denomination, unlike the various pentecostal sects, was officially recognized, Mason was the only early convert to pentecostalism who could ordain a clergy that would be recognized by the civil authorities. Ordination in the denomination allowed white pentecostal ministers to perform marriages and other functions. "So great was Mason's prestige that many white Pentecostal ministers accepted ordination at his hands. Many of the men who founded the white 'Assemblies of God' church in 1914 were thus ordained in the Church of God in Christ by Bishop Mason" (Synan 1971, 172). Their identification with the Church of God in Christ also gave them the advantage of the reduced railway rates that other officially recognized clergy received. Thus Charles Mason's decision was an important event for white pentecostal preachers in the South, although an undercurrent of racial tension remained.

The Finished Work Debate

The Midwest witnessed the first great doctrinal controversy within pentecostalism, revolving around the issue of subsequent works of grace. William H. Durham (1873–1912), a high-profile preacher at Stone Church in Chicago, championed what he called "the finished work of Calvary."[16] Durham's view was a Keswickian interpretation of Spirit-baptism that saw pentecostal experience as part of a progressive sequence of empowerment: "The living faith that justifies a man, brings him into Christ, the Sanctifier, in Whom he is complete, not with regard to sanctification only, but everything else that pertains to his salvation" (Durham 1912, 4). Durham contended that the power of sin was mastered at conversion. There was no residue of sin that necessitated distinct and subsequent experiences of sanctification. This position refuted the view of the Wesleyans in the pentecostal movement, such as Parham and Seymour, who held that Spirit-baptism was a third experience of empowerment subsequent to and entirely distinct from conversion and sanctification. Durham's argument held special appeal for non-Wesleyans, such as Baptists, who were coming into pentecostalism out of nonholiness backgrounds.

The finished work controversy grew in intensity after 1910. Durham became more strident over time, holding that his finished work view was central to understanding all of the New Testament. Support for Durham grew, since many pentecostals lacked confidence in the comprehensiveness of their own experience of sanctification after conversion. They were particularly discouraged by their frequent slides from what they saw as standards of moral perfection (Menzies 1971, 75).

In February 1911, Durham brought his forceful message to Los Angeles (see Bartleman 1980, 150–59). He went to Azusa Street to preach, but Seymour locked him out. Durham began to conduct his own meetings in downtown Los Angeles, with over a thousand people in attendance on Sundays. Frank Bartleman wrote of this revival:

> Here the "cloud" rested. God's glory filled the place. "Azusa" became deserted. The Lord was with Brother Durham in great power. God sets His seal especially on present truth to be established. He preached a gospel of salvation by faith. He was used mightily to draw anew a clear line of demarcation between salvation by works and faith, between law and grace. This had become very much needed, even among Pentecostal people (ibid., 146).

In January 1912, Charles Parham accused Durham of committing an unspecified sin unto death. Parham predicted that Durham would be dead in six months. Durham did contract a head cold upon his return to Chicago from Los Angeles and died of pneumonia in July 1912. Upon hearing this report, Parham remarked: "How signally God has answered" (Editorial 1912, n.p.).

The pentecostal movement became severely divided over the finished work issue (see Boddy 1912, 6). Initially, the Assemblies of God did not adopt a definitive position. But, almost without exception, the independent ministers and congregations that joined together to form the new denomination adhered to Durham's belief that complete and progressive power over sin's effects was received at conversion (Menzies 1971, 76–77).

The Emergence and Growth of the Assemblies of God

Early Organization

By 1913, it became evident to pentecostal leaders that their movement was not going to be accepted in the evangelical churches. The need for some independent national coordination was also obvious. The early Assemblies leader, Howard Goss, noted that the Latter Rain movement suffered from its anarchic style:

> It was becoming increasingly apparent that something would have to be done, if we were to preserve the work. . . . As our numbers increased, the influx brought with it leaders who did not believe in organization at all; some even preached that anything of that nature (when committed to paper) was of the devil. Opposing this viewpoint was the definite system existing in the New Testament Church under the apostles (Goss 1958, 163).

Related to the general need for order was the problem of controlling unscrupulous ministries, as pentecostals were increasingly victimized by charlatans who posed as traveling evangelists. Doctrinal conflicts, exemplified by the finished work debate, were another element that threatened division. It was felt that a move toward denominational identity would provide pentecostal groups with a more recognizable status in society. These were some of the considerations that brought pentecostal leaders to rethink their original ideal of complete autonomy (see Goss 1958, 163–74; Menzies 1971, 80–84).

Four regional associations of pentecostals emerged. Two of these, the Texas-Arkansas group and the Southern association, joined together in June 1913 and dropped the traditional Apostolic Faith appellation. Eudorus Bell (1866–1923), editor of the new association's publication, *Word and Witness,* sent out a call for a general council of pentecostals to be held in Hot Springs, Arkansas, in April 1914.

Bell proposed five topics for discussion:

> First—We come together that we may get a better understanding of what God would have us teach, that we may do away with so many divisions. . . .
>
> Second—Again we come together that we may know how to conserve the work, that we may build up and not tear down. . . .
>
> Third—We come together for another reason, that we may get a better understanding of the needs of each

foreign field, and may know how to place our money in such a way that one mission or missionary shall not suffer, while another not anymore worthy, lives in luxuries. Also that we may discourage wasting money on those who are running here and there accomplishing nothing. . . .

Fourth—Many of the saints have felt the need of chartering the Churches of God in Christ, putting them on a legal basis, and thus obliging the laws of the land. . . .

Fifth—We may have a proposition to lay before the body for a general Bible Training School with a literary department for our people (E. Bell 1913, 1).

Although not part of the original pentecostal vision, racial exclusivity seems to have resurfaced. Bell and his cosigners— A. P. Collins, H. A. Goss, and D. C. Opperman—did not mention a sixth point, the matter of whites separating from African-American pentecostals, which had become a matter of mutual consent (R. M. Anderson 1979, 189).

Bell's call to meet represented the desire for a fundamental shift in pentecostalism toward formal organization. With this came the need for defined and well-publicized goals. Also, proposed codes of behavior began to emerge to aid pentecostals in establishing a group ethos.

Bell's proposal to organize drew a strong response. Many pentecostals felt they had been victimized by church structures in the past and viewed the new effort with suspicion. Others feared that formal organization would quench reliance upon the direct leadings of the Holy Spirit, making pentecostalism indistinguishable from the holiness churches they had left behind (Brumback 1961, 58). The majority, who promoted forming a general council, countered the opposition's arguments with an appeal to 1 Cor. 14:40, "Let all things be done decently and in order." Citing the precedent of the apostolic church, they argued that serious conflicts over direction could only be dealt with structurally (Menzies 1971, 96).

The potential for serious conflict was obvious when the council opened on April 2, 1914. The first three days of the Hot Springs meeting were devoted exclusively to prayer, preaching, and fellowship. This helped defuse some of the inherent distrust. On the morning of April 6, Eudorus Bell opened the first official session. Since there was no fixed agenda, the initial order of business was to select a resolutions committee. This committee received suggestions and chose the subjects for the convention's further deliberations.

A smaller, unofficial group was meeting secretly. They gathered to strategize against any attempts to regiment the pentecostal movement. But the potentially explosive situation took a surprisingly conciliatory turn:

> The next day they [the secret group] unexpectedly read their proposal from the floor. This was a surprise to us [the organizers], but as we listened, we heard to our great joy your [God's] own ideas being read out. The proposal they read is now part of the preamble of the Assemblies of God (Goss 1958, 176).

When the unofficial proposal for pentecostal unity carried unanimously, a resolution for formal incorporation was also quickly passed.

Church polity became the central issue for this first Assemblies of God gathering. A sense emerged among those in the group that the loose confederation of congregations should be preserved. J. Roswell Flower (1888–1970), the first denominational secretary, wrote:

> It was agreed by all not to organize or charter a church, denomination, or sect, but to have an ANNUAL COUNCIL made up from all Pentecostal Assemblies, Churches and individuals to meet once a year to advise scriptural methods of unity and to attend to business for God (n.d., 10).

The council also decided to combine this congregational style of governance at the local level with an advisory presbytery that would provide continuity between the annual councils.

This First General Council of the Assemblies of God adopted the Preamble and Resolution on Constitution, which incorporated the group.[17] Since no denominational statement of faith was adopted until 1916 and no constitution was formalized until 1927, this document became the primary unifying agent during the denomination's early years.[18]

The newly formed Assemblies of God held the Second General Council within seven months. This meeting was held November 15–29, 1914, at the Stone Church in Chicago. It was called to decide how to organize missions, and it addressed other issues of practical concern. The Executive Presbytery was enlarged at this point and given power to make administrative decisions, although its ability to interfere with local autonomy was carefully prescribed. St. Louis was chosen as the denomination's temporary headquarters.

The Oneness Issue

In April 1913, a "worldwide" pentecostal camp meeting was held at Arroyo Seco, a small suburb of Los Angeles. Before the normal baptismal service, Canadian preacher Robert McAlister (1880–1953) announced that the baptismal formula found in Acts 2:38, "In the name of Jesus," was preferable to that found in Matt. 18:19, "In the name of the Father, and of the Son, and of the Holy Ghost." McAlister's message was believed by many to be the confirmation of an earlier prophetic revelation that claimed that God would do a "new thing" at the camp meeting.

Such special revelations were common in early pentecostalism: "A preacher who did not dig up some new slant on a Scripture, or get some new revelation to his own heart so often; a preacher who did not propagate it, defend it, and if necessary be prepared to lay down his life for it, was considered slow, stupid, unspiritual" (Goss 1958, 155). This attitude represented the primitive biblical literalism of many early pentecostals, who yearned to return to the imagined simplicity of the apostolic age. McAlister had been warned by a fellow minister of the dangers involved in promoting his new baptismal message (Ewart 1947, 75–77). He may have made his remarks casually, but the response was overwhelming.

John Scheppe (1870–1939), an itinerant preacher, was particularly moved by McAlister's new message and spent the night praying through its implications. Early in the morning, Scheppe received his own revelation. He ran through the sleeping campground yelling that all power was in the name of Jesus. Scheppe's so-called fuller revelation caused others to search the Scriptures on the baptism issue. By the end of the

Arroyo Seco meeting, McAlister, Glenn Cook (1867–1948), and Frank Ewart (1876–1947) had begun a crusade in Los Angeles announcing the absolute necessity of being rebaptized in the name of Jesus only.[19]

This Jesus Only faction quickly proclaimed itself nontrinitarian. They asserted that the truth of the absolute unity of person in God had been surrendered to pagan influences in the early centuries of the church. The result had been the polytheistic doctrine of the Trinity.[20] Rebaptism in the name of Jesus only was understood to be necessary, both to have right standing with the one God and to facilitate the physical return of Christ.

The Oneness group held to three necessary steps in a person's salvation: faith in Jesus Christ, water baptism in his name, and subsequent baptism in the Holy Spirit. Thus, salvation did not consist of having faith in the substitutionary atonement of Christ alone, but in fulfilling the new baptismal imperative (R. M. Anderson 1979, 180) and undergoing pentecostal experience. By 1914, this Jesus Only, or Oneness, revelation was being promulgated to pentecostals throughout the country.

In January 1915, the Jesus Only preacher Glenn Cook began an eastern tour to explain the new revelation. After a stop in St. Louis, where J. Roswell Flower openly opposed him, Cook went on to Indianapolis. There he rebaptized G. T. Haywood (1880–1931), the foremost African-American preacher remaining in the newly formed Assemblies of God. Other leaders soon joined in the Oneness surge. The Jesus Only view swept through the Assemblies ranks and seemed about to win over the new denomination (Synan 1971, 156).

A great shock came to Flower and his supporters in July 1915, when Eudorus Bell defected to the Jesus Only position. Bell underwent rebaptism, not as a theological statement, but as an act of personal piety. Writing five months later, he displayed the intensely emotional nature of his decision: "I can say today, before God and all men, that His joy is rolling in my soul now as never before. As I write, His glory convulses my whole physical frame, and I have to stop now and then and say 'Glory' or, 'Oh glory' to let some of it escape" (E. Bell 1915, 5). As more Assemblies ministers embraced the new enthusiasm, Flower held firmly against it and began to organize the opposition.

The Third General Council of the Assemblies of God met in St. Louis in October 1915. Both sides in the dispute sent delegations, and debate over the Jesus Only question dominated the meetings. The resolutions committee appealed for "the spirit and liberality of the Hot Springs Constitution to be applied to the discussion regarding the formula of baptism" (Assemblies of God General Council 1915, 5). The resolutions adopted by the convention did emphasize the persons of the Trinity and thus represented a limited victory for Flower's side. Still, allowance for personal conviction in the matter indicated that the dispute was far from resolved.

The Assemblies' policy was to avoid controversial stands on new doctrines until these positions could be tested, but to the majority of pentecostals, the Oneness position was too extreme to ignore.[21] In the months following the Third General Council, the strength and reputation of the Jesus Only advocates, who did not have access to the denomination's major communications systems, eroded. A key victory for Flower and his group was the return of Eudorus Bell to the fold, as he became convinced that the Oneness position was a subtle but dangerous deviation from Christian orthodoxy. Emboldened by this retraction and the perceived extremism of many Oneness advocates, Assemblies of God Chairman J. W. Welch (1858–1939) called for a Fourth General Council to decide the issue.

This crucial meeting opened at Bethel Chapel, St. Louis, on October 1, 1916. The trinitarian group was in complete control. Chairman Welch appointed a committee to draft the Statement of Fundamental Truths, and Bell was assigned to the committee. Any move toward a formal statement was bitterly opposed by the Jesus Only minority. So when a strongly worded trinitarian statement came out of committee and was adopted by the convention, the estranged group walked out and made plans to form their own denomination.[22] They met later in Indianapolis, under the leadership of G. T. Haywood, to form a new alliance, the Pentecostal Assemblies of the World (Synan 1971, 158).

The result of the Oneness controversy was that the Assemblies of God, barely two years old, lost 156 of 585 ministers and nearly 100 congregations (Flower n.d., 28). This bitter conflict was a watershed event in the history of the denomination. It clarified the Assemblies' self-definition along recognizably orthodox lines. Although the 1916 Statement of Fundamental Truths was doctrinally imprecise, it did serve to provide a basic framework upon which to build a self-perpetuating denomination.

The Initial Evidence Controversy

The question of whether tongues should be the only initial evidence of pentecostal baptism has been an internal question of the Assemblies of God from the beginning. The issue first became prominent shortly after the resolution of the Oneness controversy. At the Fourth General Council in October 1916, the delegates stated that Spirit-baptism should be understood as subsequent to salvation and that tongues should be seen as validation of the experience: "The baptism of believers in the Holy Ghost is witnessed by the initial physical sign of speaking with other tongues as the Spirit of God gives utterance" (Assemblies of God General Council 1916, 12–13).

This statement was adopted in large part to refute the Oneness position, which held that the trinitarian baptismal formula was invalid. If one was baptized in the name of Father, Son, and Holy Ghost, and then evidenced Spirit-baptism by speaking in tongues, the power within the traditional formula would be harder to dismiss.

Frederick F. Bosworth (1877–1958), a highly respected pioneer of the pentecostal movement and a prominent healer and evangelist, openly disputed the claim that tongues must inevitably follow upon Spirit-baptism. Bosworth's pentecostal credentials were impeccable. He had been identified with the restorationist impulse early on and directed John Alexander Dowie's musical band in Zion City. He had also been a delegate to the First General Council in Hot Springs. As a pentecostal preacher, he had endured ridicule and even physical assault. His Dallas-based healing ministry was considered one of the most successful pentecostal works to be found (see Etter 1916, 159–60, 172–75; Perkins 1927).

Fred Bosworth believed that the initial evidence position, which had been adopted in 1916, was too dogmatic and not scripturally supportable. In his 1918 pamphlet *Do All Speak with Tongues?* Bosworth summarized his position by saying that tongues was one gift among many. Any of the other charisms mentioned by Paul in 1 Cor. 12 were equally valid manifestations of Spirit-baptism. Requiring a physical manifestation destroyed the need for faith, which was the surest sign of the Holy Spirit's infilling. Bosworth concluded: "Proper instruction followed by consecration and prayer will in every instance bring down the baptism in the Holy Spirit, but it will not always bring down the manifestation of tongues" (1918, n.p.). Bosworth's outspoken views and high standing in the denomination made an implicit problem over the central importance of tongues explicit. Until Bosworth made tongues an issue, pentecostals had avoided conflicts over reconciling their view that Spirit-baptism was evidenced by tongues with Paul's long list of evidential gifts (R. M. Anderson 1979, 163).

When the 1918 General Council met at their new denominational headquarters in Springfield, Missouri, the question of initial evidence dominated the discussion. A majority of delegates decided it was necessary to distinguish the *sign* of tongues from the *gift* of tongues. They refused to accept Bosworth's view that there was no such distinction. The prevailing position was that tongues was a necessary initial sign of Spirit-baptism, although it might not be retained as a permanent spiritual gift.

A revised Statement of Faith included this sign-gift distinction. All Assemblies of God ministers were required to agree to the qualification. The ongoing insistence upon tongues as the initial evidence of baptism in the Holy Spirit has distanced the Assemblies from other pentecostal groups, such as the Church of God in Christ, which have held to a less definitive understanding (see Flower 1920).

Developments in the 1920s and 1930s

In the two decades following the Oneness and initial evidence controversies, the Assemblies experienced consolidation and considerable growth combined with noticeable isolation from other Christian groups. During this time, the denomination moved into early stages of maximum efficiency (see Moberg

1984, 120). This was marked by the emergence and growth of a leadership cadre that defined and emphasized long-term institutional goals while also limiting more extreme types of behavior. These limitations did not signal a loss of initial pentecostal energies, but rather a balancing of enthusiasm with the denomination's new internal structures.

In terms of ecumenism, a small attempt was made in 1921 to establish working relations with other pentecostal groups, but this effort never materialized.[23] The Protestant fundamentalists, another group with whom the Assemblies dearly wanted to identify, showed consistent antipathy toward all tongues speakers and dismissed them as wild-eyed sectarians. Tongues and other extraordinary spiritual manifestations were incompatible with the fundamentalists' more definitive worship styles. Moreover, many of the fundamentalists were strict dispensationalists who believed in a permanent cessation of the extraordinary charismata following the apostolic age. Thus they regarded tongues and the other pentecostal gifts as impossible in the present time.

In 1928, the World Christian Fundamentals Association adopted a resolution that declared pentecostalism to be both fanatical and unscriptural.[24] Stanley Frodsham (1882–1969), the editor of *Pentecostal Evangel,* responded quickly and without rancor: "Although we Pentecostal people have to be without the camp, we cannot afford to be bitter against those who do not see as we do. . . . So our business is to love the Fundamentalists and to pray, 'Lord, bless them all'" (1928, 7). Apart from negative reactions by many in the holiness and fundamentalist camps, pentecostals were generally ignored by the rest of the church world.

With the end of serious internal differences after 1918, the 1920s and 1930s proved to be a time of stabilization. In 1927, the General Council finally adopted a constitution, comprising a reformulation of various past resolutions. In 1929, Ernest S. Williams (1885–1981) began a twenty-year period as superintendent. During this long tenure, there was a large increase in membership and a consistent move toward greater centralization (Assemblies of God General Council 1941, 73–75).[25]

Missions have always been a denominational passion. As early as 1921, the General Council deliberated on criteria for missionaries receiving financial support (Assemblies of God General Council 1921, 16). Despite the proposal, missionaries remained independent for years and were expected to raise their own funds. In 1927, Noel Perkin (1893–1979), a missionary from England, took over the newly formed Missions Department and remained in charge until 1959. This extended leadership allowed for long-term strategies and successful indigenous church planting (McGee 1986, 97).

After a failed attempt at starting a denominational school in Nebraska in 1920, the Central Bible Institute was opened at Springfield, Missouri, in 1921. It was modeled upon the Christian Missionary Alliance school in Nyack, New York. There was opposition to the Central Bible Institute from those within the denomination who saw the Assemblies as sacrificing simple faith for formal education. Despite this early criticism, the Central Bible Institute survived. During the next twenty years, the Assemblies also extended ministerial recognition to graduates of other nondenominational schools. In 1937, the newly formed Department of Home Missions and Education oversaw the development of a number of regional Bible schools and began to coordinate national Sunday school programs (Menzies 1971, 151).

There was also a complete consolidation of denominational publications in 1919, with *Pentecostal Evangel* becoming the sole weekly voice (Assemblies of God General Council 1919, 24). The magazine's stability was ensured by the Englishman Stanley Frodsham, who was editor from 1919 to 1948. *Pentecostal Evangel* quickly developed the largest readership of any pentecostal publication in the United States. In 1936, the denomination also began daily broadcasts over Springfield's KWTO radio station.

The 1940s to the Present:
From Isolation to New Encounters

Increased Contacts

World War II brought the Assemblies of God out of isolation and into greater involvement with both the pentecostal and evangelical worlds. Young men and women from the denomination joined the military in large numbers, and Assemblies ministers served as military chaplains, a unique venture for a formerly pacifist denomination (see Robins 1984). These new contacts opened lines of communication between the Assemblies of God pentecostals and other Christian groups.

The Assemblies people in the military demonstrated their solidarity with evangelical Christians by helping to publish *Reveille,* an interdenominational newspaper. Open cooperation increased evangelical tolerance for pentecostalism's seemingly eccentric claims. Many evangelicals were also impressed with the denomination's commitment to foreign missions (Menzies 1971, 188–89). Nearly four hundred Assemblies of God missionaries were stationed in forty-three countries.

In April 1942, the Assemblies of God was one of several pentecostal groups invited to participate in a general evangelical gathering in St. Louis. This exploratory meeting was called to look into the possibilities of creating an organization that would define and aggressively represent evangelical interests. The result was the establishment of the National Association of Evangelicals. Some Assemblies leaders were skeptical that they would be coopted by fundamentalists in the new group. But Harold Ockenga (1905–1985), the prime architect of the National Association of Evangelicals, assured them that their views would be respected.

This opening by moderate evangelicals to the pentecostals led to a split between the National Association of Evangelicals and ultrafundamentalists. The fiery radio preacher, Carl McIntire (1906–), had formed his own group, the American Council of Christian Churches, in 1941. This organization attracted the most reactionary elements that had been forged by the fundamentalist-modernist controversy of the early twentieth century. McIntire made an overture to merge with the National Association of Evangelicals, but refused to agree to pentecostals being in the group.

In a tone reminiscent of some earlier critics, McIntire said:

"Tongues" is one of the great signs of apostasy. As true protestant denominations turn from the faith and it gets darker, the Devil comes more into the open, and people who are not fed in the old line denominations go out to the "tongues" movement, for they feel that they have some life (1944, 8).

Ockenga's group had to decide whether to accede to McIntire's demands or to allow the pentecostals in. By choosing for the pentecostals, the moderate evangelicals created a rift with the ultrafundamentalists that remains to this day. The Assemblies of God response to this show of support was one of gratitude, and they authorized a full voting delegation to the 1943 organizational meeting of the National Association of Evangelicals.[26]

During the late 1940s, pentecostal groups also concentrated on better communications among themselves. On May 7, 1948, leaders from the Assemblies of God met with representatives of seven other pentecostal denominations in Chicago. Following a second meeting in August 1948, the formal organization of the Pentecostal Fellowship of North America was announced in Des Moines. This alliance has never had more than advisory power, but it has helped project a united pentecostal voice on many issues (Synan 1971, 209), although Oneness and African-American pentecostals have never been involved.

The Assemblies of God emerged from the 1940s a vastly transformed group. They had moved from almost complete isolation to strongly identify with moderate and conservative evangelical interests. They had also moved to entertain certain common witness concerns by virtue of their new associations. But these were carefully prescribed concerns. There was both gain and loss in coming out of strict isolationism. The denomination lost its image of being ultrasectarian and gained a hearing in religious debates. With increased contacts, theological sophistication increased. The price to be paid for this move toward inclusion was the temptation to compromise classic pentecostal beliefs in the name of joint cooperation. Also, certain evangelical concerns, such as their insistence on the inerrancy of the Bible, came to dominate pentecostal consciousness. Finally, ecumenical contacts with mainline churches were precluded, since the National Association of Evangelicals adamantly refused to engage in conciliar efforts with either liberal Protestants or Catholics.

The New Order of the Latter Rain

By the late 1940s, the Assemblies of God gave every appearance of being a successful denomination. But success brought with it the problem of dissent, as serious disagreements grew over how to interpret the purposes of the movement in a changed situation. Dissenters believed the denomination was abandoning its pentecostal roots, and they wanted a return to what they perceived to be the original sources of glory and power. By doing this, they were reacting against increasing institutionalism and appealing to the restoration of a primitive ideal. The major expression of this idealism was the New Order of the Latter Rain, an extreme manifestation of the post–World War II phenomenon of revival and religious awakening (Hollenweger 1972, 353–76).

Other influences helped created an environment favorable to the New Order of the Latter Rain. Chief among these were the pentecostal ideal of local autonomy; the proliferation and popularity of controversial healing ministries; a stress on the transfer of power through the direct laying on of hands; a fascination with the spiritual benefits of asceticism and extreme fasting; and a renewed interest in the promise of the "new thing" prophesied in Isaiah 43:19, a favorite scriptural passage from earlier pentecostal revivals (see Riss 1979, 1988; Holdcroft 1980).

In 1947, George Hawtin (1909–), a Bible teacher, left the Pentecostal Assemblies of Canada in a dispute over doctrine. With some friends he formed his own school, the Sharon Bible Institute, in North Battleford, Saskatchewan. The Sharon Bible Institute, like earlier Bible schools, was devoted to "waiting on the Spirit," accompanied by extended periods of prayer and fasting. In the midst of an intense time of seeking on February 12, 1948, Hawtin reported that

> [God moved] in a strange new manner. Some students were under the power of God on the floor, others were kneeling in adoration and worship before the Lord. . . . The Lord spoke to one of the brethren. "Go and lay hands upon a certain student and pray for him." While he was in doubt and contemplation, one of the sisters who had been under the power of God, went to the brother saying the same words, and naming the identical student he was to pray for. He went in obedience and a revelation was given concerning the student's life and future ministry. After this a long prophecy was given,

with minute details concerning the great thing God was about to do. The pattern for the revival and many details concerning it were given (1949, 3–4).

Routinization had become common in pentecostal groups by the late 1940s, and many congregations lacked the depth of worship or the display of extraordinary gifts seen in the early days. The North Battleford Camp-Meeting Conventions were quickly promoted as a revived Feast of Tabernacles, where sagging pentecostal spirits could be revived. Within weeks, claims of extraordinary healings and predictive prophecy aroused popular interest. As Azusa Street had before it, the North Battleford revival attracted thousands of people from across Canada and the United States.

The comparison with the Azusa Street revival is apt. Both manifestations of spiritual enthusiasm arose in relation to larger evangelical awakenings. Both emphasized the laying on of hands to transmit spiritual gifts and powers. There were also strong eschatological tones in each revival. And, as many pentecostals had done with Azusa Street, they looked to the New Order of the Latter Rain to correct the deadening trend toward institutionalism (Brumback 1961, 331).

What began as an attempt to recover earlier sources of pentecostal power developed its own dynamic. The ability to transmit spiritual gifts, originally left to the sovereign initiative of the Holy Spirit, was soon said to reside in human beings. These individuals were prophetically revealed to be a new line of apostles. It was also claimed that a "blaze of prophetic light" gave these people the power to unveil the lives and innermost thoughts of others simply by the laying on of hands (Riss 1988, 533).

Claims to present-day apostolic authority grew ever bolder, challenging even the primacy of Scripture with claims to special revelation. The North Battleford group answered their critics simply, by denouncing them as apostate. As the Canadian group became more sectarian, it shifted its energies from evangelism to a discerning of the elect. This inward look caused even some of the most fervent early supporters to back off. For most pentecostals, extreme claims discredited the New Order of the Latter Rain.

The New Order of the Latter Rain had its strongest backers among independent pentecostal groups. But concerns about potential defections by Assemblies of God congregations caused the leadership to react directly. In 1949, General Secretary Ernest S. Williams wrote two essays in the *Pentecostal Evangel* defending the Assemblies against the Latter Rain charges of lukewarmness (Williams 1949a; 1949b). He argued that the primary purpose of prophetic office was to teach and not to direct. In what appears to be a faulty exegesis, Williams said that the biblical laying on of hands was better understood as a democratic "showing of hands" for public ordination. He pointedly questioned whether it was possible for present day apostles to exist and expressed concerned that embracing such a novel doctrine would lead to a loss of prudence:

> It [Scripture] teaches that there is a sense of reverent dignity that attends a properly conducted worship service. God help us that divine things may never become commonplace. Let us look to God that He may come forth by the Spirit in our midst, but let us not feel that this gives license for excesses or abuses (1949a, 2).

On April 20, 1949, Assemblies ministers were informed by the Executive Presbytery that the New Order of the Latter Rain was a fringe group that had strayed from the truth by insisting upon their own understanding of revelation and apostolic office. The movement was to be assiduously avoided (see Assemblies of God Executive Presbytery 1949).

The Salvation-Healing Movement

Although the New Order of the Latter Rain did not cause the Assemblies of God nearly the degree of strife that the Oneness issue had, it did present a potentially serious challenge. There were some, such as Stanley Frodsham, the long-time editor of *Pentecostal Evangel,* who resigned from the denomination to avoid further conflict. The controversy also raised the question of the extent to which the denomination should allow independent expression under its name. This question had never been adequately addressed. Assemblies-licensed ministers in the postwar Salvation-Healing movement helped bring the issue to a head.

The pivotal figure in igniting the Salvation-Healing movement was an impoverished Baptist preacher from Kentucky,
William Branham (1909–1965). He claimed that on the night
of May 7, 1946, he was visited by an angel who told him that
he would have a unique healing ministry. The sign that healing power was to be upon Branham would be a warm tin-
gling in his left hand. He reported the essence of the angelic
message as follows:

> Fear not. I am sent from the presence of almighty God to
> tell you that your peculiar life and misunderstood ways
> have been to indicate that God has sent you to take a
> gift of divine healing to the peoples of the world. If you
> will be sincere, and can get people to believe you, noth-
> ing shall stand before your prayer, not even cancer
> (Lindsay 1950, 77).

Branham claimed to be under constant angelic guidance. This
voice also helped him name the sins and the sicknesses of
those attending his meetings. His presence was mesmerizing.
At times, he was crowned by what appeared to be a halo, a
phenomenon that "remains a legend unparalleled in the history of the charismatic movement" (Harrell 1976, 162).

Gordon Lindsay (1906–1973), an Assemblies of God pastor
from Ashland, Oregon, was especially moved by Branham's
healing message. Lindsay quit his pastorate in 1947 in order to
manage Branham's growing ministry. In 1948, he began to
publish *Voice of Healing* in order to promote the ministry.
Soon Lindsay expanded the scope of the magazine to include
reports from other healing ministries, most of them conducted
by Assemblies of God ministers. This move toward greater
inclusion alienated Branham, and he and Lindsay broke off
relations. In the spring of 1950, Lindsay founded an association of healing evangelists, also known as the Voice of
Healing, which became the principal vehicle for promoting
Salvation-Healing revivals worldwide as well as for reporting
alleged healings.

The Assemblies of God initially welcomed the Salvation-
Healing movement as a source of new vitality among pentecostals. But concerns grew over both the claims and the

actions of many extremists within the movement. A special concern was that the popular, Assemblies-licensed independent healers were becoming too extravagant in their claims and life-styles.[27] A more systematic concern was the growing sense that signs and wonders were being promoted as the summit of Christian achievement (Beuther 1952, 11). By the spring of 1952, the Assemblies of God began a concerted campaign to promote sanctity as more important to Christian living than spectacular displays of supernatural power. Criticism increased to the point that *Pentecostal Evangel* refused to print independent reports of healings after 1953 (Brumback 1961, 331).

Lindsay worked to prevent an open split between the organizational Assemblies of God and Assemblies-licensed healing evangelists. Some of these ministries were conciliatory (Harrell 1976, 109). But an open break took place in 1953 when Jack Coe (1918–1956), a highly controversial independent healer, was informed that the Texas district was withdrawing its support: "Your methods and activities bring reproach upon the General Council Ministry, indicate a spirit of insubordination, constitute a breach of fellowship, and show a lack of proper appreciation for Council fellowship" (Flower 1953, 26). The denomination censured Coe and suspended his ministerial license. This increased pressure upon all licensed independents to either conform to standards or leave.

A. A. Allen (1911–1970), another prominent healing evangelist, chose to join Coe in castigating the moribund state of the Assemblies of God, which "instead of the old time revival service which brought men face to face with doom . . . offers form, ceremonies, rituals, ordinances and . . . 'inoffensive' preaching" (Allen n.d., 28). Repelled by such severe characterizations, even many Assemblies supporters of Coe, Allen, and the other independents joined the leadership in endorsing only those healing revivals sponsored by the denomination.

The General Presbytery reaffirmed belief in divine healing in 1952 (Assemblies of God General Presbytery 1952, 14–15) but later rejected the "unscriptural, unethical, and extravagant practices" of many independent ministries (Assemblies of God General Presbytery 1956, 20). Other ministers were discouraged from joining nondenominational associations, such as Lindsay's Voice of Healing. Many licensed independents refused to abide by these new restrictions and severed their denominational ties.

By the 1950s, the Assemblies of God had begun to formalize a style of reaction to dissenters. This was basically a bureaucratic response, in which decisions about new views were made by an inner circle (see Moberg 1984, 121). A force behind increasingly centralized decision making was General Superintendent Thomas Zimmerman (1912–) who oversaw the denomination from 1959 to 1985. Zimmerman became known for his hands-on and, at times, overbearing leadership style.

This bureaucratic approach had increased markedly by the 1960s, along with the tendency to identify the denomination's interests with those of conservative evangelicals. By this point an argument could be made that many Assemblies leaders, while maintaining a nominal allegiance to the pentecostal heritage, in reality were operating in ways divergent from the original ideals of the movement.

The Ecumenical Issue

By joining the National Association of Evangelicals, the Assemblies of God adopted that group's attitude toward ecumenism, namely that interdenominational efforts such as the National Council of Churches were attempts to create an apostate world church. That anti-ecumenical stance was openly challenged by one of the denomination's best known ambassadors for Spirit-baptism, David du Plessis (1905–1987) (see Robinson 1987).

Du Plessis directed his early ecumenical energies at fostering unity among classical pentecostals; that is, those groups who traced their origins back to either Charles Parham or the Azusa Street revival. In 1952, du Plessis met John Mackay, the president of Princeton Seminary. Mackay introduced him to the organized ecumenical movement, as represented by the National Council of Churches. Du Plessis was well received. Hearkening back to the original pentecostal call for unity— based in the shared experience of Spirit-baptism—du Plessis insisted on the importance of Spirit-baptism as a norm for Christian living. His persistent message earned him the title "Mr. Pentecost."

Du Plessis's reputation as a pentecostal ecumenist increased, and his denomination became extremely critical of him. In 1962, the Executive Presbytery "disfellowshipped" du Plessis for his ecumenical activities (see du Plessis 1979).[28] General Superintendent Thomas Zimmerman had just been elected president of the National Association of Evangelicals. Du Plessis long held that the revoking of his ministerial license was connected to Zimmerman's attempt at placating evangelicals and pentecostals who were incensed by du Plessis's ecumenical activities. By the early 1960s, the irrepressible du Plessis was actively meeting with mainline Protestants and had been invited as the only pentecostal observer to the third session of Vatican II.

Du Plessis maintained his membership in the Assemblies of God throughout this difficult period. He was reinstated as a minister in good standing in 1980, although denominational reaction to his ecumenical efforts remained ambivalent at best. The Assemblies has maintained an official stance against ecumenism to this day, although some individuals are deeply involved in the movement informally. For his part, du Plessis maintained the unofficial status of ambassador for Spirit-baptism until his death in 1987.

Recent Challenges

Since the 1960s, the major challenges to classical pentecostalism have come from new charismatic groups with differing doctrinal emphases. The Assemblies of God had virtually assumed that its interpretation of pentecostal experience was normative, and the charismatic surge caught many in the denomination off guard. In particular, traditional pentecostal mores (such as abstaining from drinking, smoking, and dancing) were called into question by some of these new groups. The evident fact was that pentecostal gifts were being experienced by Christians who did not embrace the classical pentecostal ethos with its strongly held holiness standards.

Assemblies leaders reacted cautiously to the new pentecostal surge, although most were anxious to identify with what "God was doing in the world" (Blumhofer 1988, 28). There were obvious signs of this ambivalence at the 1963 General Council, which condemned ecumenism while also giving measured support to the charismatics in the mainline denominations, offering them the wisdom of a senior movement (Assemblies of God General Council 1963, 41). The numerous charismatic groups have remained a source of perplexity, and charismatics continue to be considered divisive and emotionally unbalanced by some classical pentecostals.[29]

In 1968, the Assemblies of God held special meetings to discuss their evangelistic mission to a changing world. These were pivotal gatherings, representing an active attempt to respect and reach out to other pentecostal expressions, including the Catholic charismatics. At that time, there was even a tentative acknowledgment that certain aspects of denominational theology might be open to reexamination. But no specific proposals were advanced or acted upon (see Council on Evangelism 1968).

More recently, the Assemblies has had to face a powerful alternative voice in new independent charismatic groups, which affiliate with neither classical pentecostalism nor the historic churches. These independent charismatics have provided a challenge that is potentially as severe as any of the historic controversies. The challenge lies not only in the independent charismatics' more exuberant worship styles but also in their new theological emphases.

People who came into pentecostal experience in the 1960s realized that they could not express themselves openly in traditional church settings. Some joined charismatic movements within their denominations. Some embraced classical pentecostal options, particularly the Assemblies of God. Still others chose to affiliate with independent charismatic fellowships. The pursuit of spiritual fulfillment accompanied by a nomadic moving from meeting to meeting came to characterize many of these early charismatics. By the late 1960s, this pattern became a matter of concern to some Protestant charismatic leaders. The decisions of these leaders primarily affected their own charismatic groups but indirectly strongly influenced individual Assemblies of God congregations.

The Shepherding-Discipleship movement attempted to reverse nomadic patterns. It was closely identified with the Christian Growth Ministries of Fort Lauderdale, Florida, a group that published the popular Protestant charismatic magazine *New Wine*. The members of Christian Growth Ministries became convinced that a tighter system of accountability among charismatics was essential. Their attempt to gain greater control of behavior was intended to perfect Christian discipleship through submission.[30]

In 1969, six of the Christian Growth people—Bob Mumford, Derek Prince, Charles Simpson, Ern Baxter, Don Basham, and John Poole—claimed to have received a special anointing from the Holy Spirit directing them to define the lines of authority for other charismatic groups. They covenanted together in a relationship of mutual submission and offered themselves as a panel of elders to help organize a nationwide network based upon patterns of strict submission.

Although this group claimed to be reluctant to form a new denomination, there was soon a pyramidal structure organized around rigid lines of authority. Abuses were soon reported, such as an Oral Roberts University student "shepherd" (that is, one who exercised authority over another in the movement) who began collecting tithes for personal use from his fellow students. Bob Mumford, perhaps the most vocal of the group, was reported to have told his followers: "Go into your church, look around, and get yourself four new [disciples]. Steal them out of your own congregation" (Lattin 1984, 1). Thus a concern also grew that people were being proselytized out of existing churches and into a new Shepherding structure.

The controversy came to a head in 1975. On May 22, Pat Robertson, the founder of the Christian Broadcasting Network, issued a memo describing Shepherding as a cult "vastly worse than anything I could have conceived of." He ordered that all videotapes featuring the six leaders be erased immediately. On June 27, Robertson wrote Mumford an open letter, charging that the leaders were putting their alleged revelation on an equal level with Scripture. Robertson also claimed that the Shepherding system had become extremely oppressive, forcing individuals to divulge intimate details of their lives.

Robertson's open accusations reflected the private concerns of many pentecostal leaders over the increasing influence of the new movement. David du Plessis organized a meeting at Ann Arbor, Michigan, in December 1975 in an attempt to resolve the problem, but his effort failed. By early 1976, the issues surrounding the Shepherding movement were threatening to erupt and split the entire pentecostal-charismatic world.

Leaders from numerous pentecostal and charismatic groups met again March 8–12, 1976, in Oklahoma City, Oklahoma, and a consensus emerged. All participants agreed that allegations of heresy against the Christian Growth Ministries group were unfounded. There was a call to end public attacks upon the Shepherding-Discipleship position. For their part, the Fort Lauderdale group issued a conciliatory statement:

> We realize that controversies and problems have arisen among Christians in various areas as a result of our teaching in relation to subjects such as submission, discipline, shepherding. We deeply regret these problems and, insofar as they are due to fault on our part, we ask forgiveness from our fellow believers whom we have offended.
>
> We realize that our teachings, though we believe them to be essentially sound, have in various places been misapplied or handled in an immature way; and that this has caused problems for our brothers in the ministry. We deeply regret this and ask for forgiveness. Insofar as it lies in our power, we will do our best to correct these situations and to restore any broken relationships (Charismatic Leaders Conference Report 1976, n. p.).

The Assemblies of God was not formally represented at the March 1976 Oklahoma City meeting because the leadership viewed the Shepherding controversy as basically a charismatic problem. The official reaction of the Assemblies to the pentecostal newcomers may indicate the degree to which the denomination had moved toward identifying its interests with conservative evangelicalism. Nevertheless, the General Presbytery released a major statement entitled "The Discipleship and Submission Movement" in August 1976 dictating a real concern over the disruptive potential of the movement (Assemblies of God General Presbytery 1976).

The report acknowledged that Shepherding's disciplined principles filled a vacuum in the spiritual lives of some new believers. But it warned against the danger of overt guidance, where a convert could fail to develop any ability to discern the Scriptures personally and could thus fall prey to false teachings. Shepherding's central problem was its over-allegorization of the image of the church as the body of Christ, which led to an inflated emphasis on submission to the Shepherding head. The Shepherding-Discipleship leaders were not accused of false doctrine, but their model for subordination was portrayed as too rigid and thus as injurious for Assemblies of God congregations: "No one is to take arbitrary authority over others even to protect them" (Assemblies of God General Presbytery 1976, 10).

The influence of Shepherding-Discipleship had waned to near nonexistence by the late 1970s. But, in the early 1980s, another very strong challenge to the traditional values of the Assemblies of God began to come from an informal collection of Positive Confession thinkers. These views again became strong among many independent charismatic churches and began to influence classical pentecostals. Positive Confession proponents (Kenneth Hagin, Kenneth Copeland, Fred Price, Charles Capps, and others) have their ideological roots in the teachings of E. W. Kenyon (1867–1948), an early twentieth-century evangelist and Bible teacher.

While attending the Emerson College of Oratory in Boston, Kenyon encountered the claims of the new mind sciences such as parapsychology and hypnosis. He rejected what he saw as the scientific shamanism of this New Thought philosophy and maintained a belief in the central truths of Christianity. But Kenyon's contact with New Thought ideas caused him to elevate his view of Christians' ability to influence their own circumstances. He began to promote the potential available in the positive confession of the word of God (see Kenyon and Gossett 1981).

Positive Confession has been further developed by Kenyon's modern-day disciples. Chief among these is Kenneth Hagin (1917–), whose Rhema Bible Training Center in Broken Arrow, Oklahoma, has become a center for the movement. Hagin has argued that in order for Christians to be heard in prayer they must come to God with absolute confidence and creative imagination:

[Positive Confession] centers around five things. First, what God in Christ has wrought for us in the plan of redemption. Second, what God through the Word and the Holy Spirit has wrought in us in the New Birth and infilling of the Holy Ghost. Third, what we are to God the Father in Christ Jesus. Fourth, what Jesus is doing for us now, at the right hand of the Father, where He ever liveth to make intercession for us. Fifth, what God can do through us, or what His Word will do through our lips (Hagin 1979a, 82–83).

In Positive Confession, the burden of performance for fulfilled prayer shifts from God to the believer. Through the power of the tongue the believer influences situations and creates results. It is incumbent to ask without doubt, first confessing one's status as a redeemed child of God. After the claim has been established, the believer is to hold fast to scriptural promises concerning the effects of unwavering faith (such as Mark 11:23–24). Finally, upon receiving that which has been claimed, the believer is to proclaim and praise the power of God (Hagin 1978, 82–83). Thus Positive Confession involves what Hagin has called the *rhema,* or "now word," principle, meaning that whatever a Christian speaks forth in the present and with confident faith is creatively inspired and comes to pass.

Many proponents of Positive Confession have even insisted that faith-filled Christians can confess themselves into financial prosperity. Hagin echoed this view when he wrote that "our lips can make us millionaires or keep us paupers" (Hagin 1979c, 5). The key principle in play here is that all that has been promised under prior covenants is understood to be contained and activated within the New Covenant. Thus Christians are considered as direct beneficiaries of the material promises of the Abrahamic Covenant. A key Scripture cited is Galatians 3:13–14:

Christ hath redeemed us from the curse of the law, being made a curse for us: for it is written, cursed is every one that hangeth on a tree: That the blessing of Abraham

might come on the Gentiles through Jesus Christ; that we
might receive the promise of the Spirit through faith.

This blessing, released through Christ's atonement, is understood to include both material and spiritual well-being.

Kenneth Copeland (1937–), whose ministry is based in Fort
Worth, Texas, has maintained close ties with Hagin. He puts
an even greater emphasis upon the material benefits to be
gained from Positive Confession and has written of the potential for using this device for a radical economic revolution:

> The largest miracle [in coming world revival] will be in
> the area of finances. God will make Godly men and
> women more wealthy than people serving Satan. The
> Bible says that the wealth of sinners is laid up for the just.
> . . . There's going to be a financial revival (1979, 23).

Positive Confession advocates have a traditional pentecostal
belief in divine healing, but they push their claims much further. Since healing was provided for in the Atonement, the
believer has a claim upon health. Divine healing is not only
available, it is to be expected. When summoned forth with
full faith, physical health can be positively claimed as a right
(Hagin 1979b, 15). By extending the argument, poor health
can be said to show an inadequate measure of personal faith.

The Assemblies of God Executive Presbytery reacted
strongly against this popular new teaching with a position
paper on August 19, 1980. "The Life of Faith" recognized the
importance of faith to Christian living, but it characterized the
Positive Confession movement as extremist. The basic concern was that such reckless thinking could tempt people to try
to manipulate God in order to get results. This was seen as a
vain attempt to make human beings sovereign and God a servant of their wandering desires. Another concern was that
scriptural passages were being isolated and thus distorted:

> When the positive confession teaching indicates that to
> admit weakness is to accept defeat, to admit financial
> need is to accept poverty, and to admit weakness is to
> preclude healing, it is going beyond and is contrary to

the harmony of Scripture (Assemblies of God Executive Presbytery 1980, 8).

A particular aberration described was Positive Confession's tendency to substitute confession for traditional petitionary prayer. The Assemblies' position was that importunate prayer should be understood as a sign of obedience and faith rather than of weakness and doubt.

Because *rhema* and *logos* are used interchangeably to indicate the Word of God in Scripture, the special *rhema* ("now word") doctrine was dismissed as insupportable. In summary, Positive Confession promoters were chastised for being "more concerned with making the Word mean what they want it to mean than in becoming what the Word wants them to become" (ibid., 21). A preeminent concern of the Assemblies of God was that such an extreme teaching would disillusion those that became enamored of it and destroy legitimate trust in God's promises.

The Assemblies has encountered yet another external challenge from what is called Kingdom Now thinking.[31] This is not a pentecostal phenomenon per se, but it has gained an audience among pentecostal churches. Kingdom Now advocates believe that a postmillennial eschaton has already begun and that the newly militant church will usher in social and political transformation. At the center of their beliefs is the concept of theonomy, which is understood to be a state of universal adherence to Old Testament laws and practices, especially in the area of judicial decisions. The stress is on orthopraxy rather than orthodoxy, with faith being understood more in terms of externalized practice than internalized belief:

> It [theonomy] proclaims that through the exercise of saving faith and through ethical conformity to God's revealed law, regenerate men will increase the extent of their dominion over the earth. It is a religion of conquest—conquest through ethics (North 1987, 45).

Bishop Earl P. Paulk, Jr., is the most visible Kingdom Now spokesperson. Paulk grew up in a classical pentecostal household, the son of an overseer in the Church of God of Cleveland, Tennessee. In 1960, he began the Gospel Harvester Church in inner-city Atlanta. This church experienced immense growth and moved to the Atlanta suburbs in 1973. In 1982 Paulk became a bishop in the International Communion of Charismatic Churches. This alignment of pentecostals has an episcopal government and emphasizes the aggressive transformation of society. Paulk actively promoted his Kingdom Now views through a nationwide telecast, "Thy Kingdom Come."

The Assemblies of God leaders began to question Paulk's Kingdom Now teachings in December 1986, when he attended a Christian Leadership Summit Conference in Springfield, Missouri. At that time, Paulk's theological views were publicly refuted. In August 1987, the General Presbytery issued a white paper on Kingdom Now thinking. They expressed special concerns with what they saw as deviations from the Assemblies of God's Statement of Fundamental Truths. The presbyters were also disturbed by what they interpreted as Paulk's manipulation of the Scriptures in order to promote his Kingdom Now views.

Specific criticisms included (1) Paulk's diminishment of the primary authority of Scripture, as when he wrote, "A prophet is not to be judged" (Paulk 1984, 125), thus seeming to put modern-day revelations beyond normal scrutiny; (2) the position that the millennium has already begun; (3) the assertion that God had abrogated the covenant with the nation of Israel; (4) the transferral of scriptural references concerning Israel to the church; and (5) the argument that believers were "little gods" and could even conquer death: "Until the mature body of Christ challenges death as a group of people, the end cannot come" (Paulk 1985, 255) The presbyters argued that Kingdom Now insistency upon the primacy of present revelation left it open to constant variation, much as the New Order of the Latter Rain had done.

In his defense, Paulk claimed that Assemblies of God leaders had been unwilling to dialogue with him honestly on the issues. He argued that his views were misrepresented in the Assemblies of God white paper and that the special nature of the times demanded extreme measures:

The urgency of this hour will not permit men of faith to be intimidated by accusations and misunderstandings. There is a curse upon one's silence when God has

commanded boldness in our witness. There is a time to
be silent and a time to speak. The trumpet of God is
sounding around the world in this hour. God is saying,
"Sound the alarm! The Kingdom is at hand!" If we do not
speak, the stones will cry out (1985, 5).

There has been no official dialogue between the Assemblies
and Paulk since the issuance of the white paper.[32]

Conclusion

From the beginning, the founders of the Assemblies of God
realized that their common spiritual identity was tied to their
narratives of personal experience. Thus they were reluctant to
impose a standard of pentecostal orthodoxy upon all; they
envisioned the Assemblies as a vehicle where all could witness
to pentecostal experience in a loosely unified but non-doctri-
naire fashion. But they quickly suffered for this aversion to formal organization when they became embroiled in the Oneness
furor. The resulting loss of about a fourth of the denomination's membership pointed out the need for more order.

What followed was a deliberate move toward formalizing
church structures and defining common goals. Such an
approach, once begun, was repeatable. Challenges to the
emerging organizational style, usually based on so-called
special revelations did emerge from time to time. But these
challenges were overcome, both through the General Councils and, increasingly, through the pronouncements of the
Executive Presbytery. The congregational aspect of the
Assemblies of God polity, where autonomy was designed to
offset too great a reliance on centralized decision making,
often did lessen the impact of these formal positions.

In the 1920s, 1930s, and well into the 1940s, major doctrinal
disputes were rare. The Assemblies of God moved, with a
high degree of internal efficiency, toward maximum self-
definition. Increased contacts during World War II brought the
Assemblies new admirers, evangelical Christians who were
impressed with the denomination's commitment to missions
and its overall zeal to proclaim the gospel. These new contacts led the Assemblies out of isolation and into formal identification with the newly formed National Association of

Evangelicals. The result was a limited type of common witness with conservative evangelicals.

The move outward in the 1940s had mixed results. It brought the Assemblies of God from the margins and into the midst of certain contemporary religious debates. Such increased contacts, with their formal and informal alliances, could be viewed as beneficial. But acceptance in the evangelical world also tended to obscure the Assemblies of God's original mission. This was tied to the proclamation of the special transformative powers of Spirit-baptism and, particularly, its capacity to unite all Christians. That unique proclamation was compromised to the point of silence in an effort to identify with conservative evangelical interests.

After World War II, the Assemblies again found itself confronted by radical doctrinal claims. These came from restorationist elements such as the New Order of the Latter Rain and the Salvation-Healing movement. By the late 1940s, these dissenters were charging that the Assemblies of God had grown lukewarm and overly institutionalized. These claims amounted to an accusation that the leadership cadre had forgotten the original purposes of the pentecostal movement. Institutional forces, of course, vigorously refuted these charges and excluded the dissenters.

Since the 1960s, a new and even more complex set of challenges has come from the outside and influenced individual Assemblies of God congregations. The various charismatic views have proved to be especially perplexing. Some classical pentecostals see them as a positive challenge to denominational complacency. Others, while not denying the validity of the charismatics' pentecostal experience, question what they see to be suspect doctrines, extravagant worship styles, and frequent departures from traditional holiness standards. Questions about how—or whether—to relate with these charismatic groups remain.

By the 1970s and the 1980s, independent forces such as Shepherding-Discipleship, Positive Confession, and even Kingdom Now thinking began to affect the Assemblies of God. These new challenges have led to further attempts to elaborate the denomination's self-understanding as well as to establish the relevance of the classical pentecostal tradition for the present.

This current atmosphere of rapid change has a bearing on pentecostal common witness efforts. A key challenge for pentecostals with an ecumenical vision approaching Assemblies of God pentecostals (aside from the present probability of outright rejection) involves helping them understand and then recover their historic vision of transdenominational unity.

Such an appeal will not be easy, especially given the present ambiguity about internal identity in the denomination. The questioning begins with whether the members still see themselves primarily as classical pentecostals or whether, in practice, they have become indistinguishable from conservative evangelicals.

Edith Blumhofer, the foremost historian of the Assemblies of God,[33] described another most formidable internal issue in a 1987 essay. This is the question of affluence. The traditional pentecostal stance has been one of radical separation from contemporary social values. This position has declined since members have been exposed to other pentecostals who advocate a prosperity gospel, where material blessings are considered a sign of divine favor and not as a moral dilemma. The result has been a gradual and barely conscious embrace by many of a secular values system.

Blumhofer wondered whether the very nature of the denomination's basic witness is not in the balance: "The Assemblies of God is at a crossroads and must choose which style and identity to embrace. . . . But that could involve the splintering of the denomination" (1987, 431). What she portrays is a tension that could become a preoccupation. Added to this is the free-spirited approach, which marked the Assemblies in the first place, coming into conflict with the frequently bureaucratic way in which the leadership now speaks. The crucial question for the Assemblies of God today is, what will be the agreed standard that can bind all of these disparate energies together?

The Catholic
Charismatic Renewal

The early history of the Catholic charismatic renewal is closely identified with Vatican II reforms. During the first decade of their existence, the Catholic charismatics underwent a shift from extreme optimism concerning the potential for pentecostal common witness to an attitude of much greater forbearance. Despite this move to restraint, Catholic charismatics have generally been much more open to ecumenical possibilities than have classical pentecostals. This spirit of openness to ecumenism, coupled with a largely positive history of relating with other pentecostals, distinguishes charismatic renewal attitudes from those of the Assemblies of God.

The Early Years, 1966–70

Revival Breaks Out

Catholic charismatics trace their origins to a series of events at Pittsburgh's Duquesne University during 1966 and early 1967 (see Ranaghan and Ranaghan 1969; O'Connor 1971). In August 1966, William Storey, a lay history instructor at Duquesne, attended the National Congress of the Cursillo movement, a high-commitment encounter group intent on enhancing specifically Catholic spirituality. Of the antecedents to the Catholic charismatic renewal, none has been more significant than the Cursillo movement (see O'Connor 1975). Steve Clark and Ralph Martin, coordinators for student activities at a parish in East Lansing, Michigan, were also at the meeting and introduced Storey to two books that they found provocative.

David Wilkerson's *The Cross and the Switchblade* described the ministry of a small town Assemblies of God clergyman from North Carolina who had felt the call of God to preach to street gang members and drug addicts in New York City. The latter part of Wilkerson's book dramatically testified to the spiritual powers available in Spirit-baptism. The other book, *They Speak with Other Tongues,* was written by John Sherrill, a reporter for the *New York Times.* In his book, Sherrill gave an account of the pentecostal explosion among mainline Protestants and witnessed to the reality of pentecostal experience in terms similar to Wilkerson's. Sherrill's research led him to experience Spirit-baptism, and he described his subsequent involvement with the Episcopal charismatic renewal.

Storey purchased a copy of *The Cross and the Switchblade* and passed it on to Ralph Keifer, a friend of his who taught in the Duquesne theology department. Keifer later purchased *They Speak with Other Tongues,* which he then gave to Storey. Both men had been involved in campus apostolates associated with various Vatican II reforms. They had become disillusioned by the sense of spiritual powerlessness that they felt in their ministries. Both were also convinced that the Catholic Church needed a fresh experience of spiritual empowerment if it were to effectively witness to the faith. They were anxious to find out if Spirit-baptism could be that special source of power.

Storey and Keifer became increasingly convinced that they needed to look seriously into pentecostal claims. Because of past bad experiences with classical pentecostals, in which they had felt pressure to conform to fundamentalist theology, they sought out a gathering of Protestant charismatics in the Pittsburgh area. Their search led them to William Lewis, an

Episcopal rector, who put them in touch with an interdenominational prayer group led by Florence Dodge, a charismatic Presbyterian.

On January 13, 1967, Storey, Keifer, and two other Catholics attended an interdenominational pentecostal prayer meeting but left with a sense of ambivalence. The following week, Keifer and Patrick Bourgeois, a Catholic graduate student at Duquesne, returned to the prayer group. They asked that hands be laid upon them to receive Spirit-baptism. Keifer broke out in tongues immediately and, several days later, both Storey and Bourgeois experienced tongues as Keifer prayed over them.

The three men discreetly began to describe their experience to friends at Duquesne. By the middle of February 1967, approximately thirty students from the Chi Ro Society, a campus fellowship, had read *The Cross and the Switchblade*. The group decided to spend a weekend together to pray over the validity of the book's pentecostal claims.

On Friday, February 18, they gathered at a rural retreat house. As Charles Parham's group had done in 1901, they decided to begin by studying the first two chapters of Acts of the Apostles. Saturday night, February 19, had been set aside for a birthday party for one of the priests on the retreat. During the celebration, an engaged couple approached Ralph Keifer, asking whether he would pray with them to receive Spirit-baptism. The three went upstairs, and both the young man and the young woman began to speak in tongues.

At the same time, Patti Gallagher, another student, left the party to visit the camp's chapel. There she reportedly "felt the almost tangible presence of the Spirit of Christ" (Ranaghan and Ranaghan 1969, 22). Gallagher left the chapel and urged others to join her there, which they did by ones and twos. Storey and Keifer, who had been privately ministering in another part of the building, also decided to see what was going on.

In the chapel, they found twenty-five persons in various states of fervent prayer. Spiritual enthusiasm ranged from small group exclamations of praise and song to full-length prostrations on the floor. Keifer and Storey prayed with students and several more broke out in tongues. This impromptu prayer meeting went on from nine that night until five the next morning. This event became known as the Duquesne Weekend, and it was the first Catholic charismatic revival meeting.

The Early Spread

It is essential to note that a web of informal relationships had developed during the 1960s among young Catholics who were involved in various apostolates at Notre Dame, Duquesne, and other universities. This intercampus networking was an essential aspect in the early spread of the renewal (O'Connor 1971, 44–47). These young people, in the spirit of post–Vatican II experimentation, were open to religious experience and new ideas. Throughout 1967, the Catholic charismatic renewal spread mainly on college campuses, which also provided the nucleus of the early leadership (see Connelly 1971, 211–32).

Keifer, a part of this intercampus network, sent a letter relating the events of the Duquesne Weekend to several of his acquaintances on other campuses (Keifer 1972, 1). In early March 1967, a meeting was held to discuss the import of this letter at the South Bend home of Kevin and Dorothy Ranaghan, graduate students in theology at Notre Dame. Both were active in campus ministries, especially the liturgical movement. Storey, who was interviewing for a teaching job at Notre Dame at the time, was also present at the gathering. He reported the events at Duquesne and got a friendly, if somewhat cautious, reception.

The next evening, Storey met with those who wanted to know more about what was happening at Duquesne. They gathered at the home of Ray Bullard, the president of the South Bend Full Gospel Businessmen's chapter and a deacon at the local Assemblies of God church. Bullard was concerned about his ability to communicate to a group of university-educated people and asked other experienced pentecostals to attend the meeting and help him with any explanations.

During the course of the evening, the nine Catholics attending asked to be prayed over for Spirit-baptism. After imposition of hands, seven of the nine began praying in tongues (see O'Connor 1971, 47–48; Ranaghan and Ranaghan 1969,

41–42). Kevin and Dorothy Ranaghan described the sense of unity they experienced that night as follows:

> The people with whom we were meeting were mostly from an evangelical background. They spoke with a scriptural and theological fundamentalism that was very foreign to us. Furthermore, the way they spoke and prayed, the type of hymns they sang—all this was so different that at first it was very disturbing. . . . Yet, in spite of these personal differences, we were enabled to come together in common faith in Jesus, in the one experience of His Holy Spirit, to worship our Father together. That was no human achievement. The Holy Spirit simply cut across these cultural barriers to unite us as brothers and sisters in Christ (1969, 41–42).

In the next few weeks an interdenominational prayer group emerged, composed of interested Catholics and classical pentecostals. News of an outbreak of Catholic pentecostalism at Notre Dame grew by word of mouth. By Easter 1967, thirty Catholics were actively involved in the new prayer group.

Keifer also reported the events of the Duquesne Weekend to Steve Clark and Ralph Martin, the two youth coordinators from Michigan State who had introduced the Wilkerson and Sherrill books. In March 1967, Clark and Martin traveled to Duquesne, where they experienced Spirit-baptism. They returned to East Lansing and immediately formed their own charismatic prayer group.

Clark and Martin had extensive ties with Notre Dame, since both had been active in the Antioch Weekend ministry there during their student days. Antioch Weekends were developed by the Cursillo movement in order to initiate Notre Dame undergraduates into the movement. Antioch Weekends offered Notre Dame students an intensive retreat experience followed up by weekly meetings to reinforce their newly formed commitments (see Word of God community 1969; Manney 1973).

In April 1967, Clark and Martin were invited to bring an entourage of forty-five people from East Lansing to join a group of a similar size at Notre Dame. Their purpose was to seek divine guidance for the new movement; beyond that there was no planned agenda. Word of this meeting got out to the local pentecostal community in South Bend, and many classical pentecostals joined in.

At this point, disputes over doctrine had not yet emerged to dim the glow of shared exuberance over the Spirit-baptism experience. Traditional denominational barriers between Catholics and classical pentecostals seemed to come down quickly and the nightly prayer sessions became free-wheeling marathons, with participants being Spirit-baptized, praying in tongues, and prophesying. The unexpectedly large size of the gathering forced the participants out of the confines of Notre Dame's Old College to larger classrooms on the campus. There were also several informal gatherings held on the campus lawns. Charismatic masses also were held daily at the outdoor grotto of Our Lady of Lourdes.

The public nature of these meetings drew the attention of the campus community, and the student media began to investigate the new phenomenon. *The Notre Dame Observer* misrepresented its import with the headline "Spiritualists Claim 'Gift of Tongues' at Exorcism Rites" (M. Smith 1967, 1; see also O'Connor 1971, 61–83). Within a matter of weeks, the Catholic charismatics had drawn the attention of the *South Bend Tribune,* the *National Catholic Reporter,* and *Our Sunday Visitor.*[1] With such exposure, the numbers attending the weekly prayer meetings began to grow dramatically.

The renewal's visibility was further enhanced by the novelty of pentecostal prayer meetings being held under Notre Dame's Golden Dome. Much like the Azusa Street revival, hundreds of people, some ardent seekers and others merely curious, came from across the United States to visit the campus prayer group.

In May 1967, Clark and Martin, both of whom had been fired from their youth ministry at East Lansing for their open espousal of pentecostalism, moved to Ann Arbor, Michigan. There they began a youth outreach ministry at the University of Michigan. They were joined by Jerry Rauch and Jim Cavnar, two other veterans of Notre Dame's Antioch Weekends. The four began to hold regular Thursday night prayer meetings in their apartment, located above a drugstore a few blocks from the University of Michigan campus.

This gathering quickly grew into a large and committed prayer group that met at St. Mary's Chapel at the Newman Center of the University of Michigan. Ann Arbor soon became identified with Notre Dame as a main center of the Catholic charismatic renewal.[2] It also became apparent that a cooperative and influential South Bend–Ann Arbor leadership axis was beginning to emerge.

By 1968, there were at least fourteen Catholic charismatic prayer groups in the United States (Connelly 1971, 221).[3] The networking in the movement, exemplified by the close relations between Notre Dame and Ann Arbor, was aided nationally by local Days of Renewal. These exuberant gatherings, which continue to be a pertinent factor in the renewal, began in Michigan in October 1967 and were seen as opportunities for mutual encouragement, prayer, praise, and Bible study (Connelly 1971, 220). Help in dealing with special pastoral problems was given at leaders' workshops, which were held just prior to the Days of Renewal.

In March 1968, a special Holy Spirit Weekend was held at Notre Dame in order to recall the dramatic events of the previous year. Approximately 150 people from across the United States attended. This gathering became a prototype for the annual national conferences that became a major force in promoting the renewal's early image of rapid growth and increasing diversification.[4]

The Early Church Response

Early Protestant reactions to pentecostals in their midst ranged from reserved caution to overt hostility (see K. McDonnell 1980, vol. 1). Despite their real concern over potential excesses, the Catholic hierarchy did not want to develop the level of hostility seen in some of the early Protestant responses (see Bess 1963). This tolerance may have been an extension of the Catholic Church's historical tendency to allow for new religious orders and expressions of spirituality in general. The main concern of most Catholic leaders was that Catholic charismatics not embrace non-Catholic doctrines, especially given the close working relationships many Catholic charismatics were developing with both classical and Protestant pentecostals.[5]

Kevin and Dorothy Ranaghan, in an early apologetic for the Catholic charismatic movement, addressed this concern. They described the Catholic charismatics as wanting, above all else, to remain in the heart of church life:

> It is most important to note that the outpouring of the Holy Spirit in these days has occurred to Catholics *within* the Catholic Church. The pentecostal movement has not separated or excluded Catholics from their church. Rather it has renewed their love of the Church and has built up a lively faith in the Catholic community. . . .
>
> We must not confuse the baptism in the Holy Spirit with the cultural forms of religious expression common in pentecostal denominations. . . . In its own cultural setting and development, this religious style is quite beautiful, meaningful and relevant. But it is not essential to nor desirable for baptism in the Holy Spirit, especially among people of far different religious backgrounds. . . .
>
> It should be obvious that we have not adopted the methodology of fundamentalism. Too often in the past Christians experiencing baptism in the Holy Spirit have adopted not only the cultural environment of denominational pentecostalism but also the thought categories of the fundamentalist milieu (1969, 55, 154–55, 261).

The Catholic bishops, "mystified, cautious and basically unhappy" with the potential disruptiveness of the renewal, were unclear about exactly what to think (K. McDonnell 1968a, 203; see also K. McDonnell 1970). Most were not categorically opposed to the charismatics' confessed experience of the miraculous; indeed, the Catholic Church had been historically willing to grant such incursions of the supernatural into the natural order (Dolan 1985, 233–35, 387). But the bishops were concerned that the charismatics might interpret Spirit-baptism as being on a level with or superior to the sacraments. This type of interpretation had to be avoided.[6] The bishops were also concerned that charismatics not develop the sectarian tendencies that had sometimes been seen among Protestant charismatics.

In 1969 the National Conference of Catholic Bishops charged their Committee on Doctrine to look into the matter of the charismatic renewal. Bp. Alexander Zaleski of Lansing, Michigan, headed up this effort. Zaleski had ongoing contacts with the renewal through his relationship with George Martin, his diocesan director of adult education and a prominent charismatic leader. Zaleski deliberately enlisted the help of reputable, yet sympathetic, theologians, such as Edward O'Connor, C.S.C., and Fr. Kilian McDonnell, O.S.B., who knew something about the renewal and could provide a balanced assessment of it.

The Zaleski Report was notable both for its brevity and its tolerant spirit.[7] The charismatics were described as self-consciously distancing themselves from classical pentecostal theology. The report noted that the title *pentecostal movement* was probably a misnomer, since the charismatic renewal had no cohesive national organization. The term *movement,* with its suggestion of central planning, was inaccurate. The Zaleski Report suggested that, despite its potential to attract emotionally unstable individuals, decisive judgments about the charismatic renewal should be withheld.

Instead, final evaluation was to rest on long-term observation of the fruits of the participants' lives. The Vatican Council had affirmed the present operation of the Holy Spirit in the church; therefore, theologically the movement had legitimate reasons to exist. The report concluded by saying that the renewal seemed to be having a good impact and should be allowed (see O'Connor 1971, 291–93).

The Zaleski Report was a cautious, at best rather neutral, statement. But the renewal leadership seized upon it as an opening to legitimation. They proclaimed their intrinsic loyalty to the Catholic Church and characterized the report as an open endorsement of the renewal's efforts. With this particular interpretation in place, the rate of growth began to soar (Connelly 1971, 228–30).

Covenant Communities

By the fall of 1968, 250 young people were regularly attending prayer meetings at the University of Michigan's Newman Center. Within a year, the number had grown to an unwieldy total of about one thousand. A core group within these prayer meetings wanted to make a deeper commitment to one another. During the summer of 1970, a prophetic message was delivered calling for a covenant agreement that would stabilize the transient student population. As a result, the Word of God covenant community* was begun in September 1970 under the leadership of Ralph Martin, Steve Clark, and others.[8]

Later that fall, 170 persons agreed on a public, one-page covenant statement. This statement pledged those involved to mutual love and service, respect for community order, financial support for the community, and involvement in community events. A particular service of the Word of God community became its promotion of Life in the Spirit seminars, which helped to initiate thousands of Catholics into an understanding of Spirit-baptism (Hocken 1980, 404–8). The leadership of the Word of God community was Roman Catholic, but an ecumenical dimension was evident from the start, since the prayer group openly drew people from diverse backgrounds. The covenant community model was widely advanced in the charismatic renewal as an effective way for prayer group members to make deeper commitments to one another.[9]

The Service Committee

By 1970, most Catholic charismatic leaders wanted to move in the direction of a more formal organizational identity. But the concern was that, if this happened, the renewal might be in danger of being seen as just another movement within the church. The prevailing belief among the leadership was that the renewal was not just another movement within the church but was the church itself in movement.[10] But this ideal was hard to sustain, since it did not lend itself to ready observation or hard factual assessment. The leadership's desire for a more recognizable structure reflected growing discomfort with the free-wheeling style associated with the earliest phases of

---

* The term *covenant community* will be encountered throughout this chapter. An initial definition was given by John Connor: "Covenant communities are groups of Christians whom the Lord has led to bind themselves to him and to one another in the form of public commitment. Membership cuts across normally accepted divisions of God's people, including clergy, religious, and lay people. Each is small enough so that it can be a body of Christians who know and serve one another, while large enough to provide effective pastoral leadership" (1972, 5).

the renewal. They did not want to be identified as being in radical discontinuity with the Catholic tradition.

The idea that the renewal needed more formal self-definition was given added urgency because of the huge numbers of Catholics who were choosing to identify with it.[11] Most of these people were neophytes to pentecostalism and needed strong pastoral direction. In June 1970, aided by the legitimation that had been assigned to pentecostalism by the Zaleski Report, the Catholic Charismatic Renewal Service Committee, later the National Service Committee, was formed. This committee was composed almost exclusively of leaders from Notre Dame and Ann Arbor. They described themselves as "national leaders . . . who could commit themselves to regular work for the committee, and who were geographically close enough to one another to be able to meet regularly" ("Advisory Committee Meets" 1971, 7). The service committee was careful to emphasize its key mission to be one of service, and disclaimed any desire to direct a renewal that God alone was leading: "Because the charismatic renewal is renewal (an unorganized movement) there can be no authority structure within it. The only authority can be the authority that comes from services well performed" (ibid., 7). Efforts to propel the renewal's identity made this an ideal more honored in the breach than the observance.

A Push toward Legitimation, 1971-77

New Covenant Magazine

An early sign that the leadership was attempting to secure an institutional identity was the transformation of the renewal's pastoral newsletter into a monthly magazine. This new publication, *New Covenant,* was based in Ann Arbor and began operations in July 1971. *New Covenant*'s announced purposes were (1) to be a clearinghouse for information about the charismatic renewal in general; (2) to represent major trends in the Catholic renewal; and (3) to serve as a vehicle for advancing grass-roots ecumenism among various pentecostal groups.[12] *New Covenant* became a major source of information about pentecostal activities in general and also helped promote an emerging charismatic agenda.

A Dominant Ideology Emerges

Despite the disavowals in the service committee statement, many charismatic leaders were attempting to direct opinion. Two particular articles of belief emerged. The first was that, with the appearance of the Zaleski Report, the renewal had matured beyond a strictly apologetic phase and had moved on to become a prophetic voice in both church and culture. Secondly, highly committed charismatic communities were vital to this prophetic task, since they represented a vanguard and a model for superior Christian life-style.

By 1971, these propositions began to be widely circulated. Ralph Martin's book, *Unless the Lord Build the House,* specifically critiqued the American Catholic Church for failing to equip its membership to encounter the challenges of the modern age. Catholics were not being encouraged to appropriate their faith personally. Because they were not firmly based, many were experiencing a spiritual identity crisis.

Martin argued that the majority of Catholics had succumbed to a dominant secular humanism, which he characterized as a worldly values system that subtly corroded traditional values.[13] He described banal attempts to manipulate the liturgy, an overpoliticized emphasis on social activism, and a blueprinted approach to church reform as parts of the problem. Martin saw these as inadequate approaches based upon a superficial understanding of the reforms intended by Vatican II. Such fashionable attempts at reform ignored the central issue, which involved the need for repentance from sin and of ongoing personal conversion. This was a core message that had to be retaught to every generation.

Martin's answer to the spiritual crisis he described was straightforward. The church needed to emphasize the primacy of the *kerygma,* the proclaiming of a personal commitment to Jesus Christ as Savior and Lord. To be heard, this message must be preached in the power of the Holy Spirit. "Only when the Church and all of us are open to all the workings of the Spirit, will we be equipped . . . to effectively be his witnesses" (R. Martin 1971, 62). Finally, it was essential to build Christian communities flexible enough to meet the needs of those involved but also strong enough to rebuff secular social standards. Proclamation and vigilance were prerequisites to forming a modern Christian identity: "While maintaining our serious commitments and responsibilities to the old order, there is a need to move with God's Spirit into the new" (ibid., 63).

Another early and influential ideological work was Steve Clark's *Building Christian Communities*. Clark's book became a charter statement for those in the charismatic renewal who wanted to stress the importance of covenant communities. He saw the encouragement of strong communities, which would eventually join together in a community of communities, as the church's main pastoral priority and an antidote to evident spiritual decline.[14]

Clark saw Christianity receding before the challenges of the modern world, and he offered two possible responses (1972, 45). One of these was an aggressive campaign to convert the secular culture and thus to obviate the threat. This answer was untenable because the church had neither the will nor the resources for the task. The second approach was to form high-commitment Christian communities, which Clark described as similar in organization to monastic groups in the early church. These would provide a fortress environment of sufficient integrity in which to survive secular humanism's assault upon Christian values:

> A person's beliefs, attitudes, values and behavior patterns (and hence his Christianity) are formed to a great degree by his environment, and therefore the normal person needs a Christian environment if he is going to live Christianity in a vital way. . . .
>
> We need to find a way of providing for people an authentically Christian environment of sufficient strength to make it possible for them to live as vital Christians if they so choose. We need to form real Christian communities (ibid., 24; 45).

Authentic renewal in the Catholic Church would be of this vital nature, fostering environments that could challenge spiritual passivity. Clark envisioned such environments as demanding but not coercive, since they would rely on voluntary adherence. Communities that embodied Clark's idea of a high-level commitment (such as his own Word of God

Community in Ann Arbor) were directed by a core leadership, invariably male (ibid., 113–27). These leaders were not appointed so much as they were acknowledged for their special spiritual gifts (ibid., 180).

Implicitly agreeing with Ralph Martin, Clark saw the contemporary church as rarely providing its members with sufficient spiritual support. As a result, unbased Christians were succumbing to sub-Christian standards of belief and conduct. This critique of modern Catholicism was widely held by other charismatics (see Byrne 1972; Keifer 1972). But South Bend's Kevin Ranaghan did voice a caution that high-level commitments should not encourage elitist tendencies within the renewal. Even the appearance of a new gnosticism could be counterproductive:

> What seems to be happening [as a tendency in the Catholic charismatic renewal] is a small but seductive in-group mentality, a seedling isolationism, that we have been largely free from in the past. If allowed to flourish, the fruit will be one-sidedness, shallowness, and a quaint sectarianism. . . . I am anxious that all Catholics experience and grow into a spirit filled Christian life. But non-pentecostals are not non-Christians (Ranaghan 1972c, 16).

Ranaghan's antidote to charismatic pride was to stay deeply rooted in the wider Catholic tradition, "rich soil in which we ourselves are nurtured into the fullness of Christ" (ibid.).

Ecumenical Attitudes

Catholic charismatics saw Spirit-baptism as an enriching experience rather than as one that endangered their denominational loyalty. Fidelity to one's tradition, moreover, need not be opposed to ecumenical contact with other pentecostals. Indeed, such ongoing cooperation was seen as a significant benefit of Vatican II and the promotion of ecumenism was not to be solely identified with liberal elements in the Catholic Church.

Because the charismatic renewal's first loyalty was to Catholicism, Steve Clark, the service committee's chair, called for teachings that were fully Catholic before they were evangelical or pentecostal. His motive was to eliminate any ambiguity over where the renewal's priorities might lie. Clark insisted that there was no inherent conflict between Catholicism and a simple proclamation of Christian salvation and pentecostal empowerment. Indeed, the message of personal conversion to Christ and the special powers coming from that decision found a home in Catholicism.

In the past, Christian conflicts had arisen, not over the message, but over its application. Fundamentalists had traditionally held that most Catholics were not saved because they did not make a public profession of salvation. Clark observed that Catholics were not used to doing this type of thing publicly and that Catholic doctrine saw salvation not as a single event but as an ongoing process. Catholics were initially saved by turning to Christ and being baptized; they continued to be saved by cooperating with the precepts and sanctifying power of Christ; and they were finally saved when they received their resurrection body. Therefore, Catholics did not differ on the basic need for salvation, but on how this salvation was to be understood (Schreck 1983).

Clark noted that the novelty of sharing in pentecostal experience with non-Catholics had dominated the early days of the renewal. A large number of interdenominational prayer groups had been formed. Many of these groups had embraced the common denominator of their experience and had skipped over fundamental areas of disagreement. He considered this a careless disregard for important differences (see Sullivan 1988).

Despite a potential for conflict over how Catholic the charismatic renewal should be, the January 1972 National Service Committee meeting, where Clark made his remarks, was lauded for its overall spirit of Christian unity. Larry Christenson, a prominent Lutheran charismatic observer, went so far as to say that the meeting exemplified the true meaning of ecumenism: "This wonderful unity in the Spirit [prevailing at the service committee meeting] far transcends any theological formulation. It seems to me that someone will have to create a theology to express the reality of this unity" ("Reflections" 1972, 5).

Intercommunion

Intercommunion had been occasionally and informally practiced since the earliest days of the renewal (see "Intercommunion" 1973), but a new situation appeared at the May
1972 Notre Dame Conference that presented a real block to
developing pentecostal unity. This involved the public application of the bishops' guideline, which said that non-Catholics
were not to receive eucharist at Catholic liturgies because they
were not in full and open communion with Rome. According
to accepted Catholic doctrine, shared communion represented
unity at several levels: in Christ, in the doctrines of the faith, in
the visible church, and in recognition of church authority. Thus
it included the aspect of institutional loyalty. Still, this sudden
insistence on restricted communion became a source of griev-
ance to Protestants who did not believe that the sharing of
communion implied making a formal allegiance to Rome.

The announcement of this restriction at Notre Dame may
have represented simple acquiescence to the bishops' request.
But, at another level, the issue became one of "how sensi-
tively they [the guidelines] were to be applied" (R. Martin
1972, 1). The question of restricted communion has remained
a sore point between Catholic charismatics and other pentecostals into the present.

By the following year, Paul DeCelles, a coordinator for the
People of Praise community in South Bend, was expressing
his concern about a "super-Catholicism" he sensed was
emerging at the Notre Dame Conference. DeCelles' worry was
that non-Catholics were being made to feel unwelcome at all
Catholic conferences. While he thought it was good to be
obedient to the bishops, DeCelles objected to any efforts to
profess mass obedience to Rome.

Indeed, such a profession was made at the 1973 Notre
Dame Conference, indicating a growing desire to be formally
identified with Rome. There may have also been a concern on
the part of conference leaders to counter even the appearance
of antinomial tendencies by an open expression of denominational loyalty. DeCelles later suggested that a measure of emotional coercion may have been used to obtain this declaration.
He wondered whether this might not signal "a trend toward

clericalism which does not reflect the Spirit-led attitude of thousands of people in the charismatic renewal" (DeCelles 1973, 25).

Vinson Synan, a classical pentecostal with strong ecumenical ties to the Catholic renewal, used the pages of *New Covenant* to express a more general concern. He openly wondered whether the chance for a united witness might not be slipping away from charismatics. Like the classical pentecostals before them, charismatics seemed increasingly content with building denominational walls rather than ecumenical bridges (Synan 1973). This was especially notable in new prayer groups that only accepted members from their own denomination. In Synan's view, any such drift toward exclusivism represented an abandonment of the special ecumenical graces given to pentecostals through the shared experience of Spirit-baptism:

> We now speak of the "Catholic Charismatic Renewal," the "Lutheran Charismatic Renewal," the "Orthodox Charismatic Renewal," and so forth. . . . If we do not pray earnestly for unity in the Spirit, we shall witness the great Pentecostal-Charismatic movement fragmented into carbon-copies of the present day ecclesiastical divisions (ibid., 2).

The best way to counter this drift away from unity was by a public reaffirmation, a "united witness to the nation . . . an explo-type rally in a great stadium" (ibid.).

In August 1973, David Wilkerson, the author of *The Cross and the Switchblade* and a regular contributor to *New Covenant,* added to the undercurrent of tension. He revealed a vision he had received during the International Lutheran Charismatic Conference in Minneapolis. In this vision, he was warned of calamities coming upon the earth, including a deepening economic crisis, famine, natural disasters, moral decay, and the increased persecution of Christians. Pentecostals have no sure criteria for deciding the authenticity of such visions. Generally, if the person giving the message is of sufficient stature, the vision is given credence. The ultimate criterion, of course, is whether what has been said comes to pass.

David Wilkerson's vision of coming hard times included a specific warning to Catholic charismatics:

> "The Roman Catholic Church is about to 'pull in' the welcome mat to all Catholics who speak with tongues and who lean toward Pentecostal teachings concerning the Holy Spirit. High level political pressure will be placed on priests to 'put the fire out.' Watch for the pope to take a negative stand against the charismatic movement within the Catholic Church" (Wilkerson quoted in R. Martin 1974a, 11).

Wilkerson's deep suspicion of Vatican intentions may have been of the type common to many classical pentecostals. But what concerned charismatic leaders was Wilkerson's high stature within the Catholic renewal, largely because he wrote *The Cross and the Switchblade.* Both Ralph Martin, representing the Catholic movement, and David du Plessis, representing ecumenical pentecostals, portrayed Wilkerson's vision as unfounded and divisive.

Prevailing Ecumenical Optimism

Despite these hints of divisiveness, the overall tone of the early 1970s was extremely optimistic. The newness and intensity of pentecostal experience fostered a visionary spirit in many Catholics and mainline Protestants. Spirit-baptism was seen to have the potential to sweep away historic differences within Christianity. The rosters at charismatic conferences during this period contained equal billing for Catholic and Protestant speakers.[15] In addition, numerous Protestants contributors wrote for *New Covenant.*[16]

The keynote address delivered by Kevin Ranaghan to eleven thousand charismatics at the 1972 Notre Dame Conference represented the high tide of ecumenical optimism. Ranaghan asserted that the Holy Spirit had launched this nondenominational pentecostal surge and thus it was divinely mandated:

> Jesus is teaching us that we are basically and fundamentally called to be one People, one holy nation, a new

humanity led by the New Adam. Regardless of our different denominations, we do know and accept Jesus of Nazareth as our Lord and Savior, we are together plunged into the mystery of his death and resurrection, and in his Spirit we share one life together which is the very life of God. It is no empty slogan that we are one in the Spirit but it is a profound reality which, praise God, is being revealed to us in these days (1972b, 1).

He impressed upon his mostly Catholic audience the need to be loyal to Rome while still remaining sensitive to the larger reality of the entire Body of Christ. He said that faithfulness to God's ordained plan required staying within one's denomination, and his long-range vision for the charismatic renewal was that it might be both a witness to and an instrument for Christian unity: "We have to accept the call to suffer the pain of separation when we long to be one, so that our fidelity in our churches may be a ringing prophecy and sign to all Christianity that we must become really one according to Jesus' will" (ibid., 1–2).

Ranaghan's language represented the more general sense that Christianity was living through a crucial moment in its history. This perception was portrayed graphically in *New Covenant* by the classical pentecostal leader, Derek Prince:

I was back in Denmark [in October 1964] at the same cliff-top overlooking the same stretch of sea when God . . . showed me what was going on in all the earth. . . . The early Church was the high tide, but then the tide went out. The waves still came in, but they never came as high as the early waves of the Church; there was still a movement of God, but it never reached the height of the early Church, and gradually the waves lost more and more of that which they had covered until the "Dark Ages," which was low tide.

. . . God showed me that there are some small waves and there are some great ones, and he gave me a brief outline of segments of church history—Luther, Wesley, Finney, the Welsh revival, and so on. Then he brought me up to the present time and spoke to me about the Pentecostal movement. He showed me that when each wave has reached its climax it checks then recedes; the same wave never comes back again. God never revives a revival, he never gives us anything warmed over.

The Pentecostal movement had been one of the great waves. It had recovered truth not recovered by previous waves, and had made an impact all around the earth. But it had reached its climax and was receding. That was almost like a physical blow. I thought, "God, am I giving my life to something that's on the way out? . . . This is the answer the Lord gave me: "The same *wave* never comes back again, but some of the water that was in the previous wave comes back in the next one." There's a new wave coming; it will not be the Pentecostal movement; it will recover truth which Pentecostals as a whole did not recover. It will be the greatest wave, and it will be the last wave (1974, 10–11).

The 1974 Notre Dame Conference represented a similar triumph of ecumenical optimism. With thirty-seven thousand people attending, it was interpreted as a watershed moment for the Catholic charismatic renewal.[17] The leadership saw their renewal as capable of transforming both church and society. In a well-received keynote address, Ralph Martin gave his own interpretation of the twentieth century's pentecostal surge. He said it was a significant "new thing" that God was doing in these times. This powerful pentecostal witness to unity was not an end in itself, however mighty that witness might already be. Rather, the shared experience of Spirit-baptism was a divine call forward into a complete Christian unity.

Martin described a "process of disintegration," which Western Christianity had suffered since the Reformation.[18] He said that the four centuries following the Reformation had been a time of serious decline, one that had depleted Christian vitality. A tragic result of many rival claimants had been confusion in the secular world over who God was and who Jesus the Messiah was.

The divine response to this history of internal conflict was to transfuse new life into the churches through the power of the Holy Spirit. This was represented in the twentieth century's pentecostal surge. Martin claimed that there would soon be a great gathering of the three great pentecostal "streams" (classical, Protestant, and Catholic) into one. This would be a "new thing" that other Christians could not quickly fathom. But they would be compelled by subsequent events to see in this convergence the beginning of the fulfillment of Jesus' prayer for unity recorded in John 17:21.

In terms reminiscent of early pentecostal restorationists, Martin said that now was the time for the convergence of the pentecostal streams to begin:

> What is happening among the classical Pentecostals today is something we can call an ecumenical shock-wave. It is a shock to the Pentecostal churches to see what God is doing in the Catholic Church. When all your life you have been trained to look at the Catholic Church as the whore of Babylon, and when the whore of Babylon preaches Jesus, what are you going to do? It shakes up your whole world view. Among the leaders in the classical Pentecostal churches now, there is a tremendous reassessment taking place. They want to see how to flow into the new thing that God is doing. . . .
>
> Renewal is too weak a word for what needs to happen in the Christian church. "Renewal" can give us a sense that we will just polish something up a little bit. Rather, I think God is moving to *restore* New Testament Christianity to all his people—that is more than renewal. Restoration means reform as well as renewal for everything that God wants to happen in his people. Much has been lost, much as [*sic*] been distorted. He wants to change the face of the Church and the face of the earth (1974b, 6).

By this point Martin, in an excess of enthusiasm, seems to have virtually dismissed the Holy Spirit's active involvement in much of the rest of Christian history.

Martin concluded his talk with an appeal to his listeners. Since God's purposes always come to pass, and since God's principal purpose is Christian unity, it was incumbent upon them to move ahead on this mandate together. The key was not to be stuck, "clutching on to today's [charismatic] gift." His words suggest that, after seven eventful years, he already saw Catholic charismatics growing too comfortable with their newly won pentecostal identity.

Given the ongoing divine initiative Martin had outlined, familiar situations such as parish, prayer group, covenant community, even traditional church forms might have to go. The audience was urged to listen closely to the voice of the Holy Spirit on these matters and to be ready to enter into the promised land of a transformed reality.

The 1975 Leaders' Conference

If the 1974 Notre Dame Conference recognized the ecumenical potential of pentecostalism, the 1975 International Leaders Conference in Rome demonstrated that Catholic charismatics wanted to live in the heart of their church (see Ghezzi 1975). Pope Paul VI had declared 1975 a holy year of renewal and reconciliation. The charismatic leaders seized the moment, organizing a pilgrimage in order to be in Rome during Pentecost week.

Large meetings were held in a tent pitched over the Catacombs of St. Callixtus, a gathering place for pilgrims through the centuries. On Pentecost Sunday, ten thousand charismatics joined the pope in celebrating mass at St. Peter's Basilica. In his homily, Paul endorsed the charismatic renewal's proclamation of empowerment through the Holy Spirit:

> The Holy Spirit, that is God-love, lives in the soul, and the soul suddenly feels itself invaded by a need to abandon itself to Love; and it is aware of a surprising and unusual courage that makes us joyful and secure, a courage to speak, to sing, to proclaim to others, to all "the wonderful works of God (Acts 2:11)" (ibid., 16–17).

Cardinal Willebrands, head of the Vatican Secretariat for Promoting Christian Unity, addressed the afternoon session. He emphasized that unity was the sign that Christ desired to bring salvation to all. This message could not be understood apart from union with the institutional church, and the charismatic renewal itself was incomprehensible outside of the church. Ultimately, Willebrands said, it was the church itself that was charismatic.

During the last day of the conference, mass was again held at the Vatican. Cardinal Suenens was given permission to use the Renaissance basilica's main altar and there he concelebrated mass with seven hundred priests. The service was a mix of traditional Roman liturgy and spontaneous pentecostal expressions such as tongues and prophecies. To many attending, it represented a perfect blending of the old and the new.

Shortly after the conclusion of the liturgy, Paul made an unscheduled visit to give his strong personal endorsement for the work of the renewal. He cautioned that there were guidelines in discerning the legitimate work of the Holy Spirit. This work would be faithful to Catholic doctrine while earnestly desiring the "higher gifts." Above all else, it would be marked by *agape* love, which alone made a person pleasing to God. He concluded his extemporaneous remarks with an appeal: "[The renewal] ought to rejuvenate the world, give it back a spirituality, a soul, a religious thought; it [the renewal] ought to reopen its [the world's] closed lips to prayer and open its mouth to song, to joy, to hymns, and to witnessing" (ibid., 15).

A commonly held view among charismatics—that they had been given a special mission to renew the face of the earth—was bolstered by the pope's impromptu talk. But a solemn prophecy given by Ralph Martin during the conference's last liturgy closed the meeting on a more somber note. Martin's prophecy spoke of success, but success at a price:

> Because I love you, I want to show you what I am doing in the world today. I want to prepare you for what is to come. Days of darkness are coming on the world, days of tribulation. . . . Buildings that are now standing will not be standing. Supports that are there for my people now will not be there. I want you to be prepared, my people, to know only me and to cleave to me and to have me in a way deeper than ever before. I will lead you into the desert. . . . I will strip you of everything that you are depending on now, so you depend just on me. A time of darkness is coming on the world, but a time of glory is coming for my church, a time of glory is coming

for my people. I will pour out on you all the gifts of
my spirit. I will prepare you for spiritual combat; I will
prepare you for a time of evangelism that the world
has never seen. . . . And when you have nothing but
me, you will have everything: lands, fields, homes, and
brothers and sisters and love and joy and peace more
than ever before (Ghezzi 1975, 19).

This caution was heeded, during the next few years, along
with many similar prophetic warnings. The consistent theme of
all of them was the need for charismatics to enter into an ever-
deepening relationship with God without counting the cost.

Reflections on the charismatic renewal's new responsibilities to the Catholic Church were prominent in the period
immediately after the Rome conference. Fr. Francis Martin, a
key participant at Rome, pondered Paul's invitation to renew
the church. Fr. Martin said that events at the conference had
truly validated the renewal: "It now runs the risk facing any
force; it can lose itself in trying to dominate everything, or it
can corrupt itself by becoming complacent" (1975, 5). Since
the renewal had moved from a tentative position of relationship to the church and had been invited in, it needed to
develop a more mature posture as quickly as possible.

Fr. Martin did not mean that the charismatics were simply
to accept the status quo, however. Following the call of Ralph
Martin's prophecy at Rome, the renewal itself was called upon
to act both responsibly and prophetically, preparing the
church for an impending collapse of Western culture: "The
resulting battle between light and darkness will take place
much more violently in the inner recesses of the human heart
than in the outer physical dimension" (ibid., 6). Despite the
gravity of this call, such a service to the church was to be
done humbly and without undue anxiety.

Fr. Martin's remarks suggest a time of intense speculation
among charismatics over what a witness to the "heart of the
church" might involve. Dominant images emerged of the
charismatics being a righteous nation, called by God to be
true and faithful witnesses. Such a theme had undergirded
Ralph Martin's 1974 Notre Dame speech. The restorationist
perspective developed, which argued that the reappearance of
pentecostal gifts in the Catholic Church was an eschatological

precursor to God's purpose of breaking into and judging history. The targeted audience for this divine warning was understood to be the many "baptized pagans" who had never personally appropriated the Christian faith.[19]

The question of how Catholic the renewal should be became increasingly prominent by the middle of the 1970s. The issue of primary loyalty had publicly surfaced during the intercommunion dispute at the 1972 Notre Dame Conference. But it came to dominate after the 1975 Rome meeting, following Paul VI's endorsement. The prevailing argument was that prior loyalty to Rome should not hinder true ecumenism, which realistically allowed for differences.[20] But, at the grassroots level, such subtle nuancing was rare. The challenge for charismatics to be devoutly Catholic and devotedly ecumenical became more difficult over time (see Hocken 1979 and 1987).

The Push for Covenant Communities

By the middle of the 1970s the Ann Arbor–South Bend axis— which controlled the information systems—had committed itself to fighting a perceived erosion in society's moral standards. This brought them to identify with several of the causes of the Far Right, although most charismatics were not comfortable being identified with extreme political agendas. The core leadership of the Catholic charismatics, although acknowledging the importance of taking political stands, did not see social activism as the most profound response that could be made to the intensifying social crisis. For this, it was necessary to enter more deeply into the building of strong, internally disciplined communities.

For many of the leaders, the desire to repristinate Christian witness by means of these communities became all-consuming. It was believed that the church itself could be restored by such initiative and example, with committed charismatic groups providing a model for refuge from a world gone awry. In such groups, one could be weaned away from serious sin and taught how to prepare for the prophesied coming hard times.

High-commitment communities flourished in the 1970s. Above all, they were intent on portraying the power of Spirit-baptism to transform Christian relationships. They usually

gave themselves names that suggested their spiritual aspira-
tions. In 1975, an association of such communities was
formed by Word of God (Ann Arbor) and People of Praise
(South Bend), with allied groups including the Servants of the
Light (Minneapolis), the Work of Christ (East Lansing), and the
Lamb of God (Baltimore).

Most covenant communities followed a pattern pioneered
by the Word of God (Ann Arbor). Their shared discipleship
experience was called the household. This might be a group
of community members living together. But more often it was
nonresidential, with households coming together frequently for
meals, prayer, or fellowship. Some residential households were
designated as brotherhoods or sisterhoods. These were groups
of men and women who vowed to live a celibate life together.

Covenant communities also pledged themselves to mutual
love, prayer disciplines, participation in small group meetings,
and financial support for the larger group. There was great
emphasis placed on submission to the authority of pastoral
heads, perhaps showing the considerable influence of the Fort
Lauderdale group's Shepherding vision upon Catholic charismatic leaders.

The question of whether or when a prayer group should
move in the direction of covenant became an important one to
many charismatics (see B. Bell 1973, 4; Ghezzi 1973). A particular viewpoint, promoted by the Ann Arbor–South Bend leadership, dominated. Despite the preferability of full covenant
commitments, this view held that premature allegiances could
cause relational and other problems. Speaking in support of the
position, Bert Ghezzi, a prominent prayer group leader from
Grand Haven, Michigan, proposed a kind of halfway covenant:

> Once they have reached a certain depth and size, some
> prayer groups have decided to start a second meeting.
> This gathering, frequently called the "community meet-
> ing" or the "core meeting," is usually open only to peo-
> ple who are baptized in the Holy Spirit. . . . Forming this
> kind of meeting is a major step and should not be done
> without the Lord's guidance. . . .
>
> The establishment of a "community" meeting does not
> necessarily mean that a prayer group has become a

Christian community. It is, however, a move in that direction. . . . Growing prayer groups ought to consider the value of calling a second regular meeting as a way of strengthening its life in the spirit (1973, 6).

Such language indicated that—in a mild imitation of earlier monasticism—exclusivism and special disciplines were being promoted as central to Christian discipleship. One potential problem with this approach was that a "dual-citizenship" mentality could emerge, with special status being given to fully covenanted charismatics.

In addition to providing an environment for discipleship training of new members, intensive communities helped sustain a high level of commitment. Many charismatics sensed that the original spontaneity of the renewal had given way to institutionalization and routine (Fichter 1975, 145).[21] For many of the leaders in particular, the temptation was great to manufacture new enthusiasms. Whatever the reasons, the powerful energies aroused by Spirit-baptism and meant to transfuse the entire Body of Christ became concentrated in efforts to build exclusive communities.

Early Dissent to the Dominant Ideology

Covenant-building ideology, with its de facto separatism, had its early critics. One of these was William Storey, an original leader of the Duquesne revival. He left active involvement with the charismatic renewal in 1970 because he distrusted its ecumenical direction. Subsequently, Storey became director of the Graduate Program in Liturgical Studies at Notre Dame. Despite his reservations, Storey had favorably characterized the charismatic renewal as late as 1972 (Storey 1972, n.p.).

In a 1975 interview, Storey described what he saw to be alarming new trends. Chief among these was his observation that the renewal, despite its claims of loyalty to Rome, was becoming increasingly sectarian:

Recent developments, including trends encouraged and established by the national leadership, have contributed to abuses and conditions which constitute very serious

dangers, theological errors and patterns of religious response which cannot be reconciled with authentic
Catholic tradition (Storey 1975, n.p.).

He described these principal abuses and errors as being
grounded in too great an openness to non-Catholic influences, particularly biblical fundamentalism and Shepherding-
Discipleship.[22] He also warned about dangerous and growing
levels of authoritarianism.

Storey tied this recent authoritarian tendency to the unexpectedly rapid growth of the renewal:

> It [rapid growth] forced the movement to organize itself.
> . . . It is necessarily a big enterprise because of the num-
> ber of people served, but also it has become a major
> instrument for the control of ideas, practices, values, and
> personalities. . . . Decisions are made that only certain
> books, certain authors and tapes by certain speakers are
> to be distributed through the Communications Center,
> and that others are to be avoided. Many, if not most of
> these decisions are for ideological reasons determined
> by the leadership. It amounts to a combined system of
> Imprimatur and Index for members of the movement
> across the country (ibid.).

The leadership, especially the Ann Arbor group, believed that
their ideas were directly inspired by the Holy Spirit. Thus, it
was essential that these ideas be implemented. This leadership
elite took it upon themselves to decide whether other claims
to special spiritual gifts were legitimate or spurious. Charismatics who did not fit the flow of the Holy Spirit as interpreted through Ann Arbor and South Bend were judged as out
of order. As there were no real alternatives to the existing
information systems, dissenting voices were not being heard.

The push toward exclusive covenant communities was
leading to a special abuse of authority. This abuse included
the exposure of private matters to group scrutiny, a coercion
of conscience:

> This [coercion of conscience] occurs not with one person
> under privacy, the method which the Church has autho-

rized and protected with the seal of confession; commonly, several of the leaders with a recognized charism will be involved in such a session. And the knowledge of sins revealed is discussed by members of the community with astonishing openness. . . . Leaders will share their concern for the faults of one of the members; the community will be asked to pray for his deliverance from his sin. And it's a frightful invasion of the internal forum of conscience (ibid.).

There was a double blast in Storey's comment. He reproved the public discussion of personal sins; but he was also coming against the personal arrogance of leaders who presumed to have a nonsacramental remedy for sin.

In Storey's opinion, the crux of the problem was that the leaders were more focused upon the renewal's separate role than upon its service to the Catholic Church. He concluded by petitioning that the bishops move in unison to investigate what was going on in the charismatic renewal, especially in the covenant communities. Storey claimed he was not advocating suppression; but he believed that the renewal's leadership would have to "oust from the movement those teachings and policies which have produced the present de-Catholicization" (ibid.).

In the fall of 1975, the National Service Committee briefly acknowledged the existence—but not the specifics—of Storey's accusations (National Service Committee 1975). Their statement on recent criticisms did admit that abuse of authority had become an issue, but it offered no elaboration. There was also a general claim that the renewal leadership was open to discussion on all issues. But the service committee said that Storey had not conducted himself in "a brotherly and helpful way" in his comments. Finally, the committee implied that Storey, having left the renewal, did not have the necessary credentials to call for an official inquiry. The logic of this last point is hard to grasp.

Another excoriating analysis of charismatic trends came from Josephine Massyngbaerde Ford, a professor of biblical studies at Notre Dame. Ford had been involved in the early Notre Dame revival but eventually dissented from the direction she saw the group taking. She had been judged disruptive by the leadership of the People of Praise community and was ultimately barred from their meetings. Ford was especially outspoken about what she believed to be the secondary status of women in the renewal and the lack of emphasis upon traditional sacramental life.

In *Which Way for Catholic Pentecostals?* Ford argued that many charismatics were forming a type of communal Christianity that had its roots in radical anabaptism. As early as 1971, the Ann Arbor–South Bend leadership cadre had begun to impose their particular interpretations upon all, an overbearing approach that she called Type I Pentecostalism:

> These [Type I] principles include a strong and rigid hierarchy to whom obedience is required, a nonprofessional teaching body which purports to speak directly through the inspiration of the Spirit, a complicated exclusion system, the subordination of women, and withdrawal from the world. The prayer group has developed from a *koinonia* (community) to an *ecclesiola* (little church) (J. M. Ford 1976, 40).

Included in these "ordinances" were secretive methods for choosing doctrinally correct leaders, the devices of admonition and exclusion ("shunning"), and an attitude of radical separation from the world (ibid., 61).

Ford argued for what she called Type II Pentecostalism (ibid., 67–70). This approach was clerically and sacramentally oriented and accepted women as equal partners. It was not threatened by the pursuit of abstract theological questions, especially those of a more "mystic type." In short, Type II Pentecostalism showed a willingness to be open to unusual spiritual experience. Subsequent events were to substantiate Ford's charges of growing ideological rigidity in the renewal, even if her claims of a rigid sectarianism were open to serious challenge.

The 1975 Bishops' Statement

The 1975 Bishops' Statement on the Charismatic Renewal was a pastoral attempt to direct the renewal, despite the fact that few bishops were personally involved. This new directive was more involved than the 1969 Zaleski Report, although it echoed that earlier document's cautionary tone (see K. McDonnell 1980, 2:104–14).

The statement acknowledged that the charismatic renewal had produced positive spiritual values in the areas of prayer, direct awareness of divine activity in individual lives, and encouragement to deeper participation in the life of the church. But—with more specificity than the Zaleski Report— the statement cautioned against tendencies to distrust the intellectual foundations of the Catholic faith, an attitude often associated with biblical fundamentalism.

The statement also warned against a "closed-circle" elitism that, combined with an overemphasis on private experience as the grounds for assurance of one's spiritual status, could lead charismatics away from identification with the Catholic Church:

> It cannot be denied that such phenomena [extraordinary charisms] could be genuine manifestations of the Spirit. These things, however, must be carefully scrutinized and their importance, even if genuine, should not be exaggerated (ibid., 109).

There were other concerns. One of these was the lack of contact between prayer groups and local parishes. Since "association with priestly leadership is clearly essential to the healthy development of the charismatic renewal" (ibid., 110), the bishops urged priests to become more involved. In addition, there was a concern with how ecumenical relations among pentecostals were conducted, since "continual or exclusive participation in ecumenical groups runs the risk of diluting the sense of Catholic identity" (ibid.).

Finally, the bishops had misgivings about the degree of exclusivity being evidenced in some of the covenant communities. The report cited a general caution given by Paul VI:

> This hope [of intimate relationships in the Holy Spirit] would be truly stunted if their ecclesial life, in the organic unity of the single Body of Christ, were to cease or be exempted from legitimate ecclesiastical authority or be left to the arbitrary impulse of individuals (ibid., 111).

The bishops made clear their concern that such a thing must not happen with the charismatic renewal. For their part, the charismatic leadership chose to represent the statement as a further sign of support and inclusion, much as they had the earlier Zaleski Report (National Conference of Catholic Bishops 1975, 26).

The 1976 Notre Dame Conference

A solemn tone dominated the 1976 Notre Dame Conference (see Perrotta 1976). Recent prophecies were on the minds and hearts of the leadership,[23] and they wanted to impress the thirty thousand attending with the gravity of those messages. During the rain-soaked sessions in the football stadium, several major prophecies were given, including the following:

> Ways you have responded to me in the past, that have seen you through and brought you thus far, will no longer see you through. What I call you to is something new, something totally new: and where there is resistance in your hearts and in your groups, lay down that resistance that I might bring you further along.

and

> My beloved, you my people who stand before me now: hear my word. I will set my house in order. I will purify my people. I will purify my church. I shall set aside the deceiver, the false prophet, and the false teacher. I shall set aside anything and anyone who stands in the way of my kingdom.

and

> The Lord says, I raise my voice, but who listens to me? I cry out, but who heeds my word? This is a time of building up and of wasting away. This is a time of unravelling. This is a time when I establish my kingdom and every other kingdom collapses. . . . Anything that is not built by my hand will be washed away. Anything that does not come from me will not survive (ibid., 19).

The principal speaker for Saturday night was the Franciscan priest, Fr. Michael Scanlan (see Jahr 1979; Manney 1985; Tifft 1988). Scanlan was a rising personality associated with the Ann Arbor group. He was known among charismatics for having turned the Franciscan College of Steubenville in Ohio into a school with an openly pentecostal commitment. Scanlan endorsed what was by now a veritable chorus of prophecies, urging those assembled to prepare for coming hard times:

> The problem [in society] is not in some rotten fruit on a tree, the problem is the rottenness in the roots of the tree. The problem is that we are in a post-Christian society, and in some ways we are Christian exiles in it. . . . I believe the Lord is now calling us to settle in, to base ourselves solidly in the kingdom of God, so that we will be able to meet the trials and difficulties ahead of us (Scanlan 1976, 6).

This message was a new one and difficult for many charismatics to accept. Most of their pentecostal experience had been optimistic, upbeat, and centered in exuberant self-expression. The prophecies they were used to hearing were messages speaking of God's gentle solicitude and love. Despite assurances that God would be with them through every adversity, the new emphasis upon crisis and deprivation was discomfiting and even incomprehensible to many (Perrotta 1976, 16).

Kevin Ranaghan, the director of the National Communications Office, later attempted to interpret the message for the general charismatic population. Citing Ralph Martin's 1974 "Three Streams" speech he said that the renewal had moved on from an apologetic ("the *fact* that God is acting") to a prophetic ("*what* he is doing") stance (Ranaghan 1976, 23). Ranaghan presumed that all charismatics would want to involve themselves in "what God is doing," which now was preparing the people for coming hard times.

In terms of ecumenical cooperation among charismatics and pentecostals, God was continuing the work of softening hearts. The potential for public reconciliation had been symbolically demonstrated when Catholic, Protestant, and classical pentecostals had joined in a foot-washing ceremony at the

Southeastern Regional Conference in Augusta, Georgia (see Bourassa 1975b). This conference was widely publicized as an indication of the growing importance of local conferences. The decision to hold a joint Catholic-Lutheran charismatic conference in Minneapolis was another instance of growing grass-roots cooperation.

Representing a dominant point of view among the Catholic leadership, Ranaghan urged that any "summons to unity" be balanced by a strong drive to be fully integrated into the Catholic Church. Strong charismatic representation at the 41st International Eucharistic Congress exemplified this drive for inclusion.

Ranaghan claimed that the renewal's continued success depended upon a resolve to fathom God's mysterious intentions. To do this, prayer had to become more "humbled and broken before the mighty God." Ranaghan also urged a move away from materialism and toward a simple life-style. Charismatics called for the creation of networks of support in order to prepare for coming calamities. These networks would include covenant communities, associations of communities, joint prayer groups, and pastoral teams.

Some charismatics reacted against the new message coming out of Ann Arbor–South Bend. A group of these dissenters, whose orientation might best be described as approximating Ford's Type II Pentecostalism, began an alternative publication to *New Covenant* in the spring of 1976. *Catholic Charismatic* magazine, produced by Paulist Press, was a forum for points of view that were either underrepresented or totally ignored by the renewal leadership cadre. Because of this exclusionary policy, the minority faction believed that *New Covenant* was giving its readership a carefully mediated version of what was happening. The maverick publication sought to "relate the charismatic experience to the wealth of Catholic tradition . . . in order to strengthen and broaden the quality of life experienced by Catholic charismatics" (Verhalen 1976, 4).

In the first issue Fr. Joseph Lange, *Catholic Charismatic*'s editor, told the readers that the magazine's purpose was to "look beyond the charismatic movement to encounter the Spirit in the other ways He is working—much more to praise God for!" (Lange 1976, 2). *Catholic Charismatic* portrayed the charismatic renewal as one of several important manifestations of God's present workings in the world. The reality was that God worked in many ways: "The question is not one of covenant community or parish, but of both and much, much more" (Lange 1980, 2). Lack of funds and a small circulation forced the cancellation of *Catholic Charismatic* within three years.

Kansas City 1977: An Ecumenical Main Event

A call for a general conference of pentecostals was issued by Catholic charismatics and representatives from the other pentecostal streams in 1976. The result was a massive five-day rally held in July 1977 at Kansas City's Arrowhead Stadium. This event represented the high-water mark of early efforts at unity.[24]

Forty-five thousand charismatics and pentecostals came together with the simple affirmation, "Jesus is Lord." During the keynote address, Kevin Ranaghan euphorically proclaimed to those assembled that they were the largest ecumenical gathering in eight hundred years. He spoke of their past divergence and their present display of unity in Christ:

> We don't exactly have a reputation for mutual love, unity, and brotherhood. We're known to think differently, to act differently, to pray differently, to sing differently, to dress differently. Frankly, we have tended over the years to hold some very firm opinions about and against one another. . . . Yet on all of us, in spite of our divisions and separation, God has poured out his Holy Spirit (Blattner 1977, 5).

Thursday's principal speaker was the Lutheran charismatic leader, Larry Christenson. He emphasized that pentecostal renewal was God's "today-word" to the churches (that is, God's present proclamation). He leveled a challenge to the renewal's (presumably absent) opponents:

> We did not choose these gifts; the Lord Jesus has chosen to come knocking at these doors, and we have responded to his knocking. Your controversy, if you have one, is not with us but with him. . . . The issue is not

spiritual gifts. The issue is the lordship of Christ. This is his work, his initiative, his renewal. He will welcome you into it, but he will not account to you for it, nor trim it to fit your theological prescription. He is Lord, to do in his church as he pleases (ibid., 7).

Christenson concluded by challenging his listeners to move forward together. They were not to cultivate a "nice, cozy, well-insulated Episcopalian or Lutheran renewal. The Lord has not brought this renewal to prop up and bless the status quo" (ibid.).

Friday night's talk was delivered by the independent charismatic evangelist, Bob Mumford. Mumford began by exhorting the crowd to holiness. Hindrances to holiness included pervasive secular humanism ("when the world evangelizes the church"), excessive individualism, loss of vision, and disunity. The antidote was recognition of

"a victorious Lord. . . . In the early days of Pentecost, we had a siege mentality, content to get inside our four walls, nail the door shut, and wait for Jesus to come. The Lord said, 'No, I want you to take a sneak look at the back of the book,'" and Bob pantomimed opening a book to the last pages and gasping at what he discovered there. "Hey!" he shouted to the furthermost rows, "How many of you know that if you take a sneak look at the back of the book, *JESUS WINS!*" And the stadium rang [for fifteen minutes] with cheering, as if Jesus had just won the Super Bowl! (Manuel 1977, 143)

When the crowd finally quieted, Mumford shouted: "You just had a Holy Ghost breakdown" (ibid., 143).

The Saturday session cut across the mood of the previous evening like a knife. Two heavy prophecies were given by Catholic leaders Bruce Yocum and Ralph Martin, both from Word of God (Ann Arbor). Yocum prophesied:

The Lord has a word to speak to the leaders of all the Christian churches: . . . You are all guilty in my eyes for the condition of my people who are weak and divided and unprepared. I have set you in office over them, and you have not fulfilled that office. . . .

This a hard word, but I want you to hear it. You have not come to me and made important in your lives and in your efforts those things which were most important to me, but instead you chose to put other things first. You have tolerated divisions among yourselves and grown used to it. You have not repented for it or fasted for it or sought me to bring it to an end. You have tolerated it, and you have increased it. . . .

I know your hearts, and I know that many of you love me, and I have compassion on you, for I have placed you in a very hard place. But I have placed you there, and I call you to account for it. Now humble yourselves before me and come to me repentant, in fasting, mourning and weeping for the condition of my people (Blattner 1977, 10).

Martin's prophecy was equally grave:

Mourn and weep, for the body of my Son is broken.
Mourn and weep, for the body of my Son is broken.
Come before me with broken hearts and contrite spirits, for the body of my Son is broken.
Come before me with sackcloth and ashes, come before me with tears and mourning, for the body of my Son is broken.
I would have made you a light on the mountaintop, a city glorious and splendorous that all the world would have seen, but the body of my Son is broken.
The light is dim. My people are scattered. The body of my Son is broken.
Turn from the sins of your fathers. Walk in the ways of my Son. Return to the plan of your Father, return to the purpose of your God.
The body of my Son is broken (ibid.).

After a time of confusion over the full import of these messages, the leaders of the various denominational groups led the entire crowd in a prayer of repentance and intercession for unity.

The Kansas City meeting was a dividing point in the history of the entire pentecostal movement. Given the enthusiasm generated and the prophetic calls for unity, this meeting could have propelled the movement forward into an unprecedented era of cooperation. This did not happen. In a pattern similar to the faltering ecumenical efforts among the churches in general, Kansas City became an apex of unrealized desires.

After Kansas City there was a deepening realization that intractable problems remained that unity rallies alone would not resolve. These problems, most of them rooted in long-standing denominational differences, discouraged many pentecostals and charismatics once they became fully apparent. This frustration with the big picture led them to focus upon more manageable parochial concerns. Although never formally acknowledged, relations among pentecostals were not as close after Kansas City. The trend was away from other displays of unity as each stream pursued its separate agenda.

Fragmentation and the Search for an Identity, 1977–87

John Haughey's Challenge

In October 1977, Fr. John Haughey, a Jesuit theologian and major contributor to *Catholic Charismatic,* introduced the issue of competing charismatic visions to fifteen thousand people attending the Eastern Regional Conference of the Charismatic Renewal in Atlantic City (Haughey 1978; see also Moore and Wimbish 1978). His primary point was that insistence upon covenant communities to act as a bulwark against the outside world ("the Martin-Clark vision") could cut the charismatic renewal off from interaction with the larger society:

> Does Jesus have in his mind that some should be so bonded to one another in love and to him, and so transformed by him that in effect they cease to live in the culture they have grown up in and begin to create their own culture? Another way of asking the question would be: Is the new creation so that everything about us should begin to be discontinuous from the old creation? Still a third way of asking the question: Is faith-power

meant to be so powerful that it generates a completely new culture, a new style of life, a new creation? (Haughey 1978, 14).

He went so far as to question the validity of several of the recent prophecies, noting that they conveniently had "added grist to the mills" of those who advocated militant separation from the world.

Haughey proposed an alternative charismatic vision. Its lines were established by Vatican II, and it began by presupposing God's availability to all of creation. This alternative view was:

> much less confrontative and much more dialogic with the alternate religious, political, and philosophical meaning systems it finds in the world, than the first vision would be. It is more nuanced in its evangelism because it acts from the premise that the world itself proclaims the presence of God in both nature and its diverse peoples (ibid., 16).

Despite his apparent preference for the dialogic model, Haughey insisted that he was not opposing the two visions and saying that one was wrong. In fact, both had scriptural and historical roots. But they were very different, and the charismatic renewal "must remain in the tension of being both salt and leaven" (ibid.).

Haughey called for an expanded understanding. If the inclusivist position alone were emphasized, it might lead to indifference in proclaiming the gospel. If the Martin-Clark bulwark-building approach alone prevailed, it could create schism in the church, especially since it projected the militant imagery of a separated nation:

> [A] nation, because they [Martin and Clark] see at least some portion of the renewal so internally organized that it will become for all practical purposes like a little sovereign state that develops its own customs, social life, language, understanding of authority, understanding of man-woman relations, literature, recreation, and so forth,

the way a nation does to some extent. They have obviously answered the question of whether their faith is meant to generate its own culture. They find much fruit in thinking in terms of the way the Lord created the nation Israel (ibid., 15).

Haughey concluded that charismatics needed to become mature enough to "provide ubiquitous reminders of a dialectic, one side more withdrawalist in tone, the other more immersionist" (ibid., 17).

The talk was greeted with virtual silence. This may have implied disapproval, but silence probably indicated confusion. "The majority of conference participants were not concerned about the direction of the renewal so much as the direction of their own lives" (Moore and Wimbish 1798, 64). The conflicts over competing visions were being played out behind the scenes and were not known to the charismatic public.

Haughey's talk brought an underlying tension out. His own agenda was apparent, especially in his call that a discernment process be applied to the prophecies given in recent years: "Just because we have been blessed in the renewal by remarkable leaders does not relieve us of the ongoing need to do that testing" (ibid.). Bruce Yocum wrote that by calling into question the validity of these highly regarded prophecies, Haughey was also challenging an in-group interpretation of their meaning and importance (Yocum 1978, 4).[25]

The major renewal prophecies had come from a select male leadership who appeared to have fashioned themselves into a modern-day prophetic guild. This group had developed a precommitment to the exclusivist position. At issue was whether the renewal was being force-fed the exclusivist position by having it equated with a divine mandate.[26]

The 1977 National Service Committee Report

The National Service Committee claimed to speak on behalf of the entire renewal when it addressed the American Catholic bishops in late 1977 in "The State of the Catholic Church." The tone of this statement hearkened back to the controverted prophecies and was, by Haughey's standard, highly exclusivist. The purpose of the report was to assist the bishops in their pastoral task: "We speak to crucial issues out of our strengths and out of our experience of what works in building the kingdom of God" (National Service Committee 1978b, 4).

The committee acknowledged that good did exist, but its statement was designed to expound the bad. It began by declaring that millions of Catholics were "baptized pagans," without meaningful access to Christian fellowship. Moral teaching had been neglected and "the denial of sin and the lack of its correction have become common" (ibid., 5). They felt that this was no surprise, since many Catholic ministries had a weak moral foundation and, consequently, were misguided.

Contemporary theologians were frequently seen to deny the authority of the Bible and the traditions of the Church. The service committee's conclusion was that "we would be better off with seminaries and religious houses of formation closing for lack of vocations than to be attracting people to the ministry and forming them on the basis of questionable principles and values" (ibid., 6).

Restoring the integrity of the message required reaffirmation of the Scriptures as authoritative. There was also a need to embrace "the consistent prophetic word in the Catholic charismatic renewal for the past several years" (ibid.) The Catholic Church was entering an era of deprivation, opposition, and persecution. Catholics must become "disciplined, trained, holy, righteous, sacrificing people ready to endure all sorts of difficulties" (ibid., 7).

The National Service Committee called for a special recognition of new and renewed ministries.[27] The bishops "should be open to ordaining those [leaders] trained in them [charismatic programs for educating in spiritual, intellectual, and pastoral formation] to official ministry in the church whenever possible" (ibid.). The programs used to train these new leaders should be kept separate from existing seminaries and pastoral institutes because of their deficiencies.

The National Service Committee proposed a specific campaign to evangelize adult Catholics. The principal components needed for this campaign were adult catechesis and—as a directed goal—the incorporation of Catholics into a fellowship of committed believers. There was an obvious promotion of the covenant community ideal:

The Catholic charismatic renewal has been the seedbed
from which many renewal communities have developed
in recent years. These communities are perhaps the best
hope for effective evangelization and catechesis in the
Church today and ought to serve as models for the
development of similar communities, whether in parochial or non-parochial environments (ibid., 8).

Finally, strong men were needed to lead the turnabout.
"Strong and mature men" would make it possible for "strong
women" to serve the church in "genuine complementarity"
with men.[28]

The service committee concluded its report by implying
that, unless the recommended steps were taken, the Catholic
Church would continue to suffer a serious decline in influence.

An Increasing Sense of Crisis

Did the Holy Spirit initiate the "The State of the Catholic
Church"? Or was it the work of people, breaking the mold of
the divine referendum for the charismatic renewal? The statement to the bishops could easily be interpreted as overbearing. At the least, it was an unusual message from a group that,
seven years before, had denied any desire to direct other people's views.

In sharp contrast to the aggressive tone of the report was a
growing sense among the leaders that the renewal had
entered its own time of confusion and crisis. By the end
of the 1970s, the period of rapid growth in membership
appeared to be ending.[29] The circulation of *New Covenant* was
staying at about sixty thousand and the era of mass meetings
appeared to be ending. Most significantly, a lot of Catholics
who called themselves charismatic made no claim to personal
pentecostal experience.[30] Many prayer groups, although they
acknowledged the reality of the pentecostal gifts, did not
operate in them.

A joint meeting of the National Service Committee and their
Advisory Committee convened in January 1980 to explore
their deep concerns about stagnation in the renewal.[31] During
an all day session of prayer, the combined groups asked the

Holy Spirit to give them insight into the current situation. Sr. Ann Shields, a National Service Committee member, described her sense of a deadening factionalism:

> I think we can say that we see the renewal slowing down and/or fragmenting and in the fragmentation has come a dilution of God's word, dilution of the direction that God has given us over the past several years. . . . Because we have lost sight of the vision, or because we're not clear on what the vision is, we've turned in and we settled, perhaps, for much less than what God wants for us. There was a call of God to us as individuals and as a people to mourn and weep and we have not done it. . . . We know we have to stop seeing disunity as an unfortunate set of historical circumstances. We must see disunity as an abomination in the sight of God, as a blot on God's honor and as a disgrace to his name (National Communications Office 1980, 4).

Fr. Michael Scanlan had a prophetic word that seemed to offer a further reason for the sense of disarray. It sounded remarkably similar to other controversial prophecies of that time. The essence of the message was that the early period of blessings in the renewal was being replaced by a baptism of fire. This baptism was a corrective that was needed to combat a growing spirit of compromise and accommodation:

> I will not tolerate the situation that is going on. I will not tolerate the mixture and the adulterous treating of gifts and graces and blessings with infidelity, sin, and prostitution. My time is now among you.
>
> What you need to do is to come before me in total submission to my word, in total submission to my plan, in total submission to this new hour. What you need to do is to drop those things that are your own, those things of the past. What you need to do is to see yourselves and those whom you have responsibility for in light of this hour of judgment and purification. You need to see them in that way and do for them what will best help them to stand strong and be among the faithful servants.

> For there will be casualties. It will not be easy, but it is
> necessary. It is necessary that my people be, in fact, my
> people; that my church be, in fact, my church; and that my
> Spirit, in fact, bring forth the purity of life, the purity and
> fidelity to the gospel (Ranaghan and Ranaghan 1980a, 15).

This strong call to repair damaged personal relations and submit to divine leading was first embraced and then disregarded.

Debate intensified over where, if anywhere, the charismatic renewal was heading. In 1980, the long-simmering conflict between the Ann Arbor–Steubenville and South Bend leadership cadres broke into the open. This began as ideological differences over how covenant communities should relate to modern culture.[32] It soon became a personality and leadership struggle. The Association of Christian Communities broke up, with most of the member groups realigning with either Ann Arbor or South Bend.

Not surprisingly, more recent events are the hardest to interpret. A strong argument can be made that years of internecine struggle (especially within the National Service Committee) forced the flow of renewal leadership to begin to move away from the power centers in Ann Arbor and South Bend. As these groups became preoccupied with gaining control of the movement, there was a sense of drift nationally. It is safe to say that the period of the late 1970s and early 1980s was marred by competing visions, incessant quarreling, and a general sense of malaise.

The result was a shifting away from a national charismatic identity, a tenuous concept at best. There was a type of vacuum, and groups within the renewal appear increasingly to have gone their own ways. Lacking a clear direction from the top, local charismatic leaders moved to protect their independent and regional interests, often by becoming more closely identified with their diocese. This is not to say that they became fully immersed in the institutional church, but their identification increased markedly. This new regionalism was being asserted through the influence of bishop's liaisons and other locally based leaders.

By the early 1980s, the whole renewal badly needed cleansing and a new direction. Many of the leaders had become fixed on their own views and were overly competitive. A Spirit-led effort cannot have a clear vision when human nature interferes to this extent. The sense was developing that the renewal needed a second chance, a renewing of the renewal.

Diocesan Basing

The most powerful new trend in the renewal was "diocesanization" (see Sullivan 1988). By the middle of the 1970s most local bishops, following the directives of the 1975 bishops' statement, had appointed liaisons to keep them apprised of local charismatic groups. These appointees were usually priests or nuns who had significant personal involvement with the renewal. Initially, these liaisons had little power. In 1978, they met to form an independent national association, and their influence began to increase. With intensification in the conflicts between Ann Arbor–Steubenville and South Bend, these liaisons became a stabilizing factor. With the 1980 dissolution of the Association of Christian Communities, they became a dominant factor and are now significantly represented on the National Service Committee.[33]

One diocesan success story, countering the general sense of decline, occurred in Rockville Centre, Long Island (see Aridas 1977 and 1987; Boucher 1988). In the early 1970s, an aggressive strategy for parish renewal had been pursued there through the creation of pastoral training centers, which have become very popular in recent years. In distinction from many other places, the Long Island charismatic renewal developed through the emergence of a large number of small prayer groups instead of a few larger ones. This posed the special problem of small group leaders burning out. Under the leadership of Fr. Chris Aridas, the charismatic renewal in the Rockville Centre diocese was split into seven regions. Prayer group leaders were encouraged to meet with others within their own region for mutual support.

In September 1979, the lay pastoral team for the diocesan renewal received a directive prophetic word: "Unite my family on Long Island." In response to this challenge, the leadership began a special effort to support and help coordinate over one hundred prayer groups, thirty-six intercessory prayer groups, and five renewal centers across the diocese. In addition CHARISM, a spiritual growth institute that provides ongoing formation for lay leaders, was established.

Father Aridas described the rationale for this high level of local initiative as a desire to keep charismatic ministries alive throughout the whole diocese. In addition, there was the hope of keeping the image of the charismatic renewal as a move of the Holy Spirit to the entire church:

> Ministry without supervision becomes anarchy. Ministry implies supervision and accountability. [The charismatic renewal] is not a special interest group. . . . The charismatic experience is part of the fabric of the church ("CHARISM" 1987, 30).

The process of diocesanization has been less comprehensive nationally,[34] but the Rockville Centre model has often been pointed to as a way to maintain charismatic vitality.

The 1981 and 1982 National Conferences

Between 1979 and 1981, annual attendance at the national conferences fell below ten thousand, and there was talk that the meetings would not continue. Some refused to interpret the drop in numbers negatively, but saw the decline as part of the divine sifting and winnowing process prophesied by Fr. Scanlan in 1978 (Reimers 1983). At the 1981 conference, the nine thousand attending pledged to "embrace the cross" and do whatever was necessary to meet the demands of a changed situation.

Declining attendance may simply have reflected the effects of institutional acceptance by the Catholic Church, which diminished in many the sense of being part of a new and radical movement. Also, and perhaps more importantly, divisions among the national leadership had thwarted a sense of overall direction and allowed many to drift away from vital identification.

The 1982 Notre Dame Conference drew thirteen thousand people. This sudden increase in numbers was interpreted as a sign that the renewal was entering into a new and more hopeful era: God was going to renew the face of the earth and give the charismatics a second chance (National Service Committee 1982; Jahr 1982).[35] The 1982 gathering could best be characterized as a mixture of formal rededication and love feast. The key to unleashing the "fresh outpouring of the Holy Spirit" was to realize that this would require more selflessness in the future. Jack Brombach, a leader of the Servants of the Lord community in Minneapolis summarized the prevailing view: "In the early days of the renewal we focused on ourselves, our needs, our prayer life. . . . But along with that we need to be concerned about the rest of the people that God wants to save. He gave us these gifts so the church could be built up" (Jahr 1982, 36).

The National Service Committee used the apparent success of the 1982 conference to call for a back-to-basics campaign (see National Service Committee 1983b).[36] This new effort was to stress personal conversion, Spirit-baptism, the exercise of spiritual gifts and an increased emphasis upon cultivating specifically Catholic spirituality. But splits within the renewal had by now become too deep to allow for an easy return and the campaign failed.[37]

The lingering malaise may have started at the top, but frustration was felt most keenly at the local level. High-level power struggles, not uncommon when a renewal movement achieves prominence, were being experienced locally as the sense grew that the renewal was declining; that once-zealous supporters were leaving and not being replaced (Quebedeaux 1983, 233–39). This in turn led to feelings of isolation as well as the perception that established prayer groups were undergoing diminution and a slow death (Thorp 1984).

The 1984 Bishops' Statement

In March 1984, the American bishops published their third pastoral statement on the renewal. This statement was the most supportive to date, perhaps reflecting the bishops' greater personal involvement in the workings of local charismatic groups. The overall tone of the document was apparent in the conclusion:

We wish those in the charismatic renewal to know that we make our own the view of Yves Congar: "The charismatic renewal is a grace for the Church." We assure those in the charismatic renewal of the support they enjoy from the bishops of the United States, and we encourage them in their efforts to renew the life of the Church (U.S. Catholic Conference 1984, 19).

Despite their strong support, the bishops continued to caution against fundamentalism and overzealousness in the exercise of authority. They also urged better training for local prayer group leaders, observing that "the leadership issue is the most pressing problem facing the renewal" (ibid., 17).

Shortly after this statement was issued Bishop Joseph McKinney, who had chaired the National Service Committee during the worst of the troubles between Ann Arbor and South Bend in the early 1980s, was named to chair a new Bishops' Liaison Committee. This new committee, along with the diocesan liaisons themselves, became an influential new factor in the renewal. The Bishops' Liaison Committee worked closely with the National Service Committee and local liaisons to develop diocesan centers, which were intended to train leaders and inform local priests about the charismatic renewal.

New Networks Form

With the breakdown of the association of communities in 1980, Word of God (Ann Arbor) and People of Praise (South Bend) formed their own associations. The Word of God network, an international ecumenical community called Sword of the Spirit, had approximately 7,600 adult members as of 1987. The People of Praise formed a single ecumenical covenant community with twenty-three North American locations and approximately 3,500 men, women, and children as members by 1987.

A major covenant community that remained free of the controversies of the late 1970s and early 1980s was Mother of God (Gaithersburg, Maryland). This community became the home base for prominent charismatic thinkers such as Fr. Francis Martin and Fr. Peter Hocken. The Mother of God community has also been influential through the publication of a monthly pamphlet, *The Word Among Us,* which acts as a popular aid to Bible study and personal reflection (see Hocken 1988a).

In May 1983, the Ann Arbor–Steubenville group initiated the FIRE evangelistic association as their own attempt to "get back to the basics." The FIRE team was composed of Ralph Martin, Sr. Ann Shields, Fr. Michael Scanlan, and Fr. John Bertolucci. FIRE (an acronym for faith, intercession, repentance, and evangelism) proclaimed a message of personal conversion, baptism in the Holy Spirit and fire, and open allegiance to Rome (Scanlan 1988, 1).[38]

The first FIRE rally drew thirteen thousand to the Meadowlands Arena, East Rutherford, New Jersey. The alliance quickly became a source of controversy, as they appeared to others in the renewal to be attempting to create their own infrastructure, independent of the National Service Committee.[39] The charge of promoting an independent agenda was vigorously refuted by Ralph Martin, who portrayed FIRE as wanting to serve the whole renewal as well as the Catholic Church:

> We, the members of the FIRE team, see ourselves as serving the [whole] Catholic charismatic renewal by providing good teaching and materials and activities that can help nourish people spiritually. But we also see our efforts as a contribution of the charismatic renewal to the Catholic Church. Our main goal is to evangelize Catholics: to teach them how to meet Jesus personally if they have not already, and to help them sustain that relationship with teaching on faith, prayer, commitment, and many other important aspects of Christian life (Lilly 1984, 38).

By 1985, FIRE had developed a formal organizational structure with twenty-six thousand members and fifty-six FIRE chapters in twenty-two states (Shields 1986).

A sign that the Ann Arbor–Steubenville group might, in fact, be going ahead with their own renewal vision has been the increasing sponsorship of prayer group leaders' conferences at the University of Steubenville, beginning in June 1983 (Cavnar 1983). The declared purpose of these weekend meetings is to provide local leaders with an opportunity for instruction and encouragement to supplement their local groups. But an added benefit to the Ann Arbor–Steubenville group has been the continuous promotion of their views on directions in the charismatic renewal and the University of Steubenville as a spiritual and intellectual hub for the movement.

"Kansas City II"

Following Kansas City 1977, Cardinal Suenens and Vinson Synan promoted the idea of a series of ongoing worldwide rallies on Pentecost Sunday, demonstrating the unity between pentecostals and charismatics (Synan 1984, 130). Such gatherings did take place regionally in the United States from 1978 to 1981 under the name Jesus Day Rallies. The initial 1978 Jesus Day Rally drew fifty-five thousand people to the Meadowlands Stadium in East Rutherford, New Jersey. Subsequent rallies were held in different parts of the country, in order to promote a sense of grass-roots unity. By 1980, over one hundred rallies of varying sizes had taken place. But follow-up planning was not consistent and early enthusiasm waned. This led to the end of the Jesus Day concept after 1981 (see Hocken 1988b).

With the real decline in pentecostal unity following Kansas City 1977, there remained a question as to whether such a nationwide gathering would ever be attempted again. Various leaders discussed the potential for another general gathering but were dissuaded by the challenges involved. Pentecostal and charismatic leaders did continue to talk, however, about a "Kansas City II" at their annual Charismatic Concerns Committee meetings in Glencoe, Missouri. In 1985, spurred on by the irrepressible combination of David du Plessis and the Mennonite charismatic leader, Nelson Ditwiller, they decided the time had come to attempt "Kansas City II."

In May 1985, thirty-two leaders, primarily charismatics, met in St. Louis to form the North American Renewal Service Committee, a steering committee for "Kansas City II" and ongoing ecumenical projects. The committee set as its goal "to bring the majority of the human race to Jesus Christ by the end of the century."[40] They also approved a policy statement, written by Kevin Ranaghan, that grounded working relationships among pentecostals and charismatics (Ranaghan 1987, 3).

The First North American Congress on the Holy Spirit and World Evangelization was held in New Orleans in October 1986. The congress involved more than seven thousand church leaders from forty denominations and focused on the theme of world evangelization. Fr. Tom Forrest, the coordinator for the Vatican's Evangelization 2000 project, was a principal charismatic speaker. He encouraged the various pentecostal groups to unite again around the basic Kansas City 1977 proclamation, "Jesus Christ is Lord" (see Lawson 1986; Lilly 1986; Ziegler 1988).

"Kansas City II" did take place at the New Orleans Superdome in July 1987 (see North American Renewal Service Committee 1987b; Duin 1987; Lawson 1987). Unlike Kansas City 1977, which had focused upon fostering Christian unity, this meeting expressed a theme of unity for a purpose: world evangelism, accompanied with the power of pentecostal signs and wonders. Vinson Synan, the chair of the North American Renewal Service Committee, had initially projected that seventy thousand would attend the meeting (Synan 1987b, 3), but the actual number was closer to thirty-thousand. This was also well below the forty-five thousand that had attended Kansas City 1977.

This low turnout is hard to interpret. It may simply indicate a declining enthusiasm for mass rallies. It may reflect the long-term cost of fragmentation and a shift away from the focus of unity that characterized earlier days. The fact that New Orleans is an expensive city and not centrally located may also have been a factor. If numbers were down, programs were not. The agenda was more elaborate than Kansas City 1977: 110 workshops rather than 28; 40 fellowships represented rather than 10; a huge, air-conditioned domed stadium; a culminating seventeen-block-long parade through downtown New Orleans.

The exuberance of the event was tempered for some by the immensity of the task. Moishe Rosen, the founder of Jews for Jesus, told those who attended his workshop:

I'm not optimistic for the future. There are those who want to sound the trumpets of triumph, but I only see the struggle. And I see the children of God looking for an easy way out. This is a time for mourning, not for announcing Godly victory (Duin 1987, 24).

The literal last word of the congress came on the closing night, and it had a familiar tone. Fr. Francis Martin, a veteran of the early days of the Catholic charismatic renewal, solemnly prophesied:

> I have called you to preach the gospel. The word of the cross is foolishness to those who are on the way to destruction. To those who are being saved it is the power of God. My people, I have told you in my word that those who seek to be astonished find my cross a stumbling block. Those who seek to find their minds satisfied on their power find it foolishness. But I, your Lord crucified, am the wisdom of God and the power of God. . . .
>
> And I have something to say to you leaders among my people. I have chosen you. You did not choose me. I have placed you to care for my people. I have committed myself to you and my blood to you but I have this against you. You compete with one another. You rely on human resources. You are attached to money. I tell you this—I have chosen you and because you preach my name, I will not count you as being against me. But unless you seek my will, unless you pour out your life before me, unless you tremble at my word, I cannot stand by what you do. . . .
>
> It may seem splendorous in the eyes of men, but in my eyes, unless you are submitted to me and my word, it can be hay and straw. You will escape the fire of judgment as a man escaping from a burning building. But your work which seems so great can go up in smoke. . . .
>
> And to all of you I say, this is the person for whom I have regard—the one who is lowly and afflicted and trembles at my word. This is the glory I promise you (1987, 23).

Following the New Orleans meeting, planning began for a major launch-pad rally to begin a decade of world evangelization. That meeting was held at the Indianapolis Hoosierdome in the summer of 1990, but produced no long-term evangelization strategies.

Conclusion

The Catholic charismatic renewal has undergone and continues to undergo vast changes. Beginning in the relative protection of the college campuses at Duquesne and Notre Dame, it emerged within a matter of years into greater public awareness. By the early 1970s, the renewal began to catch on across the country as a powerful new way to experience the Christian life.

Immediately following its increased influence in the 1970s, the renewal began a period of serious decline. It is not clear whether this decline has even now been reversed. This situation suggests two questions: What happened to defuse the early momentum of the renewal? What is the effect upon current common witness attempts?

I believe the answer to the problem is centered in relationships. Relationships are not to be underestimated, they are a spiritual force given to people. The charismatic renewal began as a spontaneous, collective impulse grounded in Spirit-based relationships. It included the hope that this special experience could be transmitted to the entire Christian church.

Much of this early relational grace in the renewal was squandered. People who began with an unquestioned unity did not know how to disagree well. It was obvious that some attempt at institutionalization would have to occur in order to sustain the renewal. But, in many cases, this happened at the price of surrendering the unity that was originally intended. The move by Ann Arbor and South Bend to concentrate power and decision making short-circuited natural relationships by blueprinting them. There was a tendency to plunge ahead, not fully realizing that relationships are a spiritual force and not a human arrangement. As one former member of a strict covenant community told me: "We started out fresh and alive. We ended up like #2 pencils."

With such stifling of views, there was less room for the Holy Spirit to speak creatively through people. Contradictions arose that raised questions about what was of God and what was of the flesh. With such poor discernment, there was a problem with moving forward in the Holy Spirit and a tendency to ricochet from one vision to another. In my opinion, this was the main reason the renewal stalled after only ten to twelve years. This was a time when it should still have been on the ascent.

Breakdowns in relationships, especially among leaders who once were personal friends, appear to have derailed the renewal for several years. But the period of the late 1970s and early 1980s also saw new relationships begin to grow at the local level (the diocesanization of the renewal). The ultimate importance of this shift is unclear, but it may be that a healing process began that may revitalize the charismatic renewal from the grass roots up.

It seems to me that charismatic renewal flourishes best when freedom of the spirit is trusted and emphasized. This is not to say that there is to be no control or overall sense of direction. But control should be no more than what is needed for good order. Discerning leadership in such matters is needed; that is, leaders who have the type of understanding that succumbs in complete obedience to the leadings of the Holy Spirit.

The reconstituted National Service Committee has designated evangelization as the central reason for the charismatic renewal's existence. There is nothing definitive yet as to what this evangelization entails. If the Catholic charismatics are to regain a sense of unity sufficient to evangelize, they will certainly need to reclaim a common vision. But a common vision is not enough. Passing over the relational breakdowns of the past without resolving them is unacceptable. Common witness depends on moving forward in the flow of the Holy Spirit. Relational breakdowns, past or present, block that process. Without full acknowledgment of mistakes made in this area, joining together in any large common witness venture would be unrealistic.

Originally, the renewal allowed Catholic charismatics to stand shoulder to shoulder with other pentecostals to declare their unity through the graces of Spirit-baptism. This is a profoundly simple message, and the original relationships it engendered need to be restored. But to stand side by side also implies the grace to forgive past hurts and to allow present differences. In saying that God has an army, certainly one cannot insist that all God's soldiers must wear the same uniform. This is an important part of the charismatic renewal's early heritage and, along with the simplest proclamation of Spirit-baptism, it needs to be recovered.

Spirit-Baptism: Assemblies of God and Catholic Interpretations

Both the Assemblies of God and the Catholic charismatics clearly support the idea of Spirit-baptism's transforming power. The difference lies in their varied interpretations of that experience. Is Spirit-baptism understood to be part of an ongoing conversion process, or does it represent an entirely separate stage in Christian development? Catholics charismatics generally hold that Spirit-baptism is part of a single conversion event while Assemblies of God pentecostals hold to a two-stage understanding in which Spirit-baptism is separate from and subsequent to conversion.[1]

The complete phrase *baptism with the Holy Spirit* is not found in the Bible. Of course, this does not invalidate Spirit-baptism as a developed parascriptural concept since "in Scripture baptism with the Holy Spirit is no technical term" (Tugwell 1972, 269). The common biblical rendering is *en pneumati hagioi*, "with Holy Spirit" (Schoonenberg 1974). The term itself is based on the promise of Acts 1:5: "John baptized with water, but you, not many days from now, will be baptized in [with] the Holy Spirit." For the purposes of this study, I have been using the term *Spirit-baptism.*

The Assemblies of God and Spirit-Baptism

Standard Assemblies' interpretations of Spirit-baptism are found in Myer Pearlman's *Knowing the Doctrines of the Bible,* Ernest S. Williams's *Systematic Theology,* Ralph Riggs's *The Spirit Himself,* and Stanley Horton's *What the Bible Says about the Holy Spirit.* These texts have become principal resources, and, with other occasional citations, I have used them as the basis for my presentation.[2]

As a rule, the denomination's leaders avoid debates on doctrine unless they deem the subject matter to be essential. Even the 1916 Statement of Fundamental Truths can be seen more as a rough guideline than a clear confessional statement. Such latitude is not extended to divergent views concerning Spirit-baptism: the Assemblies insists that the experience is always separate from and subsequent to personal conversion. They also insist that Spirit-baptism must be initially evidenced by the sign of tongues. On these points, a form of orthodoxy has been established.

In my opinion, the Assemblies doctrine of Spirit-baptism grows out of a defensive posture. Apologists have been anxious to protect the denomination from charges of subjectivity and extremism. To do this, they developed an elaborate argument to validate their particular interpretation of Spirit-baptism. There is a reluctance to look into other interpretations, perhaps for fear of losing the sense of assured identity that a rigid definition of Spirit-baptism brought to the Assemblies. As a result, their position has hardened to the point of becoming a denominational shibboleth. But, behind the scenes, a reconsideration of the Assemblies' doctrinaire views may be going on.[3]

The Shift From Perfection to Power

Language used to describe Spirit-baptism can be traced back to John Wesley and his colleague, John Fletcher.[4]

This terminology was carried forward into the nineteenth-century–American revival known as the Second Great Awakening. Between 1845 and 1870, the idea of a special Spirit-baptism was given such prominence that emphasis upon spiritual empowerment supplanted the attention once given to Christian perfectionism (Dayton 1975, 43). The pre-eminent revivalist Charles Finney (1792–1875) used Spirit-baptism language in his memoirs (Finney 1908, 55). But the truly pivotal figure in the shift from perfection to power was the first president of Oberlin College, Asa Mahan (1799–1889) (Dayton 1975, 43–51).

The essence of Mahan's position was that if Jesus Christ had sought out special power for his salvific mission, his followers must be expected to do the same (Mahan 1870, 25). As a result of the influence of Mahan and others, a new meaning was given to the term *pentecostal*. The word came to describe a specific experience of spiritual empowerment[5] that was available to all Christians (Peters 1956, 49).

Finney followed Mahan's lead in ascribing special importance to Spirit-baptism, and issued a tract in 1872 emphasizing the distinction between the peace and the power of the Holy Spirit. Finney believed that divine peace is given at conversion but that spiritual empowerment comes with God's confirmation to serve, a calling that should be sought out by every believer: "They [the early disciples] first *consecrated themselves* to the work, and continued in prayer and supplication until . . . they received this promised enduement of power from on high" (Finney 1872, n.p.). Finney distanced himself from Mahan's stress upon the personal enlightenment and corporate union available following Spirit-baptism. He preferred to emphasize a new capacity for victorious living, which has always been the goal of holiness perfection.

This pronounced shift in emphasis from perfectionism to Spirit-baptism was "a profound transformation of theological ideas and associated concepts" (Dayton 1975, 48). It is associated with a change in emphasis from christocentrism to pneumatology, and led to an intensification in both eschatological awareness and the use of prophecy (ibid.).

Widespread Endorsement for Spirit-Baptism

With this shift in emphasis came a plethora of new teachings. Assemblies of God writers have often cited evangelical leaders such as A. J. Gordon (1828–1887), F. B. Meyer (1847–1929), A. B. Simpson, Andrew Murray (1828–1917), and, most particularly, Reuben A. Torrey, as strong supporters of empowerment through Spirit-baptism (Riggs 1949, 47–51; Williams 1953, 3:59–61).

Early pentecostals represented Torrey, the first superintendent of Chicago's Moody Bible Institute, as a special herald for Spirit-baptism (Gee 1949, 4–5). He strictly held that spiritual regeneration and Spirit-baptism should be understood as separate and distinct realities:

> The Baptism with the Holy Spirit is an operation of the Holy Spirit distinct from and subsequent and additional to His regenerating work. . . . In regeneration there is an impartation of life, and the one who receives it is fitted for service. *Every true believer has the Holy Spirit.* But not every believer has the Baptism with the Holy Spirit (Torrey 1898, 271).

Torrey believed that Spirit-baptism is imparted to the believer subsequent to regeneration. The reality of this transformation is witnessed to through victorious Christian living, an open testimony to Christ, and ongoing Christian service (Torrey 1895, 56).

But—unlike the later classical pentecostals—Torrey did not link Spirit-baptism to a climactic spiritual event. Extraordinary manifestations may accompany Spirit-baptism, but they need not do so. A simple act of faith is enough to assure the believer that the reality of Spirit-baptism is theirs. With the growing interest in the importance of the event of Spirit-baptism, it only remained for Charles Parham and his group in Topeka to ask: Is there a specific manifestation that can assure seekers of the reality of their Spirit-baptism?

Biblical Warrants

Classical pentecostals base their interpretation of Spirit-baptism primarily upon Luke-Acts (Hollenweger 1972, 336). This choice has caused some critics to claim that the source of the pentecostals' peculiar identity is a lesser theologian,[6] inferring that theological description is done better through Paul.[7]

With their predilection for Luke-Acts, Assemblies writers consistently describe Spirit-baptism in language that emphasizes special supernatural empowerment: "The point we wish to emphasize is the following: the Baptism with the Holy Spirit, which is a baptism of power, is charismatic in character, judging from the descriptions of the results of the impartation" (Pearlman 1935a, 312–13).[8] Despite the attempt to portray Spirit-baptism as a mysterious force, not a fixed concept, descriptions of its causes and effects have become formalized through time.

The terms used to describe Spirit-baptism in Acts are actually quite varied. The following list is indicative of their range. Verses in parentheses show where the original expressions are used again.

Acts	1:5	"to be baptized with the Holy Spirit"	(11:16)
	1:8	"the coming of the Holy Spirit (upon)"	(19:6)
	2:4	"to be filled with the Holy Spirit"	(4:8, 31; 9:17)
	2:17	"to pour out the Spirit"	(2:18, 33; 10:45)
	2:38	"to receive the Holy Spirit"	(8:15, 17, 19; 10:47; 19:2)
	5:32	"to give the Holy Spirit"	(8:18; 11:17; 15:8)
	8:16	"the Holy Spirit fell down on"	(10:44; 11:15)

The primary passages used to develop the doctrine of Spirit-baptism include Acts 2:1–4, 8:5–17, 9:1–19, 10–11, 19:1–7, and Mark 1:9–11 and 16:17.[9] These verses are repeatedly used by classical pentecostals to support two claims: first, that Spirit-baptism is subsequent to conversion and, second, that it is initially evidenced by the sign of tongues.

Assemblies of God apologists desire to assert the importance and reasonableness of accepting Spirit-baptism. They do this by appealing to what they see as the biblical warrants for that experience. Two audiences are addressed here: (1) other classical pentecostals, who are also searching for biblical grounds on which to base their experience and present it as a legitimate option; and (2) the evangelical subculture, with whom pentecostals sense a doctrinal and historic kinship. Many evangelicals—influenced by Reuben Torrey and others—hold to the reality of Spirit-baptism in principle. But they do not recognize specific preconditions before Spirit-baptism, nor do they expect supernatural manifestations to result from it. By developing their biblical arguments, the Assemblies apologists hope to defend not only their own right to exist but also to appeal to nonpentecostals with the reasonableness of pentecostal claims.

Subsequence Claims

The Assemblies principally use Acts to establish the doctrine of subsequence; that is, the claim that Spirit-baptism is an event that must happen after conversion. The preponderant use of one source compels these apologists to defend a lack of corroborating evidence from other parts of the New Testament. The standard assertion remains that Acts is the natural source for understanding the unique dynamics of Spirit-baptism since the gospel accounts predict a gift of the Holy Spirit that had not yet been given, while the epistles were written to Christians to whom Spirit-baptism is an established reality.[10] Such argumentation draws the response that pentecostal writers have practiced eisegesis on the text, meaning they have imposed upon it their own preordained interpretation (Bruner 1970, 68–69).

THE TEXTS USED

Acts 2:1–4 (The Day of Pentecost). Superintendent Ralph Riggs (1895–1971) argued that this incident, in which 120 disciples were "filled with the Holy Ghost," was not to be compared to the insufflation incident recorded in John 20:22. At that earlier time, Jesus breathed upon the disciples so that they might receive the Holy Spirit. Riggs interpreted Jesus' action to be a giving of his own spirit: "The Spirit of God's Son, the Spirit of Christ, as the Spirit of conversion" (1949, 4).[11]

Ernest S. Williams was another denominational leader who made an attempt to systematically defend the doctrine. He allowed that the distinction between receiving the Holy Spirit at conversion and subsequently being filled with the Holy

Spirit might cause nonpentecostals difficulty (Williams 1953, 3:39). Williams attempted to deflect such criticism by pointing out that the Scofield Reference Bible (a cornerstone of conservative evangelicalism) also makes a distinction between having the Spirit and being filled with the Spirit (ibid., 3:40). He claimed that subsequence is established in Acts 2:4, "And they were all filled with the Holy Ghost, and began to speak with other tongues, as the Spirit gave them utterance." There was every indication that the disciples were already saved on the Day of Pentecost. Thus Williams interpreted the language of Acts 2:4 as establishing the reality of subsequent spiritual empowerment (see Pearlman 1935a, 335–41; Horton 1976, 142).

Acts 2:38 (The Address to the Converts at Pentecost). Assemblies of God writers read Peter's instruction to the converts as establishing an ideal for all Christians. Riggs wrote about separate baptisms:

> At their repentance He [the Holy Spirit] would baptize them into the Body of Christ. Then they would take a public stand for Christ by being baptized in water in His name. Following that, they would receive the gift of the Holy Spirit (1949, 55).

Peter's charge, "Repent, and be baptized every one of you in the name of Jesus Christ for the remission of sins, and you shall receive the gift of the Holy Ghost," also logically and chronologically establishes subsequence (ibid.).

Acts 8: 5–17 (The Samaritan Converts). This episode reinforces earlier arguments for subsequence. Williams did not believe that water baptism is the same experience as Spirit-baptism.[12] He described the Samaritan believers as saved but not empowered (1953, 3:43). Myer Pearlman used the incident to say that "one may be in touch with Christ and be a disciple of Christ and yet lack the special enduement of power mentioned in Acts 1:8" (1935a, 309). It is notable that tongues is not explicitly mentioned in this passage. A standard response is that the exercise of extraordinary charisms is implied since

Simon Magus would not have pursued a gift that did not include special supernatural manifestations (Brumback 1949, 207; MacDonald 1964, 7).

Acts 9: 1–19 (Paul's Damascus Experience). Paul's dramatic conversion experience is understood to be prior to his spiritual empowerment in the city: "The apostle Paul was converted on his way to Damascus (Acts 9:1–6) and received his Baptism [in the Holy Spirit] three days later" (Kortkamp n.d., n.p.).

Acts 10–11 (Cornelius and His Household Convert). This incident is more problematic. Cornelius and his household experienced Spirit-baptism spontaneously and seemingly without the prior benefit of conversion, let alone water baptism.[13] Riggs maintained the argument for subsequence even as he allowed for the instantaneous nature of this one event:

> Just so it is all done in obedience to God, and to the best of one's ability, and according to the light one has. Who wouldn't welcome other sovereign interventions in the pouring out of the Holy Ghost as it happened at Cornelius' household? Could we not even consider that this visitation was God's ideal, His perfect pattern: believe Christ, receive the Holy Spirit in immediate succession? (1949, 111)[14]

Riggs went on to say that, even if there is no apparent time lapse between initial conversion and Spirit-baptism, there is a before-and-after sequential reality (see Bruner 1970, 66).

Acts 19:1–7 (The Disciples at Ephesus). This event is similar to the Samaritan incident, involving disciples who were believers but who had not yet fully received the Holy Spirit.[15] This event is used to support the assertion that one could be a Christian yet still need a further filling with the Holy Spirit.[16] Riggs represented the dominant view:

> If all disciples receive this experience of the Holy Spirit when they believe, why did Paul ask these disciples if they had done so? His very question implies that it is

possible to believe without receiving the fullness of the Spirit (1949, 54).

Mark 1:9–11 (The Baptism of Jesus). The Assemblies of God interpretation of this non-Lucan passage emphasizes that Jesus, divine and conceived by the Holy Spirit, underwent a subsequent experience of the Holy Spirit. If this was so for the Master, the same must be so for his disciples (Horton 1976, 84; Williams 1953, 2:26) since Christ serves as an exemplar for all those seeking further empowerment.[17] Apologists have held that the baptismal experience of Christ gives the doctrine of subsequence special credibility.

Initial Evidence Claims

Denominational writers believe that all Spirit-baptized Christians can and will speak in tongues. Tongues is regarded as the indisputable initial evidence of Spirit-baptism. Despite this unique claim, classical pentecostals insist that their principal doctrine is not tongues but salvation through Jesus Christ (Brumback 1949, 99). Still, the "secondary issue" of tongues remains an important and controverted doctrine.

A special distinction remains between tongues understood as initial evidence and tongues understood as an ongoing personal charism. The personal charism of tongues, upon which Paul remarked in 1 Cor. 12:30 ("Do all speak in tongues?"), is seen to have a different purpose. This personal gift is seen either as a private prayer language or a vehicle used to convey divine messages (through interpretation) to the congregation. The persisting charism of tongues is not considered to be a gift experienced by all pentecostals. Evidentiary tongues is considered the only universally shared experience.[18] The biblical warrants used for the initial evidence assertion are essentially the same as those used for subsequence.

THE TEXTS USED

Acts 2:1–6 (The Day of Pentecost). Assemblies apologists argue that the tongues the disciples experienced on Pentecost Day were of a unique type. This event was as much a miracle of hearing as one of speech. Thus, Pentecost Day was a formidable and unrepeatable event.[19] But pentecostals believe that ongoing spiritual insight can be obtained from it. The type of tongues displayed at Pentecost, *akololia,* represents a phenomenon in which a speaker uses one language and the audience hears another. Denominational writers see this as proleptic of a time when the people of every nation would hear the gospel message in their own languages (see, for example, Riggs 1949, 86). They stress Pentecost's symbolic universality:

> All 120 present were filled, all spoke in tongues, and the sound of the tongues was "noised abroad" (2:6). Peter also, speaking before a large group in Jerusalem after the experience at the house of Cornelius, said the like gift fell on them "as it did on us who believed on the Lord Jesus Christ." This suggests that the Spirit fell in the same way, not only on the apostles and the rest of the 120, but on the 3,000 who believed after the message Peter gave at Pentecost. Clearly, this experience was not just for the favored few (Horton 1976, 144).

This release of charismatic power, symbolized by tongues, is specifically interpreted to signify the end of the age (ibid.).

Nonetheless, the writers insist that the Pentecost Day events are relevant to the present time. The first disciples were fully Christian and had had the interior witness of the Holy Spirit prior to that day. The reappearance of tongues is seen by modern pentecostals as evidence that modern disciples have entered another dimension, one of being empowered by the Holy Spirit. Pentecost Day pointed to this future event since the first disciples were similarly "filled with the Holy Spirit" (Bruner 1970, 79).

Acts 8 and 9 (The Samaritan Converts and Paul's Damascus Experience). Neither the Samaritan episode nor Paul's conversion have a recorded incidence of tongues speaking, but pentecostals presume that evidentiary tongues was an element in both situations:

> It was not necessary for him [Luke] to write on its [tongues's] presence in every instance of the baptism

with the Spirit before we could accept it as the initial, physical evidence of that experience. Three out of five times [in Acts] are sufficient for all who read with an open heart, who do not demand an unnecessary recitation of details contrary to common practice in either secular or sacred reporting (Brumback 1949, 232).

The conclusion was that tongues was evident in other instances and should be implicitly applied to these as well.

Acts 10–11 (Cornelius and His Household Convert). This event is referred to as the Gentile's Pentecost. Here the Spirit fell upon Cornelius's household just as it had upon the 120 disciples "at the beginning" (Acts 11:15). The gift of tongues was evident and its presence was later used by Peter to argue for gentile inclusion in the church. Assemblies apologists cite this incident prominently, saying that Peter's insistence confirms tongues as a trustworthy sign of the full imparting of Spirit-baptism (Bruner 1970, 79).

Mark 16:17 (Tongues as a Sign). Writers interpret this verse as a promise that tongues would provide a prominent evidence for spiritual empowerment. The sense of the word *follow* in "these signs shall follow" is that the sign of tongues would be so close as never to be absent from Spirit-baptism (Kerr 1931, 61). Thus, the sign of evidential tongues will never end (a refutation of the argument for the cessation of charismata) but will always accompany a fully empowered Christian witness.

Gordon Fee's Challenge

Beginning in the late 1970s, Gordon Fee, an Assemblies of God minister who was trained as a biblical scholar at the University of Southern California, began to challenge the standard interpretation of Spirit-baptism (see Alexander 1988). Fee, a respected New Testament textual critic whose 1987 introduction to 1 Corinthians appeared in the New International Commentary Series, asserted that Assemblies writers have imposed their own predetermined understanding of Spirit-baptism upon the biblical text and have insisted that this personalized interpretation be considered normative (Fee and

Stuart 1982; Fee 1985). Thus the apologists are reading the text of Luke-Acts through the subjective lens of their experience.[20] Their focus upon the mechanics of Spirit-baptism cannot bear the weight of a mature exegesis.

Fee argued for a return to an earlier pentecostal simplicity. Elaborate attempts at proof-texting to support subsequence and initial evidence claims should be abandoned. Much like the early church era, proof should reside in a present-day witness to the supernatural power of the Holy Spirit:

> What we *must* understand is that the Spirit was the *chief* element, the primary ingredient, of this new existence. For them, [early Christians] it was not merely a matter of getting saved, forgiven, prepared for heaven. It was above all else to receive the Spirit, to walk into the new age with *power.* They simply would not have understood our Pentecostal pneumatology—"Spirit-filled Christian." That would be like saying "Scandinavian Swede" (Fee 1985, 93).

Pentecostals are right to stress their own experiences when talking about Spirit-baptism, but they are wrong to manipulate the text of Acts in order to make it appear that what had happened there should be normative for all time (Fee 1985, 95; Fee and Stuart 1982, 62–65).

The response to Gordon Fee's challenge has been generally restrained, although some have called for his ouster from the denomination (Moon n.d., 1).[21] Because of Fee's high standing and personal popularity, many have been reluctant to confront his views directly, even though he has challenged basic tenets concerning Spirit-baptism. There has been, however, an undercurrent of concern over where official tolerance for such views might lead.

Prior Conditions to Spirit-Baptism

From its earliest days, the Assemblies of God has established obedience, gratitude, and faith as prior conditions for Spirit-baptism (Riggs 1949, 101–2; Pearlman 1935b, 316–19). These conditions emphasize that a person must privately prepare for the experience (Wheelock 1983, 159; Bruner 1970, 57–129). For many classical pentecostals, these conditions remain as essential to the doctrine of Spirit-baptism as the claims to subsequence and initial evidence.

This emphasis upon prior conditions, meeting God's demands for personal preparedness before Spirit-baptism, has been linked to a desire to be found worthy. This concern has its roots in Wesleyan perfectionism, which emphasizes that profound spiritual transformation cannot occur apart from one's seeking it out and counting the cost:

> If you [nonpentecostals] accept our belief concerning tongues, you face the possible loss of religious reputation, ecclesiastical position, life-long friendships, and even temporal comforts. On the other hand, if you reject it, you will be rejecting that which an overwhelming amount of evidence proclaims as truth. Wherefore, brethren, we beseech you to count the cost carefully and prayerfully, and to ask God for grace to suffer the loss of all things rather than to sacrifice the priceless pearl of truth (Brumback 1949, 343).

Thus Spirit-baptism is something to be pondered before being sought.

After conversion, the believer seeking Spirit-baptism is expected to fully surrender to the will of God:

> We present our whole being to Him. Body, soul, and spirit must be yielded. Our physical bodies must be pliable under His power. The tongue is the most unruly of the human members, and the complete abandonment of that tongue to the Holy Spirit indicates that the entire being is surrendered to Him. Thus yielded to our Christ, we are taken into His wonderful charge and submerged into the great Spiritual Element which is none other than the actual Person of the Holy Spirit. This baptism is not complete until every part of one's spirit is saturated and permeated by the blessed Holy Spirit (Riggs 1949, 67).

This surrender has both active and passive aspects. The active element consists of importunate prayer:

> This is God's elimination test to determine whom He considers worthy to receive this priceless gift. It is without

money and without price, but He will give it only to those who *ask* for it. . . . Shall we ask once and let that suffice? Shall we consider that He gave the Spirit to us when asked once, even though there be no evidence then or thereafter that He came? Or shall we shrug our shoulders and say, "It's not our fault. We asked and nothing happened. What more can we do?" . . . Christ's instruction [is] to keep on asking until we receive the Holy Spirit (ibid., 104–5).

The seeker can do no more than ask and must depend on the divine response.

At this point, the element of passive obedience comes into play (ibid., 67; see also Carlson 1976, 73–74). Obedience consists in yielding to the initiatives of the Holy Spirit and waiting for God's moment.[22] This attitude of expectancy is described as "tarrying upon the Lord." Tarrying has its own positive value, taking on an aspect of sacred time. Importunate prayer at this point comes not from the seeker but from the seeker's supporters. The emphasis often shifts from the seeking individual to the entire community's readiness to respond to whatever God might want.[23]

Pentecostals have been accused of forcing a response in such situations. They generally reply that a public crying out is often the price to be paid in order to unleash the power of the Holy Spirit. Though not an absolute (some have experienced Spirit-baptism in private), this tarrying ritual is portrayed as the preferred way to experience Spirit-baptism and has even attained a quasi-sacramental status (Bruner 1970, 103).

A laying on of hands often accompanies the petitioning. This is "a symbol that the one who is praying is a channel through whom the power of the Lord is conveyed—for healing or for blessing" (Riggs 1949, 110). Despite its symbolic importance, the laying on of hands is not an absolute prior condition. But the practice is normatively associated with seeking after Spirit-baptism (Bruner 1970, 113).

Obedience also has a strong moralistic component (ibid., 93–99). That is, active obedience to God is signified by intentional separation from sin. This striving after sinless perfection (known patterns of sin are distinguished from actual though unrecognized patterns of sin) is an impetus coming from conversion and a prerequisite to Spirit-baptism: "As sinners we accept Christ; as saints we accept the Holy Spirit. As there is a faith towards Christ for salvation, so there is a faith toward the Spirit for power and consecration" (Pearlman 1935a, 318). Through the active assistance of the Holy Spirit, the seeker is seen as able to subdue sinful patterns of thought and behavior (Pearlman 1935b, 52–55).

Therefore, a measure of personal sanctity is understood as necessary. God will respond to heroic obedience by providing the measure of holiness needed for the deeper gift of Spirit-baptism. This connection between purity of the heart and spiritual empowerment is based in Acts 15:8–9: "And God who knows the hearts bore witness to them, giving them the Holy Spirit just as he did to us; and he made no distinction between us and them, but cleansed their hearts by faith."

Despite this stress on holiness, Assemblies apologists—unlike full Wesleyan pentecostals—do not hold that sanctification is a crisis event prior to Spirit-baptism (Pearlman 1935a, 307–8). Reflecting William Durham's position in the 1910 finished work debate, they regard sanctification as an ongoing process associated with conversion and as separate from the crisis moment of Spirit-baptism.

Gratitude for the anticipated gift is also understood to be an important precondition for its full reception. Assemblies of God writers understand prior gratitude to be based in an attitude of total confidence that the seeker has already been granted what they asked for. Such confidence on the part of the believer arouses a total response from God:

> Faith in God consists of utter lack of dependence on ourselves or on others and a knowledge that only God has what we need and want . . . but He will give freely as we meet His conditions and ask Him for His gifts. . . . Then we cease from our own works or efforts, and apply to Him for the gift which we seek. He is waiting for us to come to this point (Riggs 1949, 106).

There has also been an insistence upon continued faith, understood by the Assemblies to have two aspects. These two aspects roughly correspond, respectively, to the Reformed and the Wesleyan perfectionist understandings of faith. The first "apprehends Christ in his salvation." This is close to the forensic type of justification identified with evangelicalism. The second type "apprehends the Holy Spirit in his fullness" and represents an activist approach. (Bruner 1970, 104).[24]

Attempts to incorporate both approaches lead to a dissonance as the "free gift" of faith becomes subject to prior conditions.[25] The classical pentecostal movement as a whole has encountered disagreements over whether sanctification should be seen as a separate crisis experience (Wesleyan three-stage) or as a gradual consecration helping the Christian become victorious over sin (Assemblies-Keswickian). The practical result is the same, and faith is secured only through active appropriation.[26] "Faith is not just mental assent to existing facts; it is acting upon these facts" (Cantelon 1951, 26).[27]

The final emphasis of these prior conditions is not on faith in itself, but faith as a source of spiritual empowerment. Assemblies writers argued that the early Christian proclamation was not one of *sola fide* (faith alone) but of faith validated through power. Most pentecostals openly embrace traditional evangelical positions (the imputed or forensic type of faith) and want to be identified with those doctrines. Yet they put most of their primary energies into apprehending spiritual power through an activist approach to faith.[28]

The attempt to meld together distinctly different approaches to faith is defended as an enrichment of doctrine. Pentecostalism is said to be doing the Christian world the service of recovering a lost truth concerning faith's ordinances, or rules. But, given two quite different starting points, this position is difficult to maintain (Wheelock 1983, 215–18).

The term *faith alone* has a different weight and meaning for classical pentecostals than it does for conservative evangelicals. It might be better to substitute a term such as *faith entire,* since most pentecostals understand faith as a spiritual absolute. Their faith quest moves them past the faith sufficient for Spirit-baptism, which is understood as initiatory. The normal Christian life is to be lived in supernatural power, and Spirit-baptism is a gift enabling this power walk.[29] Many pentecostals pursue their goal of faith entire, willing to pay all costs and meet any conditions.[30]

One prior condition not associated with Spirit-baptism is water baptism. The Assemblies of God traditionally baptize only adult believers. Baptism is considered an outer sign of an inner identification with Christ's life, death, burial, and resurrection.[31] Water baptism is the believer's response to God's initiative and an obedient answer to a divine ordinance. As a result, water baptism is seen as an event entirely separate from Spirit-baptism.

The Catholic Charismatics and Spirit-Baptism

A Shift in Sacramental Emphasis

Catholic charismatic theologians hold that a special divine initiative is behind the twentieth-century reappearance of pentecostal gifts. But they do not accept the idea that the Catholic Church has been historically divorced from the power associated with Spirit-baptism. Instead, they believe that the Catholic tradition (especially in its sacramental practice) provides the richest possible context for exploring Spirit-baptism's implications.

In the early church, the initiatory sacraments (baptism, confirmation, and eucharist) were celebrated together, and that was when seekers might have expected to experience Spirit-baptism.[32] Confirmation had been a special moment at which to experience an outpouring of the Holy Spirit. But in the third century, baptism and confirmation began to be conducted separately. Confirmation began to be interpreted as a distinct stage in Christian growth that involved responsible perfecting of the graces first given in baptism (see Cully 1962; Milner 1970). This temporal division set a limit to expectations for the confirmation event (see Ranaghan and Ranaghan 1969, 139).

Charismatic sacramentalists have continued to see Spirit-baptism as connected with the initiatory sacraments and even as the primary benefit of these sacraments. Spirit-baptism's special help may become a factor in spiritual consciousness later or not at all, but it is nonetheless available. At the point of conscious personal appropriation, the abiding reality of Spirit-baptism surfaces. The contemporary Catholic Church lacks sufficient empowerment because most Catholics have limited their expectations of the Holy Spirit. It is this lack of anticipation that constrains the Holy Spirit from operating with full power (McDonnell 1980, 3:6; S. Clark 1976, 56–58).

Materials describing Catholic views on Spirit-baptism are abundant but of uneven quality. There is no dogmatic party line, as with the Assemblies of God. Also, greater allowances are made for variant interpretations. I have chosen to examine the three theologians who have spoken most thoroughly and in greatest depth on the Spirit-baptism issue. Kilian McDonnell, O.S.B., a theologian at St. John's University, Collegeville, Minnesota, represents the main sacramentalist view of Spirit-baptism. He has written extensively on the experience, especially exploring its ecumenical potential. Donald Gelpi, S.J., a professor of theology at the Jesuit School of Theology in Berkeley, California, gave the sacramentalist position a personalist expression. Francis Sullivan, S.J., a professor of dogmatic theology at the Gregorian Institute in Rome, distanced himself from the dominant position and asked whether Spirit-baptism can be interpreted through Thomas Aquinas's category of independent "sendings" of the Holy Spirit. Thus, Sullivan distanced himself from a strictly sacramentalist interpretation. I chose to represent Sullivan's sendings, or missions, position because it represents the most developed alternative to the dominant view.

Sacramentalists have consistently held that the Holy Spirit resides in all baptized believers (K. McDonnell 1980, 3:8). But they also promote the idea that the Holy Spirit, whose graces are made available through the sacraments, can most powerfully be released through Spirit-baptism. Unlike classical pentecostals, they do not insist on the absolute necessity of a crisis experience, although they acknowledge that Spirit-baptism is often associated with a personal spiritual crisis.

Kilian McDonnell's Sacramentalist View

In 1974, an international team of theologians met under the auspices of Cardinal Suenens to write Malines Document I. The document is an active apologetic, intended to show that the charismatic renewal is firmly rooted in the Catholic tradition. It pleads for toleration of charismatics by the larger church, even going so far as to request a cautious endorsement. Kilian McDonnell prepared the final draft of the text, and it accurately reflects his views.

In Malines Document I, McDonnell explored the meaning of Spirit-baptism, the role of experience in faith, and the importance of pentecostal gifts within the Catholic community. He asserted that the charismatic renewal should be understood as participating in the "chronic vigor" (Newman 1894, 203–6) of the Catholic Church:

> Whatever differences there are between the charismatic renewal and earlier renewals, the charismatic renewal stands and wishes to stand in the Catholic tradition which gave birth to the itinerant prophets of the ancient Church, the preaching apostolate of the mendicant orders in the Middle Ages, the Exercises of St. Ignatius, the giving of parish missions (CIC 1349), the liturgical, and other apostolic and spiritual movements (1980, 3:18).

McDonnell saw his task as the defense of the validity of Spirit-baptism within the Catholic context. Thus he called for a tying of that experience to the rites of initiation. His view contrasts with that of classical pentecostals who generally maintain a radical discontinuity with their prepentecostal past. The concern of McDonnell and other Catholic apologists has been to stay identified with the parent tradition, rather than to strike out on their own. This represents a fundamental difference in outlook from the classical pentecostals.[33]

McDonnell made a distinction between the theological and experiential understandings of Spirit-baptism. In the theological sense it means sacramental initiation. In the experiential sense it means "the moment when or the growth process in virtue of which the Spirit, given during the celebration of initiation, comes to conscious experience" (ibid., 3:39–40). McDonnell interrelated these events by interpreting them as two separate stages within an ongoing dynamic of personal conversion. He wrote that a real, experiential transformation of one's life, recognizable as Spirit-baptism, would result when one fully embraced the spiritual powers available in the rites of Christian initiation.

The Body of Christ as a whole is charismatic and has been given special gifts. No distinction in kind exists between charisms, since all contribute to church order and growth. The pentecostal gifts should be understood in light of this fact. McDonnell portrayed the early church as operating with a complete panoply of the gifts of the Holy Spirit:

> By way of example, imagine for the moment that the full spectrum of how the Spirit comes to visibility in a charism extends from A to Z. . . . A to P are such charisms as generosity in giving alms and other acts of mercy (Rom. 12:8) and teaching activities of various kinds. . . . The section of the spectrum which extends from P to Z is supposed here to include such charisms as prophecy, gifts of healing, working of miracles, tongues, interpretation.
>
> It is evident that in the life of the early Church the communities expected that the Spirit would manifest himself in ministries and services which might fall within the spectrum from A to P, but they also expected the Spirit to manifest himself in the other ministries and services within the section of the spectrum which extends from P to Z. . . . Communities in the Church today are not aware that the charisms in the spectrum which extends from P to Z are possibilities for the life of the Church. . . . To that degree they are not really open to them, and in most communities charisms are, as a matter of fact, not operative (ibid., 3:28–29; see also K. McDonnell 1974a, 117–28).

McDonnell believed that God wants to restore the full range of these powers to the Catholic Church.

In a deliberate attempt to distance the Catholic charismatics from classical pentecostals, McDonnell insisted that Spirit-baptism need not be evidenced by tongues. Spirit-baptism "is not in any necessary way tied to tongues" (K. McDonnell 1980 3:49), and the gift of tongues "should neither be given undue attention nor despised. Since it is the lowest of the charisms, it should not be surprising that it is common" (ibid., 3:7). McDonnell felt that the undue role given to tongues had led to a convoluted understanding of the significance of spiritual gifts. He wanted to redress overemphasis on the place of extraordinary charisms as a whole and to restore confidence that all believers are charismatic.

Most theologically sophisticated Catholic charismatics use the term *baptism in the Holy Spirit* to describe "the breaking forth into conscious experience of the Spirit who was given during the celebration of initiation" (ibid., 3:40). Any view that focuses solely on the extraordinary gifts—tongues, healing, and prophecy—hinders a richer understanding of the Spirit-baptism experience. A broad view of Spirit-baptism places proper emphasis upon its ongoing importance rather than encourages the excesses associated with a crisis-event mentality.

McDonnell held that Spirit-baptism is not a subjective disposition but a true experience of intimacy with God.[34] It is not based in feelings, although emotions may accompany the experience and are not to be despised:

> The faith encounter or religious experience includes the emotions. The attempt to divide reason from emotions, as though the latter were unworthy, is dangerous. Experience in the sense used here is something God does in the believer, and it affects the Christianization of the whole person, including the Christianization of the emotions (ibid., 3:33).

More recently, McDonnell refined his sacramentalist argument by appealing to early church sources.[35] He argued that Spirit-baptism is understood to be integral to Christian initiation in the early centuries and that "a probability exists" that New Testament references to baptism dealt with an event more involved than water baptism alone (K. McDonnell 1989, xiii–xiv). To support his contention, McDonnell used—among others—Tertullian's (A.D. 160–220) treatise *On Baptism*, excerpts from Cyril of Jerusalem's (b. A.D. 350) sermons at the Church of the Holy Sepulchre, and Hilary of Poitiers' (A.D. 315–367) description of the activity of the Holy Spirit in his commentary on Psalm 64 (65). He argued that the evidence supports the understanding of Spirit-baptism as a part of shared public liturgy:

Specific elements which are associated with baptism in the Holy Spirit as understood in the charismatic renewal today are present in the ancient rites of Christian initiation . . . . This would indicate that baptism in the Holy Spirit does not belong to private piety but to public, official, corporate liturgy of the church. What the charismatic renewal today understands as baptism in the Holy Spirit is an integral part of the initiation of all Christians. . . .

This places baptism in the Holy Spirit in a wholly new light. Baptism in the Holy Spirit is not a special grace for some, but common grace for all. Baptism in the Holy Spirit is integral to those sacraments (Baptism, Confirmation, Eucharist) which are constitutive of the deepest nature of the church. . . . The reality of the baptism in the Holy Spirit belongs to that spiritual reality which makes the church to be church (ibid., xxiv).[36]

Through his more recent research, McDonnell has suggested that Spirit-baptism properly belongs to the whole Body of Christ and should not be regarded as an eccentricity relegated to the margins of the church. If Spirit-baptism originally was a public event, it should not become solely identified with private renewal. Indeed, Spirit-baptism should generate a strong public posture by a whole church that declares "Jesus is Lord," especially through evangelization and demands for social transformation (ibid., xxv–xxvi).

Donald Gelpi's Personalist View

During the 1970s, the key period during which Catholic charismatic positions on Spirit-baptism were being defined, Donald Gelpi, S.J., wrote extensively on the subject (see especially Gelpi 1971 and 1976). Gelpi joined Kilian McDonnell in tying the sacraments of Christian initiation with Spirit-baptism, but Gelpi's sacramentalism focused upon the inner dynamics of conversion. He built upon a sacramentalist base to examine Spirit-baptism's impact upon personal spiritual growth. Gelpi also challenged tendencies among charismatics to attempt to domesticate the Holy Spirit, which diminishes the element of mystery and fails to fully recognize the complexity of spiritual life (Gelpi 1978, 1).

In his unique (occasionally opaque) style, Gelpi described Spirit-baptism as comprising several elements. Their operation in unison depends upon the spiritual maturity and receptivity of the individual involved. For fully conscious, sacramentalized people, Spirit-baptism represents God responding to their desire to cooperate more completely with the graces conferred. For those who have only been baptized in water, Spirit-baptism represents the fulfillment of their request for further transformation and their desire to embrace the mysteries of the sacramental life. For the completely unsacramentalized, Spirit-baptism dramatizes their desire to live a full life in the church (Gelpi 1971, 180–83).[37]

Gelpi also tied Spirit-baptism to the graces conferred in the sacraments, but he believed that it is only in the context of a mature spiritual life that these graces can be fully understood (Gelpi 1976, 252) and that Spirit-baptism enhances this insight. Although the Holy Spirit is not bound by ritual and is free to distribute grace in any manner, the normal arena for giving and receiving is the Christian community.[38] Gelpi assigned a special sanctifying grace to the sacrament of baptism. The powers imparted to the new Christian through water baptism are based upon an act of faith, either their own or, in the case of infant baptism, the faith of the community:

> As a ritual act, baptism is a kerygmatic and prophetic challenge to the Christian neophyte to respond in faith to the God who has revealed Himself in Jesus and to do so as a member of the Pentecostal community He founded. The sacrament is also an intercession that the neophyte will respond each day to the transforming presence of the Spirit until (s)he shares fully in the glory of the risen Christ. . . . Every other sacramental act reaffirms and further specifies one's original baptismal covenant (ibid., 141).[39]

Because the covenant sign of baptism mediates what it signifies, it is linked to subsequent graces, especially "lifelong growth in the gifts of sanctification" (ibid., 142). The consent to saving faith implicit in the act of baptism brings certain results. Consent opens the neophyte to whatever charisms the

Holy Spirit might distribute, which is "an unavoidable consequence of integral conversion to Christ" (ibid., 149).

Opening up to a life of service is usually, though not exclusively, linked to the sacrament of confirmation. This sacramental moment is "the public profession of personal readiness to respond to whatever service gift(s) the Spirit may give" (ibid., 146). Confirmation also further specifies the intent of the original baptismal covenant. Citing the Council of Florence, Gelpi said that confirmation, rightly apprehended, is "the Pentecost of the individual Christian" (ibid.).

At this point, the sacramentalized person becomes a full member of a pneumatic community that is charismatic. Gelpi refused any notion that there is an elite corps of charismatics within the church. Spirit-baptism is an extraordinary gift, but it is uniformly available.

Unlike many classical pentecostals but in line with Malines Document I, Gelpi said that the term *the baptism in the Holy Spirit* is misleading. It suggests a single event, whereas he believed that Spirit-baptism is a life-long experience of growth:

> The phrase "the baptism in the Holy Spirit" is also somewhat theologically abrasive. The problem is not with "baptism in the Holy Spirit" but with the article "the." For the article seems to tie Spirit-baptism to a single moment in human experience. In point of fact, Spirit-baptism is a lifetime process. It cannot be equated with any single graced experience, much less with the reception of any service gift, like tongues. . . .
>
> Every Christian is called to a Pentecostal moment analogous to Jesus' Jordan anointing. It consists in the initial reception of one or more service gifts. It affects the intensification and personalization of baptismal faith. It may be reached gradually or suddenly. But when it occurs it ought to change visibly a person's life into a public act of witness to Jesus. Such a moment may also be legitimately designated "a baptism in the Holy Spirit," that is, a deeper plunging into the Spirit received in baptism. It may be called an "experience of Spirit-baptism." But it may not be called "the baptism in the Holy Spirit," for the simple reason that there is much more to "Spirit-

baptism" than the experience of a Pentecostal break-through (ibid., 150–51).[40]

Gelpi obviously portrayed Spirit-baptism in ways more mysterious and less predictable than those with which many pentecostals would be comfortable. In keeping with the Catholic tradition's reluctance to define the ineffable, he insisted that the evidences for Spirit-baptism can never be cut-and-dried.

The problem, then, becomes one of a level of certitude: If people cannot point to the Spirit-baptism moment in their lives, can they be sure that they have entered into the experience at all? Gelpi believed a transformed life offers the best evidence of having been truly Spirit-baptized. The life of such a person is better understood as an ongoing process rather than as a series of spiritual crises, although it may well be punctuated by dramatic events.

Many classical pentecostals would express a concern that if Gelpi's peculiar understanding of Spirit-baptism were adopted, it could lead to a widespread relativization of the importance of spiritual gifts (Wheelock 1983, 297–98). The result would be a loss of the challenge presented by the present-day appearance of pentecostal gifts. This characterization of Gelpi's argument is inaccurate. He did not deny that certain spiritual gifts have special status. But his approach to life in the spirit was egalitarian, supporting the ideal of every individual's giftedness. His principal concern was that Spirit-baptism not be restricted to an elite company within the church. The issue as he saw it is not whether there is a primacy for certain charisms in certain situations, a proposition that seems certain. Rather, Gelpi (like Kilian McDonnell) was concerned that Christians recognize that they live together in a mysterious, charismatic community where all gifts should be honored and their common source acknowledged (Gelpi 1971, 182–83).

Francis Sullivan's Missions View

In his book *Charism and Sacrament,* Donald Gelpi touched upon Thomas Aquinas's description of the Holy Spirit's separate missions of *inhabitatio* ("permanent indwelling") and *innovationes* ("surprises")[41] to the Christian (Gelpi 1976, 148). Gelpi was referring to an aspect of Catholic theology that became the basis for a major nonsacramentalist description of Spirit-baptism.

This "missions of the Holy Spirit" position was developed by Francis Sullivan, S.J. Sullivan endorsed the dominant view (Sullivan 1974, 60–61) but sensed a one-sidedness in the sacramentalist theologians. He wanted to complement the sacramentalist position by seeking out other resources, most notably the work of Thomas Aquinas.[42]

Sullivan believed that the special theological graces associated with Spirit-baptism should not be solely identified with the release of present sacramental graces.[43] Catholic charismatics are encountering a baptism in the Holy Spirit not only experientially but theologically. Sullivan believed that there is an objective theological gift of Spirit-baptism that can be experienced apart from the sacraments.

Malines Document I had not made this point. Francis Sullivan believed there are three reasons for the oversight. First, there is a concern that recognizing an act of the Holy Spirit apart from the sacraments might be interpreted as alien to Catholic theology. Second, there is a predetermined commitment by charismatic apologists that any experience of the Holy Spirit be interpreted solely as a "coming into conscious experience" of what is already there sacramentally. Third, there is the related assumption that all later sendings of the Spirit were tied to the reception of a sacrament (Sullivan 1982, 69–70).

Sullivan's project was intended to focus attention on Thomas Aquinas's description of further missions, or sendings, of the Holy Spirit.[44] Since the Holy Spirit is already present within the Christian, such sendings mean that this divine presence has become apparent in a new and special way. This involves a real change in the person when he or she discovers, through divine initiative, a new intimacy with God. Since the Holy Spirit comes to dwell in the Christian at the moment of baptism, these *innovationes,* or new works of grace, are extrasacramental experiences (Sullivan 1974, 65). This is not to say that they are simply additional charisms. An authentic innovation is larger than a single gift, provoking a more intimate communion with God that "breaks out in ardent love" (Thomas Aquinas, I, q.43, a.5 ad 2um).

From his interpretation of Thomas Aquinas, Sullivan concluded that the sacramentalist emphasis upon a "total gift of grace" that is received with baptism and needs to "break through into experience" is too restrictive. It does not seem to take into account the difference between gifts of grace that make one pleasing to God (*gratis gratum faciens*) and gifts of service (*gratiae gratis datae*):

> It is not correct to think that because we receive the Holy Spirit in Person when he first comes to dwell in us, we thereby receive a "total gift of grace" including all the charismatic gifts. The Holy Spirit is not a thing, like a source of energy, stored up in us and merely needed to be released. The Holy Spirit is a Divine Person, the Lord of His gifts, sovereignly free to give them to whom He chooses, and in the measure of His choosing (Sullivan 1974, 66).

Sullivan noted that renewals of the Holy Spirit have been happening throughout Christian history among many groups.[45] Sullivan believed that any attempt to pin these renewals to an unrepeatable event, be it water baptism or a particular type of Spirit-baptism experience, is an infringement upon the rights of the Baptizer, Jesus Christ, to send the Holy Spirit as he chooses.[46] This seems to align Sullivan with Gelpi's dynamic view of the ongoing mystery of conversion.

Sullivan did not hold that the gift of tongues is a necessary sign of Spirit-baptism, but he indicated that true spiritual renewal must evidence "some kind of experienced change in that [the renewed] person's Christian life" (Sullivan 1982, 73–74). He again cited Thomas Aquinas to point out the difference between seeking and receiving Spirit-baptism. Unlike water baptism, which is based on God's definitive promise of moving one into a new state of grace, Spirit-baptism is verified by some evident change. Still, it is a fact that tongues is recognized by many as a sign-gift of Spirit-baptism and it remains a normative—though not absolutely necessary—feature of the pentecostal movement in the Catholic Church (ibid., 68; Sullivan 1975, 122–23).

Can Spirit-baptism be seen both as arising within the person and being sent from without? Sullivan seems to have wanted to maintain a correspondence with the sacramentalist position, even as he showed a preference for his own extra-sacramentalist view. But it appears that his argument portrays water baptism as a preparation that makes the believer more available for the later and independent sending of the gift of Spirit-baptism.

Conclusion

Catholic and Assemblies of God writers agree that Spirit-baptism is a dynamic component of Christian living. They disagree on how to understand and define that transforming reality.

Assemblies writers have developed a denominational ortho-doxy. The three elements of their position are that (1) Spirit-baptism is subsequent to conversion; (2) it is initially evidenced by tongues; and (3) certain other prior conditions must be met before Spirit-baptism can occur. All three elements presuppose that an individual is actively seeking the experience.

There is a danger in the Assemblies of God position. This is its potential to encourage a type of elitism. To insist on pre-conditions and absolutely predictable norms can lead adher-ents to regard other Christians' spiritual experiences as either misguided or superficial. As Dale Bruner pointed out, the insistence on such preconditions can even lead pentecostals into their own type of works righteousness, that is, salvation through one's own efforts. The reality is that other Christians (including Catholics) are experiencing Spirit-baptism without meeting the Assemblies of God preconditions. This is a fact that apologists for their rigidly held position have not suffi-ciently examined.

There is a fundamental difference in the way Catholic char-ismatics interpret pentecostal experience. From the start, they have expressed a desire to define the Spirit-baptism experi-ence in the context of their own tradition, in part to quell any misconceptions concerning their principal loyalty to the Catholic faith. Where the Assemblies of God forge their own novel interpretations of Spirit-baptism, Catholic charismatics understand that experience within the context of inherited interpretive categories.

This position reinforces a sense of the legitimacy of the Spirit-baptism claim and of its perduring relationship to the sacramental system. Charismatics are discouraged by the sacramentalists from identifying Spirit-baptism with predispositions (other than water baptism) or seeing it as a separate crisis-event. Rather, it is understood as a further fulfillment of a life already attuned to grace. For Catholics, there are two elements to consider: the theological and the experiential senses of Spirit-baptism. The theological sense is tied to the event of water baptism. Experientially, it awaits active release into the spiritual life of the believer.

Francis Sullivan, S.J., gave the issue a new spin when he brought in Thomas Aquinas's views on subsequent sendings of the Holy Spirit. Sullivan argued the reality of significant spiritual moments in which the believer is moved, sometimes by surprise, into new states of grace. These need not be implicitly tied to sacraments. Rather, they are to be understood as independent acts of the Holy Spirit that enhance the sacramental graces already present.

In my estimation, Sullivan's argument for independent sendings of the Holy Spirit is a healthy expansion upon the sacramentalist position, one that has not received enough attention from Catholic charismatics. His argument may also provide a dialogical bridge between Assemblies of God and Catholic charismatics that can help them to communicate better with one another on what really happens during Spirit-baptism. Sullivan offers an alternative to an either/or situation, in which Spirit-baptism is either seen as implicit to water baptism or as an entirely independent work of grace. I believe that both the scriptural record and Christian tradition can support the idea of subsequent missions of the Holy Spirit. Sullivan's appeal to Thomas Aquinas in support of his argument for independent sendings is provocative and should be examined seriously.

These further sendings (I prefer to call them anointings) may well be enablements, enhancing graces already made available through the sacraments. Sacraments are entrances into a new realm of spiritual life. The baptized person has the capacity for Spirit-baptism and can experience spiritual life more profoundly. Further investigations by competent theologians concerning what Spirit-baptism is and what empowerments accompany it are needed. There is a need, if possible, to integrate the sacramentalist and the further-sendings positions. There is also a further challenge to make these positions intelligible to both Catholic and non-Catholic pentecostals.

There is still not a spirit of mutual recognition among pentecostals and charismatics. Yet pentecostal common witness must begin in a spirit of cooperation. Widely differing interpretations of Spirit-baptism, the commonly shared pentecostal experience and the key point around which unity could begin, makes working together problematic. It seems clear that specific interpretations of the meaning of Spirit-baptism, if too strenuously insisted on, can only lead to further division and the abandonment of presently fragile common witness efforts.

There is also a need for ongoing enlightened dialogue on the meaning and implications of Spirit-baptism. This dialogic process involves coming together and finding out what the grounds of common witness might be and learning how to proclaim together an experience that all have shared. All involved should pray that answers to the present divisions are forthcoming and that the Holy Spirit will bring all together in God's good time.

Views of the Leadership

What do ecumenically oriented leaders of the Assemblies of God and Catholic charismatic renewal think about the possibilities for a common witness? In an attempt to answer that question, I interviewed eighteen of these leaders during the spring and winter of 1990.[1] I came away from the interviews with the sense that most believed that a common witness at the local level is both possible and desirable. At the institutional level, proposals for a common witness are generally described as premature and presently impossible.

Interviews provide a vital way to supplement written documents, which often contain institutional biases and can obscure as much as they reveal. Interviews also allow a researcher the opportunity to probe into ancillary questions that might otherwise be left untouched but that are crucial to a better understanding of the issues.

I chose these eighteen persons based on their knowledge of ecumenical initiatives as well as their willingness to be interviewed. Several others were contacted, but they seemed reticent to discuss their views. This may reflect a personal animus toward ecumenism or it may show a concern not to offend elements within their constituencies should these views become more widely known.

Given the interviewees' diverse backgrounds,[2] I did not ask a standard set of questions. But all questions were ultimately aimed at probing pentecostal common witness themes. I have divided their answers into two categories: (1) the perceived impediments to a common witness and (2) the grounds for a common witness.

Perceived Impediments: Assemblies of God Views

Traditional Separatism and Isolation

Many of the Assemblies interviewees stated that their denomination's makeup presents severe impediments to Assemblies involvement with common witness themes. Cecil M. (Mel) Robeck, a professor of church history at Fuller Theological Seminary, is sometimes described as an heir to David du Plessis's ecumenical mantle. Robeck labeled the key inhibiting factor "a decline in primary commitment" to pentecostal identity. Russell Spittler, a professor of biblical theology at Fuller, expanded upon this idea by describing the "evangelicalization" of the Assemblies. Spittler connected the decline in commitment to classical pentecostal identity to recent tendencies toward bureaucracy, in which much of the leadership is trying to model the denomination in the image of a traditional evangelical group:

> Cooptation happens in the pentecostal movement. In many Assemblies of God churches, people will tell you that it's not distinguishable from a standard evangelical church. . . . They may still have certain distinctives. Christian adventists, for example, have certain understandings of the Second Coming. Pentecostals may be seen to have certain understandings of the baptism in the Holy Spirit.

Related to this tendency toward evangelicalism, according to Spittler, is a tension between the congregational and presbyterial styles of government within the Assemblies. This includes the pressure to adopt a more centralized presbyterial model, which is commonly found among conservative evangelical denominations. Despite this tendency, Robeck said that the dominant polity is still congregational and that elements of presbyterianism are more marginal. The populism associated with the congregational model continues to counter any centralizing tendency, but battles over this issue could intensify: "Our biggest fights occur around local autonomy versus national authority. Almost inevitably you can get into an argument over that." Robeck said that this ongoing debate could be healthy, provided that a rough balance is maintained between congregational and presbyterian emphases.

In my contacts with the Assemblies, I was struck by the potential for disruption over this issue. I believe that protracted infighting over "evangelicalization" could become a consuming concern. If that happens, internal battles over the denomination's identity might well detract from attempts to encourage a common unity with other pentecostals.

Jerry Sandidge, a prominent international ecumenist and pastor of a large Assemblies church in Springfield, Missouri, emphasized the denomination's historic tendency to look inward. There are carefully defined involvements with the National Association of Evangelicals and the Pentecostal Fellowship of North America. Other than this, major decisions are made with the understanding that Assemblies of God interests are separate and paramount. This leads to a certain approach in dealing with others:

> The leadership doesn't openly oppose a group that would come and say, "Let's work together." They would just say: "Let's share what's happening with each other and keep in touch." But to have, for example, a joint committee made up of Assemblies of God people and others from an evangelical parachurch organization to work together to some common thing . . . I don't see that happening unless perhaps it's some remote mission circumstance.

Sandidge said that the results of this history of aloofness have a double edge. The Assemblies' size and traditional conservatism allow the denomination to be a stabilizing force when it does join a coalition. But retentiveness keeps the Assemblies from being a vanguard for change. "Once the issues are clear and the lines are drawn, the AG people could step in and say 'OK, let's do it.' But to forge the direction— that's for someone else," said Sandidge. I believe this concern to protect autonomy is probably the single greatest obstacle to making a common witness appeal to the Assemblies of God.

Gary McGee, a professor of church history at the Assemblies of God Theological Seminary, portrayed the leadership as isolated from charismatic groups. Pentecostalism in the mainstream churches caught them by surprise and they have never formulated an adequate response. More pointedly, there is a reluctance—largely based in the experience of persecution of their overseas missionaries—to recognize the validity of these new claims. This is especially the case with Catholics, according to McGee:

> From a foreign missions standpoint, you have to recognize that these missionary churches [that pressure Springfield not to recognize Catholic charismatics] are so caught up in their cultural situation that they can't see there has been validity to charismatic renewal.

Dick Champion, the managing editor of *Pentecostal Evangel,* noted that denominational leaders are wary of "doctrinal aberrations" by some charismatics and thus are anxious to avoid open endorsements. Concerns are especially directed toward Catholic charismatics and are centered on issues such as magisterial authority and Marian devotion. Many Assemblies leaders are surprised that Catholic pentecostals have remained in their own church. They anticipated that the Holy Spirit would move Catholics into new surroundings, but this expected exodus never happened: "The Holy Spirit will lead us only as far as we are willing to be led," Champion stated. "Whether this is error, or whether we are in error . . . I'm not saying we are perfect." Such errors are unlikely to be cleared up by either group without sufficient investigation of the other's doctrinal claims.

Proselytism

The most volatile issue blocking greater Catholic charismatic–Assemblies cooperation is proselytism, which involves the claim that classical pentecostals are actively recruiting Spirit-baptized Catholics into their churches. There is substance to this charge. Dick Champion noted that the desire to proselytize Catholics comes from a "monolithic" conception of Catholicism, which sees being Catholic as a social phenomenon rather than a valid spiritual expression. From this perspective, Catholics are deluded if they think they are truly Christian. Once converted to true Christianity, they must be saved out of their deception.

Mel Robeck agreed with Champion. Many in the Assemblies of God have a problem comprehending someone being both Catholic and pentecostal:

> They [Catholics] continued on with their pentecostal experience in place and with mores that flat out didn't fit with classical pentecostal understandings. We don't understand how heavily influenced our mores are by the culture around us and by our location within the class structure of that culture.

Gary McGee noted that ecumenically minded pentecostals like David du Plessis, who discouraged proselytism, are portrayed as practicing "a form of apostasy." This closed-mindedness has eased somewhat as Assemblies of God leaders, including Superintendent Raymond Carlson, find themselves working in common cause with Catholics on social issues such as abortion and pornography.

Conflicting Visions of the Church

The Assemblies of God model for the church differs profoundly from that found in Roman Catholicism. This is another drawback to the denomination's participation in a common witness effort. Differing understandings of the church have led to different views of evangelization. Vinson Synan, the noted pentecostal ecumenist, cited this as a most volatile issue: "That's our biggest problem to unity. . . . It's not easy and we've run up against almost every ecumenical road-block imaginable." Robeck attempted to compare institutional understandings of the church as follows:

> There definitely is the question of apostolic faith [with regard to different models of the church]. In your [Roman Catholic] tradition, it's seen as residing in the bishops and the passing on of apostolic succession. It also has to do with the curia, the teaching body of the church, having the final say. In our movement there's the tendency to produce position papers which function in much the same way. . . .
>
> [But] we have a congregationalism and not everybody has a chance to vote on it [the position papers]. My feeling is that the position papers may be helpful to a lot of people but I don't think they represent the collective membership.

A most fundamental difference between the Assemblies and Roman Catholicism is the understanding of how and to what a person is evangelized. In Roman Catholicism, evangelization is a process initiated by the church and that leads one into the church. It is begun and sustained through an ongoing series of events that happen through God's instrument, the church. A vital aspect of this ongoing evangelization involves participation in the sacraments. The dominant Assemblies of God understanding is that evangelization is a distinct event or moment rather than an ongoing process. From this perspective, a person is understood to have been successfully evangelized at a certain point. Once that has happened, the person decides how to respond to that transforming event and will choose how to assemble with other Christians.

The deep differences between these two visions of evangelization into the church are so significant that Russell Spittler, who may have been the most cautious of the respondents, said: "The best [present action] you can hope for is local and regional consultations." Such consultations might eventually provide the groundwork for select common witness activities.

Perceived Impediments: Catholic Views

The Loss of Internal Unity

Among Catholic charismatics, the loss of internal unity ranks as a major barrier to common witness efforts. The range of interpretations as to why unity has weakened suggests the complexity of the problem. Fr. Peter Hocken, a prominent ecumenist and theologian, had this to say:

> The Catholic renewal was distinguished [at the beginning] in having an unusual degree of cohesion. It had a unity in its origins that was lost. Why? Part of it is the history of the relations between South Bend and Ann Arbor. At the beginning the unity was represented by the Ann Arbor–South Bend axis. . . . Actually, Ann Arbor was more prophetic than South Bend. The ecumenical vision was stronger. Ann Arbor was always more challenging to the church. . . .
>
> Other people outwardly attacked this model of unity and campaigned against it. Among these were Josephine Ford and the Jesuit Fr. John Haughey. He argued that one model was being imposed on the renewal by Ann Arbor–South Bend. It was argued that Ann Arbor was too negative to the world. . . . It was an intellectual protest, and there was never any significant unity among the objectors. . . .
>
> What I am saying would not be well received by many of these people because pluralism is the order of the day. I'm not against pluralism because the Spirit produces variety. But a lot of these writings had an animus. . . . This is a very tricky thing. Something about the original unity was given. . . . That unity must have been intended in the Lord's plan, to produce something other than what happened later on. Therefore, if the fruit intended was not produced, it must be due to human disobedience and weakness.

The result of this disunity is increased confusion over the meaning of the term *charismatic identity* and the emergence of more and more independent interests.

Walter Matthews, a director of Chariscenter, the National Service Committee's informational arm, agreed that "disunity and conflict among the national leadership" has affected the whole renewal. These internal conflicts are combined with the fact that the larger Catholic Church is not ready to move faster in the direction of ecumenism. These factors have stalled efforts toward unity with other pentecostals: "The feeling was that we had gone as far as we could as a movement in talking, praying, and seeking unity. We were already steps ahead of the Catholic Church."

David Garaets, O.S.B., the abbot of Pecos Benedictine Monastery in New Mexico, had a different perspective. Garaets is a controversial figure in the renewal, known for his willingness to use Jungian categories, which some charismatics consider too liberal, in order to interpret spiritual experience. He spoke of a type of "differentiation" that emerged in the renewal by the early 1970s and had intensified by the 1980s. In his view, dominant forces in the renewal—such as the Ann Arbor group—retreated from an open to a defensive posture:

> There was a real shift that took place, it's hard to say exactly when . . . around the 1982 publication of Ralph Martin's *Crisis of Truth*. I would compare it to the shift in the early church when you moved out of the age of evangelization into the age of apologetics. We moved from a stage of total acceptance, of being open to all kinds of people, to a place where you almost became afraid of people.
>
> A certain amount of fear was generated, and the growth of the movement was stifled. I had a hesitancy to preach in the presence of some people, lest I be labeled a Jungian or a dream interpreter. Rather than there being a total acceptance of a person, letting God point things out, there was a real shift into apologetics and it stifled the evangelization aspect of the renewal.

Garaets attributed this shift to a national leadership cadre (many of them identified with covenant communities) that developed an ownership mentality:

> I don't know if it was explicitly said or if it was because these people were in the initial outpouring of the Holy Spirit. They unconsciously usurped the role of being guardians or protectors. The thing I didn't like was the shift where everybody was supposed to align themselves with the basic *methologum* which came out of Duquesne and Notre Dame. If you were in the Catholic charismatic renewal, you had to somehow own that *methologum*. I didn't feel comfortable to own it because I came through a different one. I came through the classical pentecostals. That style may be vaguely present in a lot of the covenant communities which would appear to be possessive or even controlling.

He stated that the major impact of this shift toward a controlling posture has been greatest in the more politicized groups in the Midwest and the East.

Sr. Josephe Marie Flynn, the charismatic liaison for the Milwaukee archdiocese and a liberal member of the National Advisory Committee, agreed with Garaets. She saw many in the leadership as averse to new ideas:

> The really vibrant and new thinkers are not being called forth. You get a rehash. . . . People hang on to leadership when they shouldn't. I don't think the National Service Committee has developed a really good way for continuing itself. They're going to have to rethink that. One of the national leaders characterized it as an old boys club, where you go behind closed doors and do things.

According to Flynn, the exclusion of new people with leadership qualities has led to stagnation, and many talented people have drifted away from the renewal. In my travels and contacts, I found that such exclusivity may well be present, although there is also an expressed desire to allow for more pluralism.

Kevin Ranaghan, an early leader in the renewal, lamented the disunity among Catholic charismatics and tied it to the more general loss of pentecostal unity. He did not attribute this to the imposition of a dominant ideology, but to a lack of relationship building among leaders:

> From the early 1970s to the early 1980s, the heart of what was going on ecumenically in the charismatic renewal was the personal relationships among leaders. Right now it seems people are investing less and less time in those relationships. They're busier and busier with doing things and are meeting together functionally rather than for the purpose of relationships. I have said to Vinson Synan and others that if we don't reinvest time in our relationships, I cannot see a future for us.

Ranaghan's comment suggests that restoration of unity rests in large part with the leadership. Adherents to this view could be seen as being in tension with those who press for a unity that will be built from the grass roots up. I believe that efforts toward restoring unity need to happen from both ends concurrently.

Sr. Nancy Kellar, a prominent evangelist and National Service Committee member, repeated the essence of a message she gave to the leaders of the international renewal in the fall of 1989:

> Probably the strongest thing I said at that talk in Rome was that, unless we do something about [restoring] unity, all of our efforts at evangelization are just going to be lost. Bringing people to Jesus is only the first part of conversion. Bringing them into a unified Body of Christ is the second. Unless we have vibrant small groups to evangelize people into, forget it. All the mass evangelization attempt is going to be wasted.

Sr. Josephe Marie Flynn joined Kellar in supporting small groups as a means to restoring charismatic unity: "I think Fr. Chris Aridas on Long Island is right. . . . The charismatics need a big, strong prayer meeting experience on a regular basis. But they also need small support groups." This emphasis upon building support groups as well as enhancing regional identities is the direction now favored by the National Service Committee. There is a danger in absolutizing any form, in this case the small group model. But these comments suggest the extent to which many charismatics connect intimate relationships with ideal unity. It is not only pentecostal experience that matters, but the sharing of that experience in an ongoing life together.

Proselytism

A widely recognized hindrance to common witness is the ongoing classical pentecostal proselytization of Catholics. Kilian McDonnell emphasized the gravity: "It is a very, very hard question. It is the big issue." Kevin Ranaghan described the effects of proselytism in this way:

> So these folks are going down to South America and proselytizing Roman Catholics into pentecostal churches. This creates a tremendous problem. . . . It gets reflected back to the Vatican and comes back to us: "How can you cooperate with these people?" That is a *big* problem. If we cannot solve it, we will experience that in the last part of the twentieth century we were able to move this far and no further.

He stressed the need for the charismatic renewal to offer its members sound instruction in Catholic doctrine. This would help Spirit-baptized Catholics to remain identified with the Catholic Church: "The evidence indicates that Catholics that have left for the pentecostal churches have done so under the influence of a pentecostalism where there is no Catholic component."

When asked about proselytism, David Garaets gave a special interpretation to the term. Proselytism goes beyond the obvious category of denominational recruitment to include an overall attitude of condescension. He said that meetings like Indianapolis 1990 promote a subtly patronizing attitude:

I'm concerned that what's going on at Indianapolis is proselytism rather than evangelization. . . . This comes out of the tonality of the preaching that is done. The people are very sincere, but whenever you get a bandwagon like that, you get caught up in a movement of proselytism. It's not a witness of each one for one, taking people where they are at. The real witness is love; proselytism is condescension.

Garaets said that Christianity is best "caught and not taught" and is shown by example before it is proclaimed.

Conflicting Visions of the Church

Several leaders identified key issues that specifically impede better Assemblies of God–Catholic charismatic relations. Fr. Kilian McDonnell, a long-time observer of pentecostalism, noted that when Catholics encounter classical pentecostals, "the key issue is that a structured church is talking with a movement." He was frank in assessing the problem of promoting a common witness:

I'll tell you what the problem is. The problem is when common witness really means evangelization. . . . There can be no common evangelization because you always evangelize into a worshipping body together. Therefore, you can't do it together.

Catholic charismatics may respect the classical pentecostals for their evangelical enthusiasm, but serious differences remain over how to interpret the nature of the church. Kevin Ranaghan summarized the issue as follows:

The pentecostals are known for effective personal evangelization. From our [Catholic] point of view, their weakness is their anthropology and their ecclesiology. Our strength is in the process of conversion and in the evangelization of culture, which is all part of evangelization from the Catholic point of view and which sometimes they exclude.

This exclusion is a direct result of classical pentecostalism's generally low ecclesiology.

Keith Fournier, the director of the University of Steubenville's Center for Evangelization, stressed that all should evangelize into their own church fellowship: "What God is about doing is not one renewal movement. God's solution for humanity is the church. . . . The tremendous challenge we all have is to reevangelize our own church." He described the decline in recent ecumenical contacts among pentecostals as salutary and pointed out a new emphasis upon denominational integrity: "We almost walked down the precarious road of a least common denominator approach. It smacked of a false irenicism."

Sr. Josephe Marie Flynn disagreed with Fournier's remarks, seeing them as too introverted and ultimately nonecumenical: "The Steubenville–Ann Arbor position is ecumenical only in a limited, evangelical sense." I found that, in the renewal as a whole, terms like *evangelization* and *ecumenical* are used loosely. This causes confusion over what is really being said, and one must constantly interpret the true import of statements. However, this is a fault common to human organizations in general and is not restricted to charismatics.

Peter Hocken pointed out that real differences exist and should not be obscured through shallow calls for unity:

> An appeal to a *koinonia* of the spirit might be seen by some as something more authentic than the sacramental fellowship of the church. I have never argued for this. What I have argued is that the spiritual unity given in the baptism in the Holy Spirit is real and highly significant. It is a seed that has to be expanded outward into all forms of church life. It is ultimately meant to produce sacramental, ecclesial, and institutional unity.

For Hocken, Spirit-baptism is an enriching ecumenical grace, not a force to supplant traditional church forms. Most Catholics interviewed said they would be open to Hocken's observation that Spirit-baptism has a unique power to unite and that "our received categories are not adequate to interpret what is happening. The tools of all our traditions are necessary to approach it; no one tradition is adequate."

Hocken expressed concern that entrenched attitudes might ultimately quench the Spirit: "The danger is that traditional Catholic categories begin to take over." He saw signs that this might be happening:

> If "moving into the heart of the church" means bringing this grace into the heart of Catholic life, that is totally correct. But often what "moving to the heart of the church" means is that you play down the ecumenical side and stress things that are less problematic to leadership. This causes a loss in the ecumenical thrust of the movement. . . . It has then developed in a way that is too political and accommodationist, therefore diminishing the prophetic and ecumenical.

Confusion about the Next Step

At this point there is a basic confusion about the future direction of the Catholic charismatic renewal. What course can the renewal take in order to avoid stasis and decline?[3] I found that some leaders believed that a number of the renewal's constituents are unwilling to move past spiritual adolescence and into maturity. Peter Hocken described the problem in this way:

> The renewal may be dramatic, but it is not strong on prayerful reflection and penetrating what the purpose of the Lord is, even if it costs us. The renewal is too superficial, because too much is at the emotional level. If you don't push down to deeper understanding, enthusiasm can only be emotional. It either becomes emotional or it becomes common sense and pragmatic, less bold, less courageous, less challenging, and very sensible. It goes with the conviction of the ecumenical importance [of Spirit-baptism]. What God is doing is bigger than any of us have yet grasped.

He observed that conflicting visions of the renewal have led to estrangement in the past and confusion in the present. Formerly clear cut differences in covenant community and other relational models have recently become quite blurred. To him, this is another indication that the renewal is in flux.

Garaets agreed that there has been too much emphasis put on immediate experience and too little reflection given to deeper meanings. He said that the implications of spiritual experiences must be examined before they are proclaimed:

> There is a commonness in the experiential. The only way to get unity is in the experiential, but we must reflect upon our common experience. We're almost to the stage now where we might be able to share our experience mutually. . . . I see a much more humble profile. It's going to be demanded of the church. Do you know that when the church gets too institutionalized the only way the Holy Spirit can move is outside the church? Then these movements develop the strength to confront the church. That has been the role of holy rollers in the past.
>
> We are in a time of transition. I had a vision of the lion, the Christ, burning the land and burning the foliage. After that, I saw a unique foliage that I had never seen before. I don't know what that foliage is, but I do know that it will be a new thing.

Calling upon his own experiences of growing in faith, Garaets referred to the "messiness" of new spiritual birth. He described this as identifying the nature of the renewal's changing mission while being in the middle of the change. Since the Holy Spirit is usually understood to be a promoter of order not messiness, I took Garaet's remark to mean that the Holy Spirit can take present conflicts and confusions and use them for creative purposes.

Both Garaets and Hocken seemed to believe that the renewal is being called to react to a new initiative by God. They differed in their assessment of the renewal's readiness to respond. Hocken seemed less optimistic than Garaets about charismatic willingness to move out and encounter new things.

By far the most guarded of the respondents was Keith Fournier, a leader in the tightly knit Sword of the Spirit network and a strong advocate for "traditional Catholic identity." He said that the term *charismatic renewal* had become rather meaningless:

Just because it's called renewal doesn't mean we can embrace it. You have your eclectic mess of those who were touched by charismatic renewal but have been siphoned off into ideologies, "isms," and borderline heresies. You have people who are protestantized charismatic Catholics and have left or are leaving the Catholic Church. The hope lies with the third group who have hung on to fully embrace the Catholic Church. There is a move on to deepen piety and love for the eucharist.

I interpret this to mean that true charismatics are those who identify with the institutional Catholic Church. This type of thinking has been characterized as a form of Catholic fundamentalism by other charismatics.

In Fournier's perspective, the institutional church is God's chosen vehicle for stabilizing the charismatic renewal. He likened present discords to problems in a dysfunctional family. Relational difficulties can be hidden for a time but eventually they surface. He hoped that a kind of perestroika might soon happen through the restructuring of the charismatic renewal under the guidance of the National Service Committee.

Grounds for a Common Witness: Assemblies Views

Changing Attitudes toward Ecumenism

Ecumenism has been an emotional term for the Assemblies of God, reflecting that denomination's long identification with the National Association of Evangelicals. Antipathy toward formal ecumenical contact was reflected in a 1961 denominational bylaw,[4] which prohibited contact with any ecumenical group seen as in any way resembling the World Council of Churches.

Jerry Sandidge characterized this hostility as follows: "Ecumenism is suspect. It's immediately associated with compromise and a watering down of faith. . . . It sets up Anti-christ. It's filled with apocalyptic visions." Vinson Synan similarly described the general classical pentecostal attitude:

All we ever heard was that it [formal ecumenism] was the apostate superchurch that was forming and was something we should be totally separate from. Their agenda was to destroy the true faith. Most pentecostals still have that residue of mistrust.

By their willingness to dialogue with mainline Christians, the leaders I interviewed can be considered an ecumenical vanguard. None expected quick or radical reversals in denominational policy, but all expressed hope that, in time, there could be more flexibility.

Both Mel Robeck and Jerry Sandidge spoke of receiving some quiet approbation for their ecumenical efforts. Robeck characterized the leadership as "living out the fact that the laws of God [in favor of Christian unity] are more significant than the laws of human beings." At a minimum, implicit allowance for ecumenists such as Sandidge and Robeck suggests a change from the chilly treatment given to David du Plessis.

Russell Spittler said that the Assemblies of God are "readier than ever" to tacitly encourage specific common witness initiatives. This comment may seem overly optimistic, given the denomination's past history of almost total disinvolvement, but it was tempered with cautions about what could be accomplished institutionally:

Active cooperation is happening at the grass-roots level. It would never happen officially if it didn't first happen there. We don't have a heavy theological tradition, so to do it on the formal level, like Robeck, is more marginal to the general style of behavior within the denomination.

By this, Spittler did not mean active involvement so much as greater toleration and perhaps a measure of public support for ecumenical ventures. He questioned whether massive efforts such as Indianapolis 1990 are the best way to get involved. Spittler interpreted the event as a "last hurrah" for leaders who had been prominent at Kansas City 1977 and other rallies. He also questioned that leadership's willingness to "pass on the baton from one generation to the next" and suggested that the large meeting format is not sustainable and needs to be replaced.

Sandidge said that the Assemblies has developed a style of being generally informed while remaining specifically disinvolved. Robeck supported this insight, indicating that the denomination lives with the "anomaly" of officially being opposed to ecumenism while quietly encouraging behind-the-scenes efforts by people such as Sandidge and himself. Robeck implied that being informed eventually requires becoming involved, even if unofficially.

There was a sense among those I interviewed that the leadership has avoided open discussion of common witness initiatives and lacks the resolve to investigate these openly. Vinson Synan described this response as not so much one of fear as a wait-and-see approach: "This is the Assemblies of God way of doing things, to hold off officially and at the last minute show up [show their basic solidarity with common witness efforts]."

Better Relations Lead to Mutual Recognition

All of the Assemblies of God people I interviewed considered appeals to spiritual ecumenism to have the best chance to open up the Assemblies of God to the idea of common witness. Spiritual ecumenism is an atmospheric concept, describing a mutual bond based in shared experience rather than in formal organization. It can be contrasted with formal ecumenism, in which the ultimate goal is organizational unity. Dick Champion correctly summarized the prevailing view: "What it [spiritual ecumenism] is in pentecostal circles is directly due to the ministry of the Holy Spirit and with those who recognize the move of the Holy Spirit in today's world." Mel Robeck, regarded as more liberal than Champion, gave an expansive view of spiritual ecumenism's potential, calling it a vital complement to formal ecumenism. Robeck said that both types are valid expressions of the Holy Spirit: "The Spirit has been busy creating two ecumenical movements. One is formally ecumenical, the other is pentecostal and charismatic." Robeck's views on ecumenism are not likely to be widely embraced. But an appeal to work together with other pentecostals—based upon a spiritual ecumenism—might gain an audience from certain Assemblies of God populations.

Jerry Sandidge asserted that the rise of the charismatic renewal has encouraged elements in the denomination to

reconsider cooperation: "Ecumenism has had some bad implications in the past, but it can be seen to have some wonderful
implications now [with the rise of the charismatic renewal]."

Dick Champion said that the charismatic movement caught
the denomination by surprise and is forcing a reevaluation of
attitudes toward Roman Catholics and others. The charismatic
surge has challenged thoughtful classical pentecostals to see
Spirit-baptism interpreted through other traditions:

> One of the things that happened, especially in the early
> days of the charismatic renewal, was that people who
> had the same experience would describe it differently.
> There would be a freshness in the description that chal-
> lenged us. It also helped us to better understand what
> had happened to us.

Champion added that the realization that "others were saying
what we [the Assemblies] have been believing all along was
true" is taking time to sink in.

Russell Spittler was more circumspect. In his view there
was still "considerable hostility towards charismatics, let alone
the third wave [i.e., evangelical pentecostals]" within the leadership. He allowed that, because of the charismatic surge,
some Assemblies congregations are becoming more open to
common witness thinking. Improved relationships would
begin with local dialogues where old attitudes could be reex-
amined and "mythologies" put to rest.

All of the Assemblies of God representatives I interviewed
said that improved relations between classical pentecostals
and Catholics are possible. Champion expressed his delight
with the local Assemblies of God–Roman Catholic dialogue in
Springfield, Missouri:

> I think that those of us outside the Catholic Church have
> our concepts of what it is. I had more the feeling of this
> monolithic structure in which the pope said things and
> everybody got in line. The thing that surprised me was
> the many, many areas of agreement between us.

Robeck saw mutual respect as a precondition to greater
tolerance:

I think the international Roman Catholic–pentecostal dialogue has found a great deal of agreement around the subject of *koinonia*. This can be a key into an understanding of ecclesiology that allows both of us [Roman Catholics and pentecostals] to bless each other. When Basil Meeking [an English Catholic theologian] addressed us in 1985 he said that Rome had come to the understanding that we were, in effect, church.

The Catholics had come to an understanding that they had done a great job of sacramentalizing people; but they had not done a good job of evangelizing them. What pentecostals were doing in bringing them to an imminent confession [was recognized as] a good thing. If that was what was meant by evangelism, the Catholic Church was all for it.

In Robeck's view, the key to creating good relations is the development of *koinonia*. The meaning of this word varies according to context. In terms of pentecostal common witness, I define it as a special sense of bonding among pentecostals that is the result of the Holy Spirit's work in their lives and that presupposes a vital relationship with Christ. According to Robeck, the attitude that nurtures *koinonia* is "not so much a change of mind as a change of heart" and involves the grace to allow and bless the other's efforts. From this perspective, respect is not earned but required.

Robeck asserted that ecclesiology is really not the main obstacle separating classical pentecostals from Catholic charismatics. Catholics and pentecostal views on the church are "closer than what is generally thought." In Robeck's view, the greatest hindrance to church unity comes from misreading one another's motives, which leads to suspicion. The result is a tendency to talk at cross-purposes over the nature of holiness: "You [Catholics] don't hold your people accountable enough. We are not at odds over evangelization but accountability and sanctification." His position represents a common Assemblies of God attitude that stresses the functional nature of the church. This view either does not perceive or refuses to accept the Catholic Church's more comprehensive understanding of the Body of Christ.

Vinson Synan talked about the need to synthesize, "taking the best of the various traditions and putting them together in a dynamic fashion." Of course, Synan's comment about the "best" in Christian traditions does not address the question of who decides what is best and by what criteria this judgment is made. In itself this would be a most involved enterprise. Synan's depiction of the "dynamic fashion" needed for pentecostal unity is clearer. It depends upon recognizing and using the shared resource available in Spirit-baptism:

> When you talk about common witness, I think that this [the experience of Spirit-baptism] is the most common denominator that the church has seen in the last thousand years. It doesn't solve all problems. [But] as far as evangelizing the non-Christian world, I think that shared pentecostal experience is what they had at Pentecost. They didn't even have denominational structures. These were just beginning to form. All they had was the common experience.

Synan's remarks represent a common pentecostal desire to repristinate; that is, to get behind centuries of church history and recover the essence that defined the early Christian experience. The success of such an enterprise, given the present complexities within the Body of Christ, remains much in doubt.

Shared Social Concerns

Russell Spittler observed that future common witness opportunities might develop around shared social concerns, once these are better defined. Finding a common opponent could help build an alliance:

> What would most likely make common witness happen is for a common enemy to emerge to unite quarreling siblings. . . . Carl Henry has talked about new verities, new clusters of loyalties taking effect, for example on the abortion issue.

Gary McGee noted that, even at the institutional level, the Assemblies of God is going through a change in attitude as

the leadership realizes that they share common social concerns with many Catholics. This is the result of more active
involvements with Catholics. "Our leaders were thrust into
committees with Catholic leaders [to deal with certain social
issues]. It's kind of like the Jerry Falwell experience with
Moral Majority," referring to that fundamentalist leader's
ad hoc alliances with members of other religious groups on a
variety of issues.

Jerry Sandidge also saw increased contacts as a factor that
could lead to a lessening in prejudices against Catholics,
which are centered on the perception that Roman Catholics
are not fully Christian. One result of these newly shared social
concerns is an increase in mutual recognition:

> The reason for that is the charismatic renewal plus a
> sense that the agenda of the American Catholic Church
> has a lot of what we might call conservative elements in
> it. . . . There's common ground on things like abortion,
> for example. The integrity of the family. Ethical actions
> by government, and so on. We're beginning to think that
> maybe the Catholics have something to say after all.

There is an inherent problem in Sandidge's comment on the
nature of the shared social agenda. The problem with uniting
in common opposition is that it can lead to a mere appearance
of unity. I think such an alliance would be hard pressed to survive a shift in focus to other issues. Nonetheless, ad hoc
alliances do have a purpose. Sustained interaction can spur the
participants, once they know one another better, to go forward
with a unity that is more comprehensive. The promotion of
more liberal Catholic justice concerns could prove to be a
problem, although a couple of the respondents (Gary McGee
in particular) pointed out that Catholics have much to teach
classical pentecostals in the area of social justice. McGee was
notably alert to the rich potential for merging Catholic and
classical pentecostal emphases: "The pentecostals are heavy on
proclamation. The Catholics are heavy on compassion. There
has to be a solid balance between the two."

Decade of Harvest's Ecumenical Potential

There is a possibility that Decade of Harvest, the Assemblies of God's key outreach program for increasing membership in the 1990s, could be coordinated with other evangelistic efforts. The domestic Decade of Harvest program has been subject to various interpretations because its goals remain poorly defined. Common witness themes could certainly be incorporated, although this is not part of the present plan.

Jerry Sandidge described Decade of Harvest as born of a simple desire to evangelize. He also noted, with some irony, that the project represents a move away from the denomination's past sense of eschatological urgency: "As soon as you talk about a 'decade of harvest' . . . the imminent return theology diminishes." Sandidge's primary problem with Decade of Harvest is not with its eschatological vision but its origins. The idea has been improperly attributed to the Assemblies of God. In fact, it is a borrowed concept, modeled from a Southern Baptist evangelistic plan for the 1990s. Sandidge said:

> The truth is that we got the idea for Decade of Harvest from someone else. But when you hear us talk, you think that God planted this all by himself just in our heart and in no one else's heart. The fact that we're doing this without reference to anyone else is very disturbing to me.

This lack of proper attribution can be interpreted as a lapse into triumphalism. If Sandidge is right, such an attitude could be an obstacle in attempting to tie Decade of Harvest with any common witness effort.

Dick Champion defended the program from charges of triumphalism. He acknowledged that there are "different views on cooperation" among the planners but said that all intend that it be one in spirit with other evangelistic efforts: "I think it's [at present] more a situation where many evangelical and pentecostal groups are doing something similar, rather than everybody coordinating in one great big thrust."

According to Mel Robeck and Russell Spittler, the planners have not begun to think in terms of a wider effort. Robeck especially expressed concern with Decade of Harvest's nonspecified nature: "I'm not sure I know what Decade of Harvest is. It has a lot of goals in terms of church planting. Beyond that, I don't know what Decade of Harvest is." He sensed that, unless a specific definition was forthcoming, the program will flounder. Spittler, however, did acknowledge Decade of Harvest as a defined effort: "I don't remember a program in recent times that has had more prominence within the denomination. It's catching on and has quantifiable goals." He did not specify these numerical goals, but he expressed concern that if these goals are not met, the failure will be subject to "creative accounting" and recast as a success.

Gary McGee characterized Decade of Harvest as an attempt to revitalize the Assemblies of God by reconnecting the membership to their pentecostal and evangelistic roots. But he noted that there is little evidence of the effort having any wider dimension. He said that it is primarily "an in-house promotional campaign for the Assemblies of God" and that its greatest strength is an emphasis upon indigenous (locally based) church planting.

Most of the Assemblies people I interviewed accepted McGee's view that the denomination traditionally has been "clannish." This clanishness is evidenced in Decade of Harvest's exclusively denominational goals. Robeck remarked: "There is a place for Decade of Harvest, but they [the planners] could be more cooperative in some of these [common witness] ventures." Decade of Harvest's Declaration of Mission has the potential to be reinterpreted ecumenically, and there is always the hope that this could happen.

Assemblies of God Strengths

All of those interviewed reflected a noticeable pride in their heritage and portrayed the Assemblies as a rich resource for helping interpret pentecostal experience. They exhibited confidence that the gifts of discernment and wisdom have been highly developed through the denomination's past struggles.

Jerry Sandidge said that the Assemblies of God bears special witness to God's faithfulness to the pentecostal movement, "a sense that, with the Holy Spirit, anything could be accomplished." Dick Champion echoed this view and cited the denomination's experience in confronting the problems of religious enthusiasm. Similarly, Gary McGee noted that a great strength in the Assemblies of God is its capacity to balance personal subjective experience with discipleship training:

> I would see us as bringing the stability the Assemblies of God has had [to any common witness effort]. I think that others could benefit, especially the independent charismatics, from our stability and caution on the extremes of subjective experience.

Mel Robeck represented the general view when he observed the Assemblies' potential to bring stability to any unity effort:

> We've been around long enough and have experienced a lot of extremes. As I think about the third-wave evangelicals, Pete Wagner, John Wimber, and everything, I look at that and say: "That's my experience of pentecostalism in the early 1950s." If only they would bother to read a little bit of the literature from there, about how churches reacted and understand the theology of why certain things took place, I don't think they'd be making the same mistakes. They look at it and say, in essence, they are ahistorical and that God has brought them into being for this moment. We said the same thing.

Grounds for a Common Witness: Catholic Views

Ecumenism and Spirit-Baptism

Catholic charismatics have considered themselves ecumenical throughout their existence. Kevin Ranaghan remarked:

> We [charismatics] have always regarded that what was going on was a pentecostal movement among Roman Catholics who were in relation to other people with the same experience in other churches. . . . There was this broad pentecostal movement that was subdivided into

smaller movements that were church-related. . . . It's important to understand that, from the beginning, the movement had that ecumenical dimension.

But there are differences over what ecumenism means.

Fr. Peter Hocken, in speculating about the renewal's ecumenical potential, went further than Ranaghan in describing its "ecumenical dimension." He described it as part of a work of God that transcends any denominational identity. Pentecostalism has no human founder, and Hocken interpreted this to mean that it is purely an initiative of the Holy Spirit. Its ecumenical grace lies in the "more immediate character" of Spirit-baptism, which is "the same for people in all different traditions and backgrounds." He also cited his belief that Spirit-baptism "is the same work of God in all the churches, not just a 'parallel movement' among Catholics."[5]

Hocken said that continued contacts among pentecostals shows a "fundamental instinct" toward unity that amounts to shared recognition: "Pentecostals encountered Catholics and saw the same thing was happening to the Catholics." Hocken later nuanced his statement when he said that certain classical pentecostals have not yet "adverted to the fact that the Spirit produces unity, although there has begun to be a reevaluation of the historic churches by some pentecostals." Among ecumenically oriented pentecostals this has begun with a recognition that Catholics can be Spirit-baptized and has gone on to the next step, a positive appraisal "of what is possible" in Catholic-pentecostal relations in general.

Kilian McDonnell was most outspoken in his reaction to Hocken's view that Spirit-baptism is a unique ecumenical grace:

Peter does not seem to believe in the unique character of the apostolic age. There's a counterpart to that [claim to special ecumenical grace] in that God is always doing new things. What God is doing now is a new thing, and what he did with the early Franciscans, which was another charismatic movement, was also a new thing. What God did with the fourth-century monastic movement was also a new thing. So you are *absolutizing* the latest new thing as though God had done no new things in the past. That's my problem, I'm concerned about history.

McDonnell also expressed concern that Hocken's reluctance to identify Spirit-baptism with his tradition was idiosyncratic: "My difficulty with Peter is that he has seemed to dismiss baptism in the Spirit's basing in the sacramental model." In my estimation, McDonnell's critique of Hocken is only partially correct. Hocken does not seem to tie Spirit-baptism specifically to the sacraments, thus suggesting that he does not see the experience as capable of being adequately interpreted through them. In defense of his position, Hocken has indicated his belief that the sacramentalist model was introduced to make pentecostalism's unique claims more palatable to the Catholic hierarchy.

During the interview, Hocken responded at some length to McDonnell's criticism. He noted that McDonnell is best described as "a sympathetic observer rather than a participant" in the renewal:

> It's the responsibility for people who are participants in the charismatic renewal to say to people like Kilian, who is one of the few theologians to see its significance, that their approach is too apologetic and not looking at the deep meaning. This produces an explanation which is divisive, being Catholic and not commended to Protestants. What happens to people when they are baptized in the Spirit is connected to what is preached to them. When you say that baptism in the Holy Spirit is an "actualization of sacramental graces," it's not that something inside of you pops out. Something is being taught and preached now which was not when they were confirmed and baptized, which is what the Spirit is now doing. An important theological datum is not sufficiently being paid attention to.

Hocken seemed to want to avoid charges of extremism. He admitted that Spirit-baptism is a "tricky area theologically" and that his views should not be construed as an argument for a supraconfessional movement. He concluded:

> My position is that we have to pay attention to our historical categories and relate what God is doing in the renewal to what we have received in the deepest

wisdom of our traditions. But we must also respect what God is doing today. Our received categories are not adequate to interpret what is happening. The tools of all our traditions are necessary to approach it; no one tradition is adequate to approach it.

Such a comment suggests that Hocken may equate tradition with the various ecclesiastical traditions. This is intrinsic to McDonnell's problems with Hocken's view of Spirit-baptism as an ecumenical grace.

Hocken's view on Spirit-baptism's ecumenical dimension has been interpreted as deficiently "Catholic" by some other charismatics. His assertion that Spirit-baptism should be interpreted in light of all the Christian traditions has also been criticized for sacrificing the charismatic renewal's mission into the heart of the Catholic Church. Keith Fournier in particular expressed concern that the charismatic renewal's Catholic nature should be emphasized. Its primary mission is to evangelize other Catholics. Ecumenical relations with other pentecostals are not of primary significance, but a secondary concern. It seemed evident to me that Fournier considered the Catholic tradition to be the best vehicle for interpreting pentecostal experience. His principal ecumenical contribution was to argue for a coalition among pentecostals "based upon my being fully in my tradition and you being fully in yours."

Walter Matthews seemed to represent something of a middle view. He indirectly supported Hocken's views on ecumenism with the qualification that he would "say it differently." He stressed the need for maintaining good relations among pentecostals and noted that the Catholic renewal has experienced problems sustaining such contacts, especially at the local level. There is difficulty in maintaining both a Catholic and an ecumenical identity. "You have people consciously or unconsciously opting for one mode or the other."

Opportunities for Cooperation

The views of the Catholic interviewees diverged considerably over what is currently possible in the area of a common witness. Kevin Ranaghan was most cautious in his evaluation. He stated that differences are so great that common witness opportunities are precluded, except on the individual level:

> I would tend to project more of a cross-pollenization of speakers and resources in denominationally sponsored events rather than kicking off more ecumenical events after Indianapolis 1990. . . . There is no agreement between, for example, the Catholic charismatic renewal and the Assemblies of God. But there are individuals who have good relationships, who are able to cooperate with and respect one another.

Informal "cross-pollenization" is an important aspect of common witness according to Ranaghan, but it falls short of the more complete identification others are calling for. Ranaghan asserted that, rather than further attempts at coalition, "there needs to be a going back and regrouping in the individual movements." Responsibilities to one's own constituents take precedence over attempts to further common witness efforts.

Peter Hocken agreed on the importance of sharing resources, but only as an aspect of a more activist approach:

> In practice, I don't think that Catholic-pentecostal cooperation is going to come out of theological reflection. It comes out of people baptized in the Spirit doing things together. Methodologically, the best thing to do is to find as many ways as possible for Cathoiics and pentecostals to do things together.

The question remains as to how complete cooperation can be without theological agreement as the basis for it. It seems to me that action and reflection will have to be combined in some dynamic way.

The interviewees expressed general agreement with Walter Matthews, who described the present time as crucially important: "We are on the verge of some move of God in terms of massive evangelization and are at the beginning of a time of mission to communion." He talked about a current "window of opportunity" for evangelization. To respond, it is essential to define and solidify a new direction.

Matthews continued by saying that pentecostals need to agree on some "convening authority" that could help sharpen their evangelizing focus:

> I think that common witness to Jesus Christ is possible. One of the values to the kind of conference that we hope Indianapolis will be is that it is a witness. People from a diversity of theological and ecclesiological backgrounds can come together in worship, praise, and prayer. . . . Different church traditions have different emphases that we can grow from.
>
> Before, the emphasis was exclusively on spiritual unity, which ran into a wall. Now, it is a matter of coming together for evangelization. That shifted the focus from internal structural unity to encouraging one another to stir the flames. . . . We're now looking at these last six months [late 1989 and early 1990] and what's going on in Europe. These are not minor changes but structural shifts. Through a historical lens, it's in those sorts of times of turmoil that God's word is clearly proclaimed.

The problem remains of how "evangelization" is to be defined.

Common Ground

Kilian McDonnell found a possible common ground between the Assemblies of God and Catholic charismatics in Christian anthropology. To do this, the Assemblies would need to rediscover their Wesleyan roots:[6]

> Wesleyan anthropology tends to be very compatible with Roman Catholics, much more so than, say, Lutherans and Calvinists. The relationship between grace and nature and the role of human effort would also be more compatible with Roman Catholicism. There's a lot we [Catholics and pentecostals] can share together in this area.

Walter Matthews noted a level of maturity in the Catholic tradition that could help common witness efforts: "Catholics know how to stabilize churches. We know how to take people after their initial [pentecostal] experiences and ground them in a spirituality that will endure the inevitable next crisis." The Catholic emphasis upon personal spiritual growth might mesh well with Wesleyan emphases on sanctification.

Peter Hocken noted other areas of convergence between Catholic charismatics and classical pentecostals. First, "both [Catholic charismatics and classical pentecostals] have a special emphasis on bodily outward signs. . . . Pentecostals have rehabilitated the body in Christian worship and ministry." It is difficult to say how this could be transferred into practice: "Whatever you come up with must have some potential for cooperation even if you can't yet see it working out in practice." Second, "both groups are more open to the supernatural [such as signs and wonders] than are most mainline Protestants." Third, Hocken described both groups as having greater freedom in the use of Scripture: "The use of Scripture in preaching and prophecy is freer than with evangelicals. . . . There are parallels between the use of Scripture in prophecy and the use of the Old Testament in the New."

Keith Fournier also noted the value in recognizing a common Christian source:

> There are certain actions we can cooperate on. The analogy I like is the allies in the trench in World War I. You had the American, the Frenchman, and the Englishman. They were in the trench together although they were different. They knew they had a common battle, a darkness that threatened all that they trusted and cherished. That kind of imagery can support the right kind of ecumenism that we see coming out of the correctives of the late 1980s. We can recognize one another as allies and look for the actions we can engage in with genuineness.

By "correctives of the late 1980s" Fournier seems to be referring to a time of retrenchment when many Catholic charismatics stood off and reassessed their relations with other pentecostals and one another.

Catholic Charismatic Strengths

Sr. Nancy Kellar described the allowance for diversity as the greatest strength that Catholic charismatics could bring to any common witness effort. She depicted the renewal as a community of movements pursuing a common mission:

> I think our move to help people form other models of community and more committed relationships at the local level, though not at as intensive a degree as we've had in covenant communities, is the way to go. . . . Unity comes about better when we focus on mission than when we focus on unity. On the ecumenical level of the NARSC committee, some of these men were thrown out of the churches of the person sitting across the table from them a generation ago. Working together on evangelization, the unity is truly being built.

David Thorp, a lay evangelist and National Service Committee member, characterized the charismatic renewal as getting stronger as it moves toward emphasizing local identity over central authority. He regarded this approach, now being urged by the National Service Committee, as a gift to the overall pentecostal movement, and he tied it to evangelization:

> The charismatic renewal needs to catch hold of the vision of concerted evangelization. It doesn't have to catch hold of it in the same way that other groups do. God has given us a particular word about evangelization. The Catholic renewal became a more diverse movement in the 1980s. There began to be a more diocesan focus for the renewal and less dependence on seeking only a national voice, although those national voices continue to be heard and sought. We also had the realization that there was ten or twelve years of leadership and experience available in the local area. We're growing up, and God can use us to bring a particular word for our area.
>
> Some movements just die out. Others rearticulate in a clear way the vision for the movement and begin to grow again. The call, as we have experienced it, is that the grace of Pentecost is the grace of evangelization.

These remarks reveal a problem. How can pentecostals work together when they do not agree on what people are being evangelized into? In this book, I have emphasized the idea of common witness based in Spirit-baptism precisely because of the problems that arise when the talk shifts to common evangelism. It is only at the level of common witness that I believe significant unity among pentecostals is possible. The thrust of all of the comments by Catholic charismatics is that Christian unity is a reality to be lived out. The remarks by Kellar and Thorp represent the absolutizing of a thematic concern, namely an allowance for diversity. This suggests to me that charismatic leaders are searching for new images that will motivate and sustain the renewal.

Current Possibilities for a Common Witness

Kevin Ranaghan suggested that Catholic charismatics could make a special contribution to common witness through their views on evangelization. He said that "effective personal evangelization" has been a historic strength of classical pentecostals, but that Catholic charismatics offered a mature understanding of what full conversion entails: "It [the traditional Catholic view] doesn't have proselytism in it. When I talk evangelization I always talk incorporation into community or into church." He also advocated "doing a lot together in evangelization cross-training." Extending this to pentecostals and charismatics working together as witnessing teams would "remain an unusual situation done by competent people, well trained in ecumenism for a specific purpose."

Walter Matthews expressed wariness of any attempt at common witness efforts when I spoke to him, but he argued for the value of engaging in a "half step" of proclaiming common faith in Jesus Christ as opportunities arise. He described such moments as passive witnessing opportunities. In such situations, theological differences among the witnesses can be spelled out at a later time. Despite the possibility that such efforts might promote a churchless Christianity, Matthews asserted that shared testimony to personal faith is "very possible and, in fact, if we don't respond to that sort of opportunity it borders on sin."

Kilian McDonnell said that, given the current secular climate, he could rejoice over the conversion of a lapsed Catholic into an active non-Catholic Christian fellowship: "The whole question [with current efforts at common witness] is, Can Catholics celebrate the conversion of a nonpracticing Catholic into the Assemblies of God? I say that I can." McDonnell's remark might appear to clash with his previously expressed concerns about proselytism. I interpret his comment to represent a preference for a lapsed Catholic to be actively involved with a classical pentecostal fellowship rather than with none at all. Active recruitment of practicing Catholics is another matter.

As did the Assemblies of God representatives, most of the Catholics I interviewed seemed to take common witness seriously. They appeared to recognize that Christian diversity is founded on a more fundamental unity and that unity has precedence over diversity. The fact is that the current interest in the possibilities of common witness have even gone beyond pentecostal circles. David Thorp was accurate in saying: "There seems to be more of a willingness on the part of Rome to investigate this common witness desire."[7]

Conclusion

It is difficult to gauge a range of subjective responses. What follows are my observations based on the evidence gathered. Many of those I interviewed expressed the belief that the experience of Spirit-baptism is a fundamental and sufficient reason for wanting to pursue a common witness. Differences arose over what that common witness would look like and how it could succeed.

As a rule, the Assemblies of God representatives seemed more cautious in assessing the possibilities. This may represent an inherent conservatism or, more likely, a realization of how far common witness themes are from their denomination's mainstream of thinking.

There are particular problems at the organizational level. The Assemblies shows signs of conflict over the denomination's future direction and pentecostal identity, such as over the "evangelicalization" issue. Should this become a preoccupation, it could be a major obstacle to anyone who wants to promote the priority of common witness. There is also the enduring frustration of belonging to a denomination that prides itself in its aloofness. This leads to a definition of Spirit-baptism that misses its ecumenical dimension.

The Catholic charismatics were generally more expansive in their views of common witness. They spoke of Catholicism's openness to ecumenism as well as to positive contacts with non-Catholic pentecostals. Yet the Catholic charismatics suffer from their own internal problems. They conceded that battling with one another has hurt them. They expressed a definite sense that the renewal has stalled and become internally pre-occupied. Strong disagreements over how to relate Catholic belief to pentecostal practice have contributed to the sense of frustration. A most obvious hindrance to greater cooperation between Catholic charismatics and the Assemblies of God involves the proselytization of Catholics by pentecostals and the harassment of pentecostal missionaries by Catholics. This is an overseas issue that impairs relationships here. On a theoretical level, there are differing senses of how the Christian faith is to be carried forth from generation to generation. Is it primarily by way of the tradition (Catholicism) or through a fresh anointing (classical pentecostalism)? These two views are not mutually exclusive. The Catholic tradition can encourage vital spiritual experience, and classical pentecostals have, in fact, developed their own transferable tradition.

Despite the problems, all of those interviewed held out some hope for the future success of a pentecostal common witness. On the Assemblies of God side, this springs from the greater tolerance that is being shown to other traditions and the growing sense of spiritual ecumenism, especially with charismatics. Many of the Catholics expressed a similar belief in the potential of spiritual ecumenism and a confidence in their group's ability to spread this message. Both sides reacted similarly when asked what special strengths they could bring to a common witness effort. The Assemblies of God representatives stressed their confidence in the denomination's stabilizing influence and the richness of its pentecostal heritage. The Catholic charismatics also emphasized the rich and stabilizing influences present within their tradition.

In terms of present possibilities for a common witness, the overall tone of the interviewees was cautious, yet allowance was made for a measured optimism. This positive appraisal can be attributed in part to the nature of those interviewed, but it also displays confidence in the Holy Spirit's ability to effect fundamental change. Several pointed out the rapid shifts in the political realm and asked whether such change could not be matched in the spiritual realm. I found this view provocative and also wonder whether transformation in the social and political realms might be matched in the spiritual.

Toward
a Common Witness

I believe that pentecostal groups as diverse as the Assemblies of God and the Catholic charismatics can find grounds to undertake common witness initiatives. To do this, past tensions over how to interpret pentecostal experiences will have to be resolved and claims to the mutual worth of their experiences will have to be brought into focus. If successful, such an effort would point to the potential for Spirit-baptism as God's gift to the entire Body of Christ, useful to unite and empower the church. I also believe that Spirit-baptism remains an underexplored support for Christian life and witness in the secular world.

Tens of millions can testify firsthand to the reality of Spirit-baptism, and to dismiss their witness out of hand is unrealistic. Numinous engagements between the human and divine are not new; the alcoves of the Vatican are filled with carvings depicting just such supernatural encounters. Is it so astonishing that God would intervene in a special way to our own beleaguered generation?

Present claims to Spirit-baptism should not be dismissed as unrealistic or too ethereal. Spirit-baptism represents entrance into a new spiritual realm and initiation into the dynamics of eternal life. For the seeking Christian, there can be no a priori dismissal of the Holy Spirit operating in such a way, since it has been witnessed to in Scriptures and is testified to in the history of the tradition.

People are spiritual beings. Once this special encounter with the Holy Spirit has been experienced, there begins an odyssey unto new spiritual horizons. Spirit-baptism is a primary way in which God lays the foundation for a person to operate in the earthly realm while still focusing upon the heavenly goal. With all its other benefits, Spirit-baptism is a special gift that prepares a more Christ-like stature; and for those who will soon face their Maker, it affords the comfort of knowing that they are at one with God. Honest seekers after the truth should be willing to investigate pentecostal claims and to proceed with prayerful caution and open minds to test the claims to Spirit-baptism's validity.

Despite general allowances at all levels, and even a measure of institutional acceptance, there has not yet been such an enthusiastic and rigorous official investigation. Rather, the tendency has been to ignore and thus effectively to dismiss this pronounced new life. Why? Perhaps avoidance reflects the fact that the extraordinary dynamics of the Holy Spirit, evidenced in the "new wine" of Spirit-baptism, are not well understood and thus not comfortably encountered. Many may be reacting out of fear of the unknown. Such a fear can cause a refusal to concede to what may seem to be a dangerous or foolish phenomenon. Excessive institutional caution leads to inertia, in which loyalty to the church is interpreted as adherence to an unchanging situation. This attitude supplants the demand for faithfulness to the Holy Spirit's own initiative: "No one having drunk old wine immediately desires new: for they say, the old is better" (Luke 5:39).

Such inhibitions, the result of human judgment, stifle and suppress the free operation of the Spirit in the church. The Holy Spirit will not be countered by human aggressiveness and demands close cooperation. God is not willing to endure a denial of this empowering initiative. If human folly persists, the Spirit will not come through in power. And when the strong presence of the Holy Spirit recedes, the church does not fire on all cylinders.

The obvious best response to Spirit-baptism claims would be for the institutional church to examine and cooperate with the Holy Spirit's initiative. To begin an exploratory process of the implications of Spirit-baptism, even among pentecostals, would require that the claims of its serious potential to unify be recognized.

Priests and ministers who have opened themselves up to Spirit-baptism can testify to the encouragement they have received. They experience a refreshing side of Christ's relationship with his family, the church. For those who look into Spirit-baptism, who overcome fear with free thought, past barriers are pushed aside. As they receive the enlightenment of Spirit-baptism, a new spiritual energy comes charging into them. This unqualified gain is in harmony with what they had known before. In company with Christ—made powerfully present through the infilling of the Holy Spirit—they have found the guiding presence of a helpmate. As they experience Christ truly "making their burden light," they no longer dread certain responsibilities as they had before. They experience the reception of a constant and ongoing power to meet their obligations.

Since the beginning, there have been skeptics—both within and without the Christian family—who have refused to open their minds to new ideas and possibilities. This is still the case today. One cannot expect an across-the-board conversion to the Spirit-baptism principle. But probing minds will find that millions have come to the conclusion that this experience is both real and transforming. Many of those who make such claims are not in mainline denominations, but they hold out the hope that one day they may belong to a universal church, actively incorporating Spirit-baptism as a principle.

Such comments are not intended to be unduly critical of the Christian churches as they are. Coping with the full implications of a radical truth claim is certainly not easy. As the evidence indicates, this difficulty has even been true for pentecostals. Within the pentecostal realm there has been a falling off when jealously, personal ambition, and mutual recrimination have begun to dominate. It is easy to lose a sense of the Holy Spirit's vision for a movement of this size and complexity. But God is a strict taskmaster when matters of human design get in the way of divine prerogatives. Fortitude, obedience, humility, and prayerful holiness in response to the promptings and messages of the Holy Spirit are all necessary virtues. They prepare the soil for the seed of God's designs to grow.

The Assemblies of God and Common Witness

On the surface, the present readiness of the Assemblies of God to engage in a pentecostal common witness appears obvious. The more ecumenically minded view the Christian family transdenominationally, and there is little evidence of open repression of common witness activity by the denominational leadership. However, only the most superficial interest is being given to common witness efforts, and there is no present intention to identify actively with such efforts.

This reflects the fact that most members of the Assemblies of God have rarely, if ever, thought in terms of a pentecostal common witness. It also represents the denomination's historic isolation, evident even in its dealings with other classical pentecostals. Important as soul-winning zeal is to the Assemblies, such passion is not translated outward.

This analysis of the present situation is correct, as far as it goes, but it needs elaboration. In the early years, classical pentecostals did not look inward as most do today. Rather, the pentecostal movement saw itself as "an ecumenical revival movement within the traditional churches" (Hollenweger 1966, 313). This pentecostal sense of mission was not well received by the dominant evangelical population, and the focus of the message began to change. It moved from an optimistic proclamation of a divinely mandated ecumenical revival to a prophetic declamation against compromised churches. Responding to rejection, many pentecostals began to describe themselves as a divinely ordained remnant, an eschatological sign to "worldly" Christians.

As with their initial call to ecumenical unity, this prophetic stance was not taken seriously. It was either ignored or openly rejected by the mainline evangelical churches. The response of these dominant groups was to view pentecostals as eccentric extremists, subject to wild claims of special revelation. *Holy roller* became a term of derision applied to pentecostals. After the Azusa Street revival, pentecostals gave up all hope of transforming their old denominations.

In addition to ostracism from without, the new movement suffered from extremists within. Serious and increasing problems forced the leadership to band together and forge a particular pentecostal identity. But, for many of those who bonded together as the Assemblies of God in May 1914, theirs was a denomination born more of necessity than desire. In its effect, the Hot Springs meeting represented a step back from an earlier vision of a pentecostal ecumenical revival that would capture and surpass the evangelical denominations.

The immediate furor in the Assemblies of God over the Jesus Only issue resulted in the 1916 Statement of Fundamental Truths. Further refinements in doctrinal self-definition were inevitable, and they came in response to external events and internal needs. These follow-up decisions were usually more protective than speculative, and the denomination took on an increasingly conservative cast. The tendency toward parochialism intensified during the isolation of the 1920s and 1930s and moved the Assemblies still further away from the ecumenical revival visions of earlier days. The original emphasis on Spirit-baptism as a special grace that could unite and then ignite churches was nearly forgotten by the end of the 1920s. Although not overtly abandoned, this original ideal of the pentecostal movement as God's special gift for Christian unity was effectively submerged.

Since the Assemblies of God's early isolation from the larger church community cut it off from the theological currents of the day, the denomination was also denied a larger context in which to interpret its experience. As a result, the Assemblies failed to develop the theological sophistication to describe the implications of Spirit-baptism for its own constituency. Nor did they depict the potentials of this concept to nonpentecostal Christians.

Another major obstacle to sharing the ecumenical potentials of Spirit-baptism came from the Assemblies' borrowed belief system, which was fundamentalism. The fundamentalist belief that extraordinary spiritual gifts had ceased operating at the close of the biblical age did not provide adequate room for pentecostal experience, let alone ecumenical outreach (see Ruthven 1989). The temptation for pentecostals, many of whom wanted to gain acceptance from the established fundamentalist culture, was to portray Spirit-baptism as an addendum rather than as a central reality of Christian life.

The Assemblies of God's ecclesial isolation eased somewhat with its acceptance into the National Association of Evangelicals in the 1940s. This placed the large and growing pentecostal denomination in a more capacious environment, and they soon became a major influence (see Spittler 1978). This new association contributed to a shift in denominational self-understanding, moving it from a strictly pentecostal identity toward a more conservative evangelical cast. Though it was not an iron-clad rule, the leadership began to respond to issues—including those concerning ecumenism—following a style learned from their new evangelical associates (Blumhofer 1990, 2: 106).

The National Association of Evangelicals has demonstrated a consistent antipathy to the term *ecumenical,* tying it to apostasy. In 1961, the Assemblies of God's General Council openly identified with this antiecumenical attitude (Robeck 1987). In fact, such antiecumenism is in tension with the little-recognized ecumenical revival themes that were prominent in the denomination's early history. This stream has continued to survive, represented by people like Mel Robeck, Jr., Gary McGee, Russell Spittler, as well as by enlightened conservatives such as Dick Champion. The inheritors of this earlier ecumenical heritage recognize that there is an ongoing pentecostal initiative of the Holy Spirit in all the churches. In terms of common witness potential, categories such as *liberal* and *conservative* may not be particularly helpful. In assessing openness to pentecostal ecumenism, better categories might be *involved* and *indifferent* or *tolerant* and *intolerant.*

Independent judgment and the ministry of all believers are perduring denominational values, despite recent, more centralizing tendencies. Even without official backing, the Assemblies church model, with its emphasis on local autonomy, would allow individual members to engage in common witness efforts if they so chose. There also remains the long-range hope of recovering some of the original ecumenical revival fervor that marked the early days of the pentecostal movement.

The Assemblies of God's present evangelistic effort, the Decade of Harvest, represents a programmatic attempt from the center aimed at increasing denominational numbers and influence. Such campaigns have been attempted periodically, but Decade of Harvest appears to be by far the most ambitious.[1] There is a tendency among many evangelicals and pentecostals to quantify the success of their programs.[2] If the anticipated numbers fall far short or are manipulated to look better, the result may well be a serious internal debate. There might also be a reevaluation of present denominational trends and calls for a new direction.

One alternative approach would be to structure Decade of Harvest differently from the present model. The program need not be developed solely to build up denominational membership. Traditional ecumenical revival motifs are not in the current plan, but neither are they systematically excluded. The broad thematic statement presented in *The Strategy for the 1990s* could, in fact, be reinterpreted to include pentecostal common witness themes.

Admittedly, this would be a radical departure, a development in the direction of greater ecumenical empathy. According to the ecumenist John Ford, in a group like the Assemblies of God

> the tendency is to answer questions of doctrine in terms of their own horizon and, in so doing, run the risk of overvaluing their own denomination's perceptions, while undervaluing and even rejecting the perceptions of other denominations. Carried to its logical conclusion, such a view makes it easy for Christians [in these particular denominations] to believe their own denominational horizon is the best way—or even the only way—for authentically perceiving the gospel message (1986, 519).

Ford's statement aptly summarizes the present attitude of large numbers of Assemblies of God adherents and accounts for instances of denominational triumphalism. Some denominational horizons are the result of circumstances, while others are self-imposed. Ignorance of the original importance of ecumenical revival themes involves elements of both; thus, pentecostal common witness initiatives from other groups can appear unfamiliar and even threatening.

Since limited perceptions inhibit many, resolving the situation requires developing a willingness to search out a wider denominational horizon. This can be begun most fruitfully by an appeal to return to the pentecostal movement's original charism, which involved an ecumenical hope for the revival of the whole Christian family.

This will probably not happen soon, at least not on a comprehensive scale. The leadership cadre in Springfield is not ready to speak clearly to the issue, let alone to act boldly. But, given the denomination's ecclesiastical model, interested individuals and congregations can actively pioneer a return to the original charism of unity and find their ecumenical revival roots there. The current leadership is unlikely to block such independent attempts and at times may even tacitly encourage them.[3]

The received categories of classical pentecostalism, already challenged by the charismatic phenomenon, have been hard pressed to interpret the events of recent years, especially as many conservative evangelicals became involved with third-wave neocharismatics.[4] Challenges to the comfort zones of tradition became full-blown when Spirit-baptism claims began to come from new groupings of Christians, who described themselves as independent charismatics. These charismatics choose to distance themselves from classical pentecostals, denominational charismatics, evangelicals, and others and do not formally identify with any of these groups (see Blumhofer 1990, 2:85–106).

To date, the Assemblies of God has responded to all of these new groups with a restrained cordiality, while trying to maintain a dual identification with its classical pentecostal and conservative evangelical influences. But present calls for a pentecostal common witness suggest the need for the Assemblies to react definitively to the changed pentecostal environment.[5]

Catholic Charismatics and Common Witness

Given the complexity of the Catholic charismatic renewal, generalizations are difficult. The evidence clearly suggests one thing. The call to one bread, one body, one Lord of all has often been surrendered to lesser agendas. The renewal initially allowed for diversity, but, as definite factions emerged, rigid views of where the charismatics should be going and of how they should get there came to dominate. Initial ecumenical hopes for the renewal were obscured by the demands of special interest groups. New calls for pentecostal unity are being heard now; but the future of these efforts is uncertain.

During the Duquesne and South Bend revivals of the late 1960s, the Catholic charismatics received help from both classical pentecostals and Protestant charismatics. Thus, from their inception, Catholic charismatics had close working relationships with other groups. In such an environment, denominational lines became less intimidating than before, and shared worship with the free exercise of pentecostal gifts was normal.

Many charismatics interpreted their powerful experience as God's way of establishing a pentecostal beachhead in the Catholic Church. In their overly optimistic appraisal, God was using Spirit-baptism to topple nonspiritual influences in all the churches. Participants believed that they were living symbols of the Holy Spirit's passion for a united and empowered Christian family.

This belief was enhanced by the Catholic Church's open commitment to ecumenism. Vatican II's *Decree on Ecumenism* had encouraged initiatives to unite Catholics with "separated brethren."[6] Many Catholic charismatics interpreted this as a mandate to seek out fellowship, and Spirit-baptism was seen as the vehicle par excellence for sharing the faith with non-Catholic pentecostals. This surprising gift of God would overwhelm traditional divisions born of apathy, suspicion, and fear.

Vatican II also issued *Lumen Gentium,* a call for a life of dedicated holiness on the part of the Catholic laity. Many in the renewal saw themselves as faithfully following this call by living out their new-found spirituality within the Catholic Church. The special benefit of pursuing pentecostal holiness in the Catholic context would be its witness to the present power of the Holy Spirit. Charismatics believed they were advancing together spiritually, using both the resources of traditional Catholicism and the special graces of Spirit-baptism. With this unique combination, they could also encourage other Catholics to join them in their pursuit of holiness.

Although their relationships were largely with one another, most charismatics were anxious to avoid any charge of sectarianism. The greatest number of them remained loyal to the Catholic Church, usually because of an inherent love they held for their traditional faith. Some early charismatics did become disillusioned with the slow rate of change they saw and the questionable level of acceptance for their pentecostal claims. These charismatics left in order to find an environment in which they were more comfortable and where they felt they could be spiritually "fed."

By the early 1970s, the situation for Catholic charismatics had changed considerably. The renewal had grown almost exponentially, and with the increase came the need for definition and a growing desire for institutional acceptance. Though probably not a deliberate policy, public identification with non-Catholic pentecostals through common worship and testimony—other than at official ecumenical gatherings—began to wane. Thus, the spontaneous relationships that had arisen through shared worship and the common exercise of the pentecostal gifts and that had formed the earliest basis for building a common witness declined.

By 1975, the Catholic charismatic leaders had succeeded in their drive for legitimation. Their desire to "move into the heart of the church" can be seen as salutary. But such a move is subject to varied interpretations. I believe that many Catholic leaders attempted to win institutional acceptance by playing down their identification with non-Catholic pentecostals. The original drive for pentecostal unity appears to have been sacrificed as the desire for institutional legitimation gained momentum.

A foreshadowing of this shift occurred at the 1972 Notre Dame Conference. In order to show public compliance with the bishops' directives on who could share in the eucharist, the Catholic leaders asked that non-Catholics refrain from coming forward. This caused consternation among many of the Protestant observers. A number were ready to attribute the source of the problem to Catholic arrogance and interpreted the request as an affront, one that portrayed non-Catholics as having a second-class status within the Body of Christ.

Most Catholic charismatics at the local level, new to ecumenical relations, were unsophisticated in interfaith contacts. They were not trained to interpret correctly such signals as those that came out of Notre Dame. Many failed to understand that *catholic* and *ecumenical* are meant to be complementary and not conflicting terms. Certainly, provocation was not the intent of what happened at Notre Dame and other places. But by 1973, Vinson Synan was openly wondering if the golden opportunity for pentecostal relations had not already begun to pass.

Catholic pentecostals might have wondered the same thing. David Wilkerson's book *The Vision* also came out in 1973. In it, Wilkerson said that God had revealed to him that the Vatican would "pull in the welcome mat" from the charismatic renewal, forcing it to choose between pentecostalism and the Catholic Church. Wilkerson's warning about the impossibility of maintaining a pentecostal witness in the Catholic Church came as a shock and drew a sharp response. As did the 1972 Notre Dame incident over intercommunion, Wilkerson's remarks had a negative impact upon Catholic charismatic–classical pentecostal relations.

Catholic leaders were still defining the renewal's identity during the 1970s. Many borrowed extensively from sources outside the Catholic tradition. In particular, the authoritarian Shepherding-Discipleship emphasis of Fort Lauderdale's Christian Growth Ministries became influential. By the mid-1970s, such imported ideas became yet another source of friction.

The Catholic charismatic renewal, the product of informal origins, was never a very well defined national movement, but, during the 1970s, many of the renewal's leaders seemed compelled to define a national structure for unity (for example, the National Service Committee). At the local pastoral level, sustained attempts also were made to create an overall direction. Most notable among these efforts were the intentional community models, such as Ann Arbor's Servant of God and South Bend's People of Praise.

Conflicts over the nature and lines of authority within the renewal intensified during this time. Fundamental differences in outlook became apparent and were exacerbated by personality clashes. Such conflicts had a deleterious impact upon both internal unity and attempts to promote pentecostal unity in general. The original allowance for diversity was sacrificed as common charismatic identity deteriorated into mutual autonomies.

In my travels, I repeatedly heard the claim that such a breakup was inevitable, that the Catholic charismatic renewal was really a collection of movements from the start. But is this a true statement of the case, and was the breakup of the charismatic renewal into separate movements bound to happen?

That is a complex question without a definitive answer. The appearance of separate movements may well have been stimulated by exclusionary principles, many of them imported. Ideological litmus tests may well have forced more laissez-faire charismatics to chart their own course. Perhaps the multiple-movements argument is an attempt to justify that which took place but could have been avoided. What might have hastened the loss of the renewal's original charism of unity was the marginalization of individuals not within the comfort zone of those who promoted the dominant ideology and controlled the major sources of communication.[7]

Internal shifts and conflicts had an impact on pentecostal relations in general. Certainly, pentecostal conferences that featured sharing of speakers remained common throughout the 1970s, indicating at least a desire to embrace a more ecumenical vision. But Protestant writers gradually began to recede from the pages of Catholic charismatic literature. Interdenominational prayer groups declined as the inward focus of the intentional community models involved the concentrated efforts of many Catholic charismatic leaders. In addition, much energy was expended upon internal debates about the Catholic charismatic renewal. Attention and energy are finite. It appears that internal issues became preoccupations that took away from the personal reflection, dialogue, and thorough commitment needed to foster a pentecostal common witness.

Kansas City 1977 was billed as a launching pad, an epochal display of the potential for pentecostal unity. As has been suggested, its true backdrop was more doubtful. Arrowhead Stadium might better be seen as an arena in which the Holy Spirit made a fervent appeal for a return to an earlier focus. Not responding to a divine summons is a form of disobedience, especially in a situation where the results of disunity were becoming so apparent. I am in agreement with Peter Hocken, who has stated that the prophetic directives of Kansas City were ultimately ignored and thus functionally disobeyed.[8]

Most of those involved ended up treating the Kansas City meeting as another pentecostal mega-event. It suffered the fate of many such meetings; namely, insufficient reflection upon the events' deeper implications. Without a wholehearted attempt to respond to the strong prophetic summons, the unity meeting ironically presaged a time of steep ecumenical decline. Despite the rhetoric of acceptance, the reality was that the various pentecostal groups—including the Catholics— never moved to act upon the Kansas City prophecies and thus muzzled the message.

Since the solemn import of Kansas City 1977 was missed or not personally applied, it became lost in a cascade of more immediate concerns. Reworking G. K. Chesterton's aphorism: It is not that the message of Kansas City failed, it was never really tried.

Following Kansas City, the Catholic charismatic renewal experienced a more pronounced shift from an evangelistic (outward looking, inclusive) to an apologetic (defensive, exclusive) stance. The result of intensifying conflicts within the renewal was an atmosphere in which one either identified with some faction or found new alliances outside.

By the early 1980s, the renewal had devolved into a number of independent groups as elements began to drift free from one another. The passions surrounding the battles of the late 1970s and early 1980s were replaced by weariness over rehashing old issues. A call for unity and a restored sense of shared purpose came most notably at Notre Dame 1982. But such calls have not really proved successful.

The 1980s saw many charismatics drifting away into private spiritualities or exiting the renewal. There was a noticeable decline in personal evangelistic zeal.[9] Like a freeflowing channel that becomes clogged with weeds, the renewal has been made stagnant through unresolved conflicts and has suffered a loss of vital circulation. Much of its retained vitality lies in strong local groups with explicit regional and diocesan loyalties.

The National Service Committee may be correct in its assessment that the present time represents a new window of opportunity for charismatics joining together in an evangelistic effort. But the needed overall unity is not yet there. The evidence is inconclusive as to whether the charismatics are going through a time of restoration,[10] or whether (as others claim) they have indeed entered a period of stasis and decline. Only God knows. But the foundation from which to proclaim a unity of purpose seems uncertain, still obscured by the swirls of independent agendas. The hope for evangelistic thrust appears at present to be hanging without visible means of support.

Divine endorsement for unity efforts does not come cheaply. The coming together of high-profile Catholic leaders at large unity meetings is somewhat deceptive. The uninitiated might believe that, by appearing together on one stage, these Catholics are demonstrating that they are, in fact, of one heart and mind. Before Catholic charismatics can appeal for unity with other pentecostals, they must repair the deep breaches within their own camp. The key blockage to many Catholic charismatics joining a pentecostal common witness is the lack of personal common witness, one to another. Common witness begins with a hard look inward.[11]

Toward a Pentecostal Common Witness

Recurring Frustration and Enduring Hopes

In January 1990, I received the following prophecy from a member of a small charismatic prayer group in northern Wisconsin:

My renewal is a victim of entrepreneurs. Someone should tell them this. "Have you got a minute?" I ask.

When so many of My children make a claim on My Godhead whom do I listen to? All, of course. But the renewal becomes fragmented. Tilling the soil is hard when the power is not available. My word to them is: "One bread, one body, one Lord of all."

Let there be common efforts to stage a rally for all. Get on your knees, My children. Do not hold back. Let there be a wailing unto God for the twin gifts of repentance and forgiveness. No song ascends heavenward unless a cleansing takes place. No incense can rise to me except through purification. Clothe yourselves in sackcloth and put all arrows to rest: the arrows that have been darting from confrere to confrere.

What a pity! I want so much to relieve you of the darkness that has cast a cloud upon My people. Yes, My people; but divided in their loyalty to what I am calling them to. I have so much to give, but your hearts must abandon the pathetic little struggles you create for each other.

Hold on to the good you have been given. A firm foundation is in place but weaknesses and human folly have substantially hurt the structure. Please, My children, announce together the word: "We will overcome through God's grace. His Holy Spirit will lead us on to victory. Alleluia!"[12]

The tone of this prophecy, which speaks of present hindrances to common witness, seems just as solemn and pointed as the those given at Rome 1975, Kansas City 1977, and New Orleans 1987. After extensive research—which included seventeen thousand miles of bus travel and visits to many pentecostal communities—I endorse this message's import. A strong bond for common witness is available to pentecostals through the "firm foundation" of Spirit-baptism, but "weaknesses and human folly have substantially hurt the structure [that is, God's shared dwelling of unity through the experience of Spirit-baptism]."

In his 1990 interview, Fr. Peter Hocken talked about a special charism of unity given to pentecostals and charismatics in the late 1960s and early 1970s, when the rich diversity of the participants enhanced the sense that God was sovereignly bringing them together. I see no reason to believe that such a special grace was given for a season only and has since been rescinded. In fact, with the advent of the 1990s, hopes for a pentecostal common witness have been revived. But a new approach seems to be needed. There is strong evidence that "pathetic little struggles" among pentecostals still continue to frustrate God's plans for unity. There are also still individual factions ("entrepreneurs") who insist upon their particular visions of what common witness should be like. If such differences again lead to infighting, they could rupture the already fragile lines of trust.

Sustaining common witness relationships requires a sacrificial spirit willing to assume the burden of discipleship. This means a commitment to an ideal of unity strong enough to survive inevitable conflicts. It also demands enough humility about one's own views to fully allow the views of others.

At the most basic level, there are numerous obstacles to understanding one another and working together. Enthusiasts for pentecostal common witness have often overlooked the degree to which their traditional settings have affected their understanding of spiritual gifts. It cannot be assumed that one person's experience of Spirit-baptism is exactly like another's. Given the distinctive ways that the pentecostal gifts are experienced in Catholic and classical pentecostal settings, shared recognition and allowance for varied interpretations can become particularly complex. For example, Catholic charismatics often operate in the gifts of the Spirit, such as tongues, prophecy, and healing, at their masses. This setting for expression would be incomprehensible to many classical pentecostals.

At this point, the gift of discernment becomes essential. Discernment is a special spiritual charism that few pentecostals have, although it is highly developed in some. This gift needs to be self-regulating. It involves recognizing what is true from what is false, and its purpose is stabilization and peace of mind concerning a course of action. Discernment is a gift hard to define but absolutely necessary in order to avoid extremes of interpretation and behavior. As such, it requires special discipline and humility.

The power to discern is not one of human judgment. One must be zeroed in to the leading of the Holy Spirit in order to exercise this gift, and it takes prayerful consideration to grow in it. Because of the responsibility associated with discernment, it is best done by confirming one's conclusions with others similarly gifted. This group approach also confirms the facts of a situation and helps the participants avoid unfounded interpretations.

As the histories of pentecostal and charismatic groups demonstrate, there is great potential for unfounded interpretations. Such volatility usually occurs when the flow of divine power is interrupted or blocked by unchecked human desire. It is particularly important not to abuse spiritual gifts for personal gain. Personality can become the seat of initiative for what might, on the surface, seem to be the legitimate use of pentecostal gifts.

To act in the flesh is to consciously abuse the charismatic gifts for private ends, acting out of personal motivations (for example, fear, competition, pride, acclaim). These actions often appear quite spiritual because they are performed in a recognizably pentecostal style. This caution regarding the flesh does not imply that gifts and leadings need always be of an explicitly spiritual nature. There is a full allowance for personality. One does not surrender one's personality when praying in tongues or prophesying. But subtle reliance on the flesh results in a short-circuiting of the spiritual gifts and the delivery of a false message.

Foundational Steps toward Unity

A foundation for pentecostal common witness can be found in an appeal to the apostolic faith ideal, which is a concept sufficiently large to encompass all major Christian groups. A consultation between the Roman Catholic Church and the Faith and Order Commission of the World Council of Churches produced the following definition of apostolic faith:

> It points to the dynamic, historical [geschichtlich] reality of the central affirmations of the Christian faith which are *grounded* in the witness of the people of the Old Testament and the normative testimony of those who

preached Jesus in the earliest days ["apostles"] and of their community, as attested in the New Testament. These central affirmations were further *developed* in the Church of the first centuries. This apostolic faith is expressed in various ways, i.e., in individual and common confession of Christians, in preaching and sacraments, in formalized and received creedal statements, in decisions of councils and in confessional texts. Ongoing theological explication aims at clarifying this faith as a service to the confessing community. Having its centre in the confession as Jesus as Christ and of the triune God, this apostolic faith is to be ever confessed anew and interpreted in the context of changing times and places in continuity with the original witness of the apostolic community and with the faithful explication of that witness throughout the centuries (Roman Catholic Church et. al 1984, 331).

The call to recover the original charism of unity associated with Spirit-baptism is one such central affirmation. It underlies many of the elements of the apostolic faith just described. The apostolic community preached Jesus Christ in the power of Spirit-baptism. Through the charismatic gifts, they experienced his continued presence. The apostolic church's inspired insights were elaborated by the first councils and creeds. Not all the elements defined in the "apostolic faith" tradition are needed for a common witness to begin, since unity can be "expressed in various ways." In fact, because of the diversity of the participants, these "various ways" must be allowed.

Apostolic faith is a valuable thematic concept. It is precisely because the apostolic faith tradition is so capacious that it could prove accessible to all pentecostals who wish to use it as a means of identifying with one another. Catholic charismatics can faithfully embrace all the elements described. But the apostolic faith is also an important term in the Assemblies of God's historic trajectory. The range within this proposed definition allows classical pentecostals to avoid being forced to embrace other groups' doctrinal decisions as their own. Differences in doctrine will have to be faced in time, but they do not have to impede a pentecostal common witness in its initial stages (see Gros 1987).

Searching out the grounds for common witness is a highly speculative task, and thus it is subject to ongoing refinement.[13] I have written this book in hope, subscribing to Yves Congar's view that "we can hope for everything, if the Holy Spirit is at work" (Congar 1967, 151). The transformed lives of millions proclaim that the Holy Spirit is powerfully at work in Spirit-baptism. Despite their testimonies, obstacles to implementing a pentecostal common witness are formidable, reflecting the long and unhappy history of general Christian disunity.

The practical foundation for building a common witness is simple. It begins with a spirit of mutual repentance and forgiveness. These virtues lead to a renewal of personal and group attitudes, including:

> awareness of the guilt and failure of Christians, readiness for *kenosis,* emptying ourselves, as the Lord emptied Himself for us, *metanoia,* a conversion of the heart, as well as prayer of penance and supplication (Willebrands 1985, 44).

For both Catholic charismatics and classical pentecostals, the allied graces of *kenosis* and *metanoia* have been short-circuited throughout their history. But past failures need not lead to present despair. It is scripturally attested that God's strength is perfected in weakness. If relational failures of the past are recognized and repented of, the renewed spiritual energy that can come through repentance becomes an unsuspected source of strength.

In his book *The Charismatic Renewal and Ecumenism,* Kilian McDonnell said that the traditional Catholic language for unity, which is based upon the idea of a "return" to Rome, is unworkable. Vatican II supplanted the traditional imagery with that of "family reconciliation" (K. McDonnell 1978, 73–74).[14] Family members share blood lines and many of the same experiences. But they do not all look or act alike. Indeed, this diversity can become a source of strength and edification. Similarly, mutual recognition by Christians of their common identity in faith can move one-time competitors from a state of coexistence—a condition in which there is only passive acknowledgment of the presence of Christ in the other—to active cooperation (Rusch 1985, 116–17).

Sharing and relating the fruits and gifts of a life lived within the graces of Spirit-baptism can even become a source of mutual hope. Fr. Peter Hocken has urged that Spirit-baptism be taken seriously as an "ecumenical grace" that penetrates the current barriers between the Christian traditions:

> The grace [of Spirit-baptism] is not different from one church to another. What is different are the varied traditions into which this grace is being received. This means that the grace given is in a vital sense more than what any church tradition now "possesses." We can glimpse perhaps how God in his infinite wisdom saw that only a grace transcending the present endowments of the churches could be a grace for all equally, and only such a transcendent ecumenical grace could summon and bring the divided churches into unity (Hocken 1987, 87).[15]

I support this understanding of Spirit-baptism, although the ecumenical grace of Spirit-baptism should never compete with nor threaten traditional understandings. It is important that grace not be confined to certain times, since such an attitude diminishes the special role tradition has played in carrying grace forward through time. But I do not believe that Hocken wants to deny either the uniqueness of the apostolic age or the enduring importance of church tradition.

Ecumenical pentecostals can begin to make a common witness within their various traditions even as they witness to one another. They can do this by recognizing, appropriating, and then sharing together, the unique charisms of their varied traditions. Deeper insights, as they come, will be forged in the crucible of shared lives and witness—both within their churches and to one another.

Pentecostals have not yet experienced enough unity to develop a theology by which to interpret their Spirit-baptism experience. Such a mature pentecostal theology is needed. It is likely to follow, not precede, initial common witness efforts to one another and to the various churches.

For a common witness to work, there must be an anchoring of the message in a basic core of doctrinal agreements. Included among these would be (1) a mutual recognition of Christian confessions, provided these are not diametrically opposed to one another; (2) a mutual acknowledgment of the legitimacy of the others' claims to Spirit-baptism; (3) a shared regard for Scripture as a norm for Christian faith and practice (Catholic charismatics, of course, will be a group that holds a similarly high regard for tradition and the magisterium); (4) a shared recognition of the validity of the others' water baptism; and (5) common acknowledgment of an irreducible set of beliefs, meaning a de facto acceptance of the tenets of the Nicene-Constantinople Creed.

Given the present level of pentecostal relations, common witness to the general public must be kept profoundly simple. This can be done through a clearly articulated message that explains the importance of the Spirit-baptism experience and locates the source of this experience in an encounter with Jesus Christ. Included in this witness should be an emphasis on the need for personal conversion, a clear articulation of the requirements for a life of Christian discipleship, and a focus on the power for Christian living available in Spirit-baptism. These emphases are all commonly held, complementary pentecostal values and are well within the reach of any beginning common witness attempt.

If the powers available through Spirit-baptism are unleashed, ecumenical pentecostals can be confident they have been put in this time and place to proclaim the message of the New Pentecost. The radical event of the apostolic faith being proclaimed in pentecostal power in our times would jar many modern sensibilities. Still, a witness faithful to the apostolic faith source could help clear a public mind so confused by conflicting claims that they see the gospel message as one more riddle to solve.[16]

Finally, ecumenical pentecostals must be confident that their claims will be validated by divine acts of power. To many nonpentecostals, this expectation of supernatural aid seems risky, foolish, or simply incomprehensible. But to pentecostals it is the life's blood of their proclamation. This confidence in direct intervention demonstrates faith in the reality of God's ongoing involvement in history. This is the assertion by which any pentecostal movement finally stands or falls. In embracing such claims, pentecostals display a flair for the dramatic not unlike that of the highwire walker who remarked: "Life is the wire. All else is waiting."

A Workable Ecumenical Model

A steady stream of images have been created to describe church unity. A popular one, promulgated by the World Council of Churches, is that of church groups revolving around Christ as planets revolve around a sun. This image has been even more extensively promoted since it was understood to be endorsed by Vatican II (Gonzalez 1967, ch. 1, sec. 2). Such a christocentric focus appears congenial to both Catholic charismatics and classical pentecostals. Following this first line of agreement, considerable diversity can be allowed in the particulars. The challenge then becomes that of moving beyond past parochialisms to discover "the limits of acceptable diversity" (Kinnamon 1988, viii; see also Congar 1981).

Oscar Cullmann's model of unity through diversity probes these possibilities and is a useful theoretical support for pentecostal common witness. Cullmann's model is worth investigating since, above all, he is not threatened by plurality, but rather sees it as strengthening Christianity.

Cullmann's thesis begins with the claim that different Christian groups retain permanent gifts that should be made available to the entire Body of Christ. It is crucial that the historic confessions remain independent in order to preserve and promote their unique gifts "for the purpose of forming a community of all those churches that call on the name of our Lord Jesus Christ" (Cullmann 1988, 33). These special spiritual strengths should never be sacrificed for the sake of "homogenization" (ibid., 9).[17] The Christian union Cullmann envisions can best be described as a community of harmoniously separated churches. Thus he has deliberately distanced himself from any hint of denominational merger (ibid., 15).

Cullmann argues for a smorgasbord approach to Christianity, with an open sharing of charisms and special insights. Since this approach does not insist upon uniformity, real differences need not lead to hostile separation. What unites Christians always remains more fundamental than what separates them. Cullmann's model foresees an association of churches in which the member groups remain autonomous, since they have the independence to choose how they will be identified with one another. However this autonomy is not entirely free, since Christ expects unity to be a primary value among Christians, and since total disinvolvement can be interpreted as sectarian.

Cullmann's proposal for greater flexibility in Christian relations has a basis in the New Testament saying "The one who is not against us is for us" (Luke 9:50). He represents the apostolic age as having had no single approach toward unity other than one based upon mutual trust and *koinonia* fellowship. Despite his emphasis upon cordial relationships, Cullmann has an aversion to an easy irenicism, which superficially smoothes over real differences (1988, 79). He believes, rather, that differences must be clearly defined, established, and allowed to exist.

The obvious cleavages between Catholic charismatics and classical pentecostals preclude even the thought of institutional unity. But a pentecostal common-witness effort falls well within Cullmann's workable alternative to institutional unity, namely ecumenical work in individual areas of common concern: "But so long as a superstructure [for Christian unity] does not exist, as is presently the case, or if it should be impossible to construct, then the only unity which can come into consideration is cooperative work in certain areas of common concern. I would like to note that even here everything need not simply remain as it has been, but that this cooperation should be constantly intensified and increasingly lead to particular declarations of solidarity" (ibid., 37).

Cardinal Joseph Ratzinger, prefect of the Vatican's Sacred Congregation for the Doctrine of the Faith, wrote an extended letter in support of Cullmann's model of unity through diversity (1988, 138–42). In his letter, Ratzinger expressed concern about "ecumenism by authority," which he described as *iuris humani* (a human declaration) rather than as the actual unity envisioned by Jesus Christ (ibid., 137). Cardinal Ratzinger represented Cullmann's model as a realistic alternative that might advance current ecumenical relations while still allowing the integrity of the individual church traditions (ibid., 138–39).

The fact that Ratzinger, with his high position in the Vatican, would point out the ecumenical potentials for Cullmann's unity-through-diversity model suggests its possible appeal.

Cullmann embraces diversity, seeing it as divinely endorsed rather than as merely tolerated. His approach is inclusive enough to allow past differences between Catholics and classical pentecostals to be redefined in a new and positive way.[18]

An Essential Moment: Renewing the Covenant

Developments in any movement are hard to evaluate. With one as involved as modern pentecostalism, real discernment is especially difficult. But the 1990 Indianapolis Congress, a meeting intended to launch an unprecedented decade of global evangelism, may have been more a matter of human design than divine intent.

The question lingers as to whether this meeting was forced to meet an artificial deadline for beginning an evangelistic campaign by the beginning of the 1990s. It has yet to be shown that the congress was blessed to accomplish its stated purpose. The problem was signaled by the fact that forty thousand were expected to attend but only twenty-five thousand showed up.[19] Given the hopes engendered before the meeting, the lack of a real evangelistic explosion at Indianapolis became a subtle source of disappointment for many of those attending.

At best, the impact of large rallies like Indianapolis 1990 tends to be rather evanescent. The main function of such gatherings is not profound insight but mass inspiration, as pentecostals join together in an anticipation of the time when all Christians will come into the *eschaton*. But mistaking a momentary collective enthusiasm for real commitment has been an ongoing problem for pentecostals.

One thing does seem clear: given the level of unresolved tensions, any call for a sending meeting—at which large numbers of people are commissioned to pursue a course of intense personal evangelism—seems premature. Establishing the spirit of fellowship and mutual service is a vital preparation for any such effort, but this has not been done sufficiently.

This is not to say that Indianapolis 1990 could not become a springboard for things to come. The Lord does not send sincere seekers away empty. Alliances were formed and individuals were trained in personal evangelization techniques. The large number of young people attending meant that a new generation was introduced to Spirit-baptism and the necessity of making a personal commitment to Jesus Christ. But this does not allay the nagging sense that the Indianapolis rally was more the result of human will than a sovereign leading of the Holy Spirit.

Pentecostals are not yet ready to launch or sustain a decade of evangelization. What is first needed is for their movement to understand and reclaim their original charism of unity. Doing this requires repentance for past divisions and a recommitment to their initial conversion experience. It also demands a deeper immersion into the mystery of Spirit-baptism. These steps will help restore pentecostals to their unusual covenant relationship with the Lord and with one another.

There is also a need for a more solemn assembly than the one held at Indianapolis. Solemnity is not to be confused with the gnashing of teeth, but pentecostals seeking unity need a time together to seek the Lord's direction for their future. Like the great Christian assemblies of the past, the needed meeting would have an air of mature deliberation. Any group wanting to commit itself to a task as daunting as a global decade of evangelism cannot afford to go into the task unprepared. Unless they do this, they could well spend their vital energies in shallow soil rather than cultivating the depths of God-given powers.

Large, fast-paced rallies do not provide a proper environment to look into the hard questions currently dividing pentecostals. These hard questions usually revolve around separate visions[20] and, even if they cannot be answered, the questions need to be fully acknowledged. Perhaps such issues of practical ecumenism should be introduced to those participating prior to large unity gatherings, in a series of smaller background briefings. With proper preparation, the general meeting could serve as a time for active reconciliation.

This needed gathering would have an agenda different from that of any meeting the participants have known before. The Holy Spirit might even give them leave and send them in surprisingly new directions.

Such an assembly for general reconciliation among pentecostals needs to be preceded by a similar meeting among the leaders (Sandidge 1987a, 30–32). Reconciliation among leaders would prepare an atmosphere that would help address and heal past divisions among pentecostals. Sincere prayer for unity and forgiveness should be the proper foundation for any such meeting. In my view, any coordinated attempt to proclaim pentecostalism's special message to the churches and the general population demands this sort of an approach.

Following this special unity meeting, specific local activities for building pentecostal unity might begin. These could include intercongregational love offerings, shared Bible studies, and doing the spiritual and corporal works of mercy together. There might even be an exploration of the potential for starting base communities where committed pentecostal ecumenists could study and live out the implications of the common witness ideal. In *Unity through Diversity,* Oscar Cullmann suggested restoring the practice of agape meals (the traditional Christian love feast) as a sign of Christian fellowship. Though certainly no substitute for eucharist, the restoration of agape meals might positively express the hope that someday full sacramental fellowship could happen.

Full intercommunion would be a powerful binding force. There are many dimensions to this issue, and a major aspect of the eucharist's sign value is its recognition of a unity already present. But there is another dimension to be considered, namely the eucharist's power to heal division. By any measure, confessing Christians are brothers and sisters in the Lord. It is in being fused to the Lord through his body and blood that Christians can begin most intimately to draw mutual strength. This being said, there will be no easy resolution to the complex questions surrounding intercommunion.

It is an important principle not to despise small beginnings. What can happen now between pentecostals, since there are no prohibitions, are specific efforts by committed alliances of individuals. A possible criterion for such attempts is God's deliverance of the nation of Israel through Gideon and his army of three hundred (Judges 7). The current application may be in God's act of collecting a band of ecumenical irregulars to witness unity to the modern world.

The Ultimate Challenge: Secular Drought

The Book of Amos describes a future plight of the human race: "Behold the days come, saith the Lord God, that I will send a famine in the land, not a famine of bread, nor a thirst for water, but of hearing the words of the Lord" (8:11). The ultimate challenge to pentecostal common witness is a society largely preoccupied with this-worldly concerns (see Ellul 1975, 18–47). This familiar condition has been called secularization. Sociologist Peter Berger defined secularization as "the process by which sectors of society and culture are removed from the domination of religious institutions and symbols" (1967, 107). Secular inroads to public consciousness are so pervasive that even many Christians have been subconsciously influenced by them.

A famine in the hearing of God's word, at least in terms of comprehending its true meaning, is threatening the American spiritual landscape. Christian views are being presented to the people; indeed, the systems for doing so are more elaborate than ever. But the dulling, cumulative press of too many voices and too many truth claims has made the Christian message seem like one more voice in the modern wilderness. To many onlookers, the church is another interested player in society, rather than an arbiter of absolute moral and spiritual standards (see Abraham 1989, 185–208).[21] In effect, what has happened is a flattening out, with the impression being given that the tread has worn off the gospel message.

Those pointing to a decline in Christian influence have a prima facie case. Christianity's impact upon the substructure of behavior and intellectual reflection has declined (see Lindbeck 1984). The result is often a type of moral relativism tantamount to moral illiteracy. The use of foundational standards as a measure for defining personal and social attitudes has begun to seem unimportant or strange to many. For the more thoroughly secularized, Christians seem to be speaking in a language with scarcely believable moral and ethical categories.

Peter Berger, in his book *A Rumor of Angels,* appraised the results of this conceptual shift:

> Whatever the situation may have been in the past, *today* the supernatural as a meaningful reality is absent or remote from the horizons of everyday life of large numbers, very probably of the majority, of people in modern societies, who seem to manage to get along without it quite well. This means that those to whom the

supernatural is still, or again, a meaningful reality find themselves in the status of a minority, more precisely, a *cognitive minority*—a very important consequence with far-reaching implications [emphases his] (1969, 5–6).

But Berger went on to assert that a life-style of total secularization is insupportable[22] because human beings cannot live meaningfully without a sense of transcendence.[23]

As traditional belief patterns break down on a wide scale, society moves in a direction that Emile Durkheim (1858–1917) described as *anomie,* a state of rootlessness resulting from the lack of an assured moral framework that an individual can count on (Emmett 1958, 146). Berger called this state "homelessness," and saw it as the main negative effect of the decline in the certitudes previously assigned to religion. A persistent question in assessing the decline of Christendom is: What can replace it?

The French sociologist of religion Jacques Ellul graphically portrays a modern society, unable to endure spiritual emptiness:

Modern man in these grandiose cities, in these feverish exchanges, in the continual chatter of radios and television, knows the human wasteland perhaps as never before. The chatter has no more meaning for him than the swarming of insects or the chirping, on every note, of millions of birds in a tropical forest. The human wasteland of the big city or the highway is even more disquieting and oppressive because new questions without number come to the lips of modern man and arise in his heart. There is no one to give him an answer. How can he talk to a computer? (1975, 130–31)

Ellul portrays a desperate search for transcendence in and through the world. Surrogates include political ideologies or nationalisms,[24] science as a panacea for human ills, and the portrayal of social sciences (such as psychotherapy and depth psychology) as sufficient to meet human spiritual needs. There are also the direct "secular religion" efforts, such as the New Age movement.[25]

The eternal message of the gospel is both simple and profound. It contrasts with the busyness of the secular world, which is marked by distraction, fear, and strife. That world's citizens are strongly affected by the hectic environment in which they live. The secular audience can be assumed to have undeclared—and probably underexplored—spiritual needs and desires (see Engel 1977).

Secularized thinking is so pervasive as to make it difficult for these people to hear the gospel message clearly or to reflect upon it profoundly. Thus, the greatest challenge to any pentecostal common witness is one of presenting the conversion message and Spirit-baptism in such a way as to penetrate modern consciousness. Perhaps what is needed is not so much a message that is intelligible as a converted intelligibility.[26]

For those who are experiencing the emptiness of disenchantment, it is important to demonstrate real empathy. There is the need to present a spiritually empowered way to interpret their experiences. Thus any common witness effort must be both compassionate to the hearer and faithful to Christian tradition. It can only convince through the force of the message and the integrity of the messengers.

Conclusion

Many pentecostals share my sense that this era is a *kairos,* a divinely notched hour. The language of revival is in the air. It is possible that, reminiscent of its beginnings, the Holy Spirit will ambush the pentecostal movement from all sides, setting it on fire and on a true course.

It may be that the participants of the ecumenical rallies of late will show that they are willing to pay the price for unity. Procedural habits die hard and they have weighed pentecostals down, sometimes making their claims of being led by the Holy Spirit sound like the echo of a disappeared truth. But it is also possible that the true cost of commitment—humility, forgiveness, and heart-rending prayer for a new anointing from on high—is still too great a price for many to pay.

Should present efforts falter, that need not be seen as a failure. There is always the confidence that the Holy Spirit will take what is worthy from the current model and build a better one, thus renewing the renewal.

I have been involved with the pentecostals for over fifteen years. Like many of them, I can testify to a range of emotions as I have tried to understand what all of this has meant. My reactions have gone from extreme optimism in the Lord's abilities to do anything, to a pained cynicism that made me see all of the problems perfectly and none of the answers at all. What has always reentered is hope. Hope recurs because hope is eternal. May those pentecostals who strive for common witness, "whose hope is in the Lord their God, who made heaven and earth" (Psalm 146:5–6), sustain their hope. Yes, may that tribe finally arrive and fully increase.

Epilogue

I completed my initial study with an analysis of the 1990 Indianapolis meeting. Since then, events of note have taken place.

In July 1991, an international consultation was held in Brighton, England, that brought together three thousand pentecostal and charismatic leaders (see *Ecumenical Trends* 1992, passim.; Blumhofer and Tinlin 1991a). As with the Indianapolis conference, the turnout for this invitational meeting was disappointingly low. Organizers had anticipated that five thousand of those asked would attend, and a financial deficit was incurred. Notably absent were significant representations from most of the major classical pentecostal groups, including the Assemblies of God.

Many high-profile personalities from North America did not come to Brighton. This seeming aloofness may—in large part—be explained by the "celebrity status" approach common to pentecostalism here. In such a case, if leaders are not invited to speak at a meeting, they do not attend.

The groups best represented at Brighton were the independent charismatics, the Anglicans, and the Roman Catholics. A

sense emerged that the center of gravity in worldwide pentecostalism had begun to shift from North America to the developing nations. As a result, social justice issues were prominent
on the agenda.

The Brighton meeting was thoroughly ecumenical in character, and Fr. Raniero Cantalamessa, the Preacher for the Papal
Household, used his plenary address to appeal for Christian
unity. This speech was a high point of the assembly and was
well received by those attending (Cantalamessa 1991).

There were also pioneering attempts to investigate diverse
theological views (see H. Hunter 1992). Workshops held during the day dealt in depth with both the practical and theoretical aspects of common witness. In particular, these meetings
helped participants comprehend the special concerns of pentecostals and charismatics from other parts of the world. The
result was a cross-fertilization of views. Through these workshops, common concerns were identified and a network of
informal global contacts established, which helped to lessen
the participants' previous sense of isolation.

Despite such hopeful signs, no explicit strategies for the
future came out of the Brighton conference. No further ecumenical events were planned, past preliminary discussions
about another international gathering in East Africa sometime
in the mid-1990s.

In terms of the Assemblies of God (U.S.A.), the Decade of
Harvest program does not seem to be catching on. Its success
in indigenous church planting has been largely restricted to
Latino and Korean outreaches. Growth in these groups has
been largely offset by declines in other areas. Examination of
the early results of the Decade of Harvest "suggests that the
Assemblies of God suffers from a numerical and spiritual
stagnation more typically associated with mainline Pro-
testantism" (Blumhofer and Tinlin 1991b, 684).

The entrenched Assemblies of God leadership does not
seem to be any more open to common witness initiatives,
although second echelon leaders appear to be more flexible.
Such an assessment needs to be nuanced, since discreet
allowance continues to be made for behind-the-scenes efforts
by Assemblies ecumenists. There are also signs that the
National Association of Evangelicals may be seeking a grace-

ful way to die out. This would be in favor of a more widely configured alliance, including classical pentecostals, evangelicals, and charismatics, including Roman Catholics. But, to this point, Assemblies of God contacts with other Christian groups continue to be limited to cooperation on specific issues such as battles against pornography and abortion.

The Catholic charismatic renewal continues to undergo significant changes. In 1991, The National Service Committee relocated its offices from South Bend to the Washington, D.C., area. This move reflects a desire to work more closely with the National Council of Bishops as well as to dissociate the service committee from any remaining identification with covenant community control.

Another significant decision was the choice to move the renewal's national conference from city to city rather than continuing to hold it at Notre Dame. This signifies the committee's current promotion of diocesan and regional renewals and shows a desire to integrate Spirit-Baptism fully into the life of the local church (see Matthews 1992). A specific instrument for promoting such local involvement has been Kilian McDonnell and George Montague's *Fanning the Flame*. This book is a biblical and historical apologetic for Spirit-Baptism as an ongoing source of Christian empowerment. The National Service Committee has sent a copy of this book to all American bishops in the hope that its teachings will be included in any preparation for the sacraments.

Many of the covenant communities have gone through a time of intensification and crisis (Duin 1992). People of Praise (South Bend) has lost both income and influence with the departure of the National Service Committee. In 1991, the Word of God (Ann Arbor) split internally over differences in leadership style and authority structures within the community. In February 1991, the Servants of Christ the King (Steubenville) were investigated by the local bishop over charges of psychological and spiritual abuse of its membership as well as withholding financial information (ibid.).

Emerging crises within the covenant communities are tied to difficulty in identifying their authentic mission. Some of these groups may, in fact, disappear. It seems to me that the notion of covenant community as the preferred charismatic renewal model has effectively ended. At the same time, the sense of mission to "the heart of the church" seems to be increasing. The ultimate impact of these shifts is impossible to predict, although there does seem to be increased caution about embarking upon new ecumenical projects. Thus the final realization of the dream of a common witness remains in abeyance.

Notes

Introduction

[1] The closest approach has been Fr. Peter Hocken's (1987) appraisal of Spirit-baptism as an ecumenical grace.

Chapter 1

[1] There is much material available on nineteenth-century revivalism. W. W. Sweet (1944) presents a number of useful insights into the nature of frontier revivalism. Melvin E. Dieter (1980) describes the National Holiness Movement and also represents the major theological streams that came to dominate. Timothy L. Smith (1962) provides a definitive history of the movement. Vinson Synan (1971) traces the link between the holiness movement and pentecostalism. Donald Dayton (1979) gives a good introduction to the elements involved in nineteenth-century pentecostalism.

[2] Much has been written about the changing urban religious climate following the Civil War. Arthur M. Schlesinger (1932) provides a good overview. For the post–Civil War intellectual climate and its impact upon the evangelical community see Henry Steele

Commager (1959, 165f). William W. Menzies (1971, 18–26), presents a pentecostal historian's understanding of the social and religious milieu following the Civil War. Another source for setting the origins of the pentecostal movement in context is Robert Mapes Anderson (1979, 28–46).

[3] A good introduction to fundamentalism is George Marsden (1980). Two other foundational texts are Ernest R. Sandeen (1970) and Ferenc Morton Szasz (1982). The last gives a good summation of the fundamentalist-modernist debate.

[4] Sandeen (1970, 114–31) traces the influence of eighteenth-century rationalism upon Princeton theology, a movement that he sees as intrinsically ahistorical. See also Mark A. Noll (1986). The history of nineteenth-century Princeton theology can be found in John Oliver Nelson (1935).

[5] There is a significant history to the concept of Holy Spirit baptism in nineteenth-century evangelicalism. A list of influential books includes William E. Boardman (1858), Asa Mahan (1870), and Robert Pearsall Smith (1870). Charles Grandison Finney (1908) describes his own interpretation of the baptism of the Holy Spirit. Reuben A. Torrey (1895) adduced the strongest arguments to that point for the baptism of the Holy Spirit as a second definite work of grace.

[6] Hardening to the holiness movement is noticeable in the 1894 issue of the *Journal, General Conference, Methodist Episcopal Church, South:* "But there has sprung up among us a party with holiness as a watchword. They have holiness associations, holiness meetings, holiness preachers, holiness evangelists, and holiness property. Religious experience is represented as if it consists of only two steps, the first step out of condemnation into peace and the next step into Christian perfection. . . . We deplore their teachings and methods in so far as they claim a monopoly of the experience, practice, and advocacy of holiness, and separate themselves from the body of ministers and disciples" (Methodist Episcopal Church, South 1894, 25–26). For an analysis of these charges of spiritual elitism, see John L. Peters (1956, 148).

[7] Gordon Lindsay (1951) remains the foremost biography of Dowie. Grant Wacker (1985) offers a good introduction to the Zion City experiment. In addition, Carl Brumback (1961, 72–73) summarizes Zion City's influence upon later Assemblies of God leaders.

[8] There are two chief accounts of Parham's life. Sarah E. Parham (1930), his wife, wrote one; a more analytical account is James R.

Goff, Jr. (1988b). A synopsis of Parham's theological views is found in Klaude Kendrick (1961, 38–45).

Several general descriptions of pentecostalism have been done. The most encyclopedic is Walter Hollenweger (1965). Part of this work has been translated as *The Pentecostals: The Charismatic Movement in the Churches* (1972). Three other comprehensive efforts are Nils Bloch-Hoell (1964), John Thomas Nichol (1966), and Donald Gee (1949).

[9] James R. Goff, Jr. (1988a) claims that Charles Parham knew upon his departure that the students would decide upon tongues as indisputable evidence of baptism in the Holy Spirit. Thus he "strategically directed" the study to a foregone conclusion.

[10] Several writers have attempted to describe the remarkable events surrounding Azusa Street. The most complete (though unabashedly biased) report is Frank Bartleman's 1925 reminiscence (reprinted in 1980). Vinson Synan (1971) contains a full chapter on Azusa Street. Openly sympathetic accounts are also given by Brumback (1961, 34–47) and Menzies (1971, 50–57). For a more skeptical appraisal, see Robert Mapes Anderson (1979, 66–71).

[11] The most widely circulated report of the Welsh revival was S. B. Shaw (1905). Another account is W. T. Stead (1905). Hollenweger (1972, 176–87) gives a good summary.

[12] For example, there is this rather jaundiced report from the *Los Angeles Times:*

> An old colored exhorter [Seymour, who was in fact thirty-six at the time], blind in one eye, is the major-domo of the company. With his stony optic fixed on some luckless unbeliever, the old man yells his defiance and challenges an answer. Anathemas are heaped upon him who shall dare to gainsay the utterance of the preacher. Clasped in his big fist, the colored brother holds a miniature Bible from which he reads at intervals one or two words—never more. After an hour spent in exhortation, the bretheren [*sic*] present are invited to join in a "meeting of prayer, song and testimony." Then it is that pandemonium breaks loose, and the bounds of reason are passed by those who are "filled with the spirit," whatever that may be.
>
> "You-oo-oo goo-loo-loo come under the bloo-oo-oo boo-loo," shouts an old colored "mammy" in a frenzy of religious zeal. Swinging her arms wildly about her, she continues with the strangest harangue ever uttered. Few of

her words are intelligible, and for the most part her testimony contains the most outrageous jumbo of syllables,
which are listened to with awe by the company (April 18,
1906, 1).

[13] The radical nature of early pentecostalism caused Robert Mapes
Anderson to locate the central appeal not in extraordinary spiritual experience but in inverted social categories. He characterizes
early pentecostalism as a crisis cult of the deprived. See Anderson
(1979, 223–40).

[14] Persistent rumors of Parham's homosexuality provided another
reason for his dismissal. The issue of Parham's sexual orientation has not been resolved. Nils Bloch-Hoell writes (probably
unfairly): "The rumour about Parham's fall from grace can
scarcely have been quite groundless" (1964, 20). See also Synan
(1971, 112–13).

[15] Two documents that give a sense of early pentecostalism are D.
Wesley Myland (1910) and B. F. Lawrence (1916). Myland's book
is a collection of sermons given at the pentecostal church he pas-
tored in 1909. It is replete with eschatological urgency, providing
elaborate argumentation (even to the point of charting rainfall
patterns in Palestine) in order to prove that the "latter rain" return
of the Lord was imminent. Lawrence's book came six years later
and represents a shift in emphasis from the Latter Rain thinking
of Myland. Though eschatological concerns remain prominent in
his book, Lawrence gives special weight to the restoration of the
powers of the apostolic age. Both works can be found in Dayton
(1985).

[16] There are several descriptions of the finished work debate. See
Menzies (1975, 90–94) and Synan (1971, 147–51). Frank Bar-
tleman (1980, 150–59) describes William Durham's visit to Los
Angeles. Edith Blumhofer (1983) reviews Durham's life and doc-
trine from an Assemblies of God perspective. Robert Mapes
Anderson (1979, 153–75) assesses the impact of the issue.

[17] The text of the Preamble and Resolution on Constitution reads as
follows:

WHEREAS, God, our Heavenly Father, sent His only begot-
ten Son, the Lord Jesus Christ, into the World, Who purchased and redeemed fallen man with His own precious
blood, and called out of the world and saved a people, of
whom He built and established His church (Assembly of
God. Matt. 16:18), upon the foundation of the Apostles and

Prophets, Jesus Christ Himself being the Head and Chief Cornerstone (Eph. 2:20), and organized and baptized it with the Holy Spirit, with its government upon His shoulders (Isaiah 9:6, 7), said "the gates of hell shall not prevail against it" (Matt. 16:18); and

WHEREAS, He gave the holy inspired Scriptures, (both old and new covenants, Heb. 8:6–13), as the all-sufficient rule for faith and practice (2 Tim. 3:16), as follows: "All Scripture is given by inspiration of God, and is profitable for doctrine, for reproof, for correction, for instruction in righteousness: That the man of God may be perfect, thoroughly furnished unto all good works," we therefore shall not add to nor take from it (Rev. 22:18); and

WHEREAS, He commanded that there should be no schism (division, sectarianism) in His body, the GENERAL ASSEMBLY (Church) of the firstborn, which are written in heaven (Heb. 12:23); and

WHEREAS, We recognize ourselves as members of said GENERAL ASSEMBLY OF GOD (which is God's organism), and do not believe in identifying ourselves as, or establishing ourselves into, a sect, that is a human organization that legislates or forms laws and articles of faith and has unscriptural jurisdiction over its members and creates unscriptural lines of fellowship and disfellowship and which separates itself from other members of the General Assembly (Church) of the first born, which is contrary to Christ's prayer in St. John 17, and Paul's teaching in Eph. 4:1–16, which we heartily endorse:

THEREFORE, BE IT RESOLVED, First, that we recognize ourselves as a GENERAL COUNCIL of Pentecostal (Spirit Baptized) saints from local Churches of God in Christ, Assemblies of God and various Apostolic Faith Missions and Churches, and Full Gospel Pentecostal Missions, and Assemblies of like faith in the United States of America, Canada, and Foreign Lands, whose purpose is neither to legislate laws of government, nor usurp authority over said various Assemblies of God, nor deprive them of their Scriptural and local rights and privileges, but to recognize Scriptural methods and order for worship, unity, fellowship, work and business for God, and to disapprove of all unscriptural methods, doctrine and conduct, and approve all Scriptural truth and conduct, endeavoring to keep the unity of the Spirit in the bonds of peace, until we all come into the unity of the faith, and of the knowledge of the Son of God, unto a perfect man, unto the measure of the stature of the fulness of Christ, and to walk accordingly, as recorded in Eph. 4:17–32, and to consider the five purposes announced in the Convention Call in the February, 1914, issue of "Word and Witness":

RESOLVED, Second, That we recognize all the above said Assemblies of various names, and when speaking of them refer to them by the general Scriptural name "Assemblies of God"; and recommend that they all recognize themselves by the same name, that is "Assembly of God" and adopt it as soon as practicable for the purpose of being more Scriptural and also legal in transacting business, owning property, and executing missionary work in home and foreign lands, and for general convenience, unity and fellowship.

[18] For a full listing of resolutions, see the minutes of Assemblies of God General Council, (1914, 5–6).

[19] A thorough discussion of Jesus Only theology can be found in David Reed (1978). Brumback (1961, 191–210) describes the effects of the Oneness teaching upon the Assemblies of God. Other descriptions of this major pentecostal eruption can be found in Synan (1971, 153–62) and Menzies (1971, 106–21). Two prominent apologies for the Oneness position are Fred J. Foster (1965) and Frank J. Ewart (1947).

[20] A more modern articulation of this Oneness view can be found in Roy H. Maki (1961). Maki writes: "The doctrine of the Trinity is an example of how paganism has obscured vital Christian doctrines. . . . The fact remains that behind the fundamental doctrine of the Trinity lies the essential pagan concept of a plurality of gods! . . . The pure monotheism inspired by the Israelites and the early inhabitants of the earth was corrupted by Nimrod. Much of the paganism, including the basic idea of a trinity of gods, found in Christianity, has come down to us straight from Babylon" (1961, 11).

[21] Menzies (1971, 116–17) discusses the interim between the Third and Fourth General Councils from a trinitarian position.

[22] The following subpoints from "The Essentials as to the Godhead" section of the Fourth General Council Minutes, October 1–7, (1916, 10–11) are relevant to the issue:

(a) The terms "Trinity" and "Persons" as related to the Godhead, while not found in the Scriptures, yet are words in harmony with Scripture, whereby we may convey to others our immediate understanding of the doctrine of Christ respecting the Being of God, as distinguished from "gods many and lords many." We, therefore, may speak with propriety of the Lord our God, who is One Lord, as a Trinity or as one Being of three Persons, and still be absolutely Scriptural (Examples: Matthew, 2:6; 8:16, 17; Acts 15:15–18). . . .

(h) Transgressions of the Doctrine of Christ.

Wherefore, it is a transgression of the Doctrine of Christ to say that Jesus Christ derived the title, Son of God, either from the fact of the incarnation, or because of His relation to the economy of relation. Therefore, to deny that the Father is a real and eternal Father, and that the Son is a real and eternal Son, is a denial of the distinctions and relationship in the Being of God; a denial of the Father and Son, and a displacement of the truth that Jesus Christ is come in flesh (John 9; John 1:1, 2, 14, 18, 29, 49; 8:57, 58; 1 John 2:22, 23; 4:1–5; Heb. 12:3, 4).

[23] A proposal to establish contact with other pentecostal groups was contained in the Assemblies of God General Council Minutes (1921, 59–60). Although an exploratory committee was formed, there is no record that it ever met.

[24] The text of the condemnation of pentecostals, reprinted in Stanley Frodsham (1928), is as follows:

Whereas, the present wave of Modern Pentecostalism, often referred to as the "tongues movement," and the present wave of fanatical and unscriptural healing which is sweeping over the country today, has become a menace in many churches and a real injury to sane testimony of Fundamental Christians,

Be it Resolved, That this convention go on record as unreservedly opposed to Modern Pentecostalism, including the speaking in unknown tongues, and the fanatical healing known as general healing in the atonement, and the perpetuation of the miraculous sign-healing of Jesus and His apostles, wherein they claim the only reason the church cannot perform these miracles is because of unbelief.

[25] Under Williams, there was a 290 percent increase in membership (from 72,143 to 209,549) between 1927 and 1941. Menzies (1971, 146–49) describes the rapid growth of the 1930s as the "Storefront Era" because of the number of pioneer efforts initiated.

[26] The Assemblies of God has fully identified with the National Association of Evangelicals since its inception. Indeed, figures from 1987 indicate that pentecostals have come to dominate the group, representing 3.1 million of approximately 5 million members. See Cecil M. Robeck, Jr. (1988, 635).

[27] Walter Hollenweger writes of the healing evangelists:

> The Healing evangelists live in a constant dialogue with demons, the Holy Spirit, and the spirits of diseases from the abyss; some experience electric currents through their hands when they pray with the sick, others have a halo around their heads when they are photographed, and others again have oil appearing on their hands when they pray. If the healing of sick persons does not take place, this can be the result of one of ten, fifteen, or twenty reasons why prayers are not heard (unbelief, sin, etc., on the part of the persons seeking healing) (1972, 357).

E. M. Wadworth notes the claims of financial extravagance on the part of independent healing ministries. He commends "these pastors and evangelists who deliberately limit themselves to a modest salary in order to avoid the appearance of covetousness" (1952, 4).

[28] The 1963 General Council Minutes pointedly affirmed the National Association of Evangelicals' position on the ecumenical movement: "1) We believe said movement to be a sign of the times and contrary to the real Biblical doctrine of spiritual unity in the church of Jesus Christ, and 2) We are opposed to ecumenicity based on organic and organizational unity, and 3) We believe that the combination of many denominations into a World Super Church will probably culminate in the Scarlet Woman or Religious Babylon of Revelation" (Assemblies of God 1963, 41).

[29] Karl Strader (1975, 13) defends charismatics against such charges of emotional extremism.

[30] Rev. Bob Mumford, a key spokesperson for the Shepherding position, gave a vigorous defense of it in his personal newsletter, *Plumbline*, in November 1975. His essay, entitled "A Defense of Shepherding," provides an introduction to the Shepherding position. See also Edward E. Plowman (1975) and Charles Farah (1975).

[31] Gary North and Earl Paulk, Jr., are among the most prolific writers of the Kingdom Now movement. R. J. Rushdoony is generally

acknowledged as the movement's systematician. See, for example, Rushdoony (1973). Other significant Kingdom Now texts include Greg L. Bahnsen (1984) and David Chilton (1985).

[32] Since the Kingdom Now position is still in formation, interpretative literature is currently appearing. An introduction to Paulk's thought is provided by William A. Griffin (1987).

[33] See her definitive work, *The Assemblies of God: A Chapter in the History of American Pentecostalism*.

Chapter 2

[1] The 17 May 1967 article by Mary Papa in the *National Catholic Reporter* is primarily a positive report on the Catholic charismatics. By contrast, an editorial in *Our Sunday Visitor*, 30 April 1967, is notable for its depiction of "hippies" who had rejected traditional Catholicism. The publication later denied any intention of connecting the charismatics with a youth drug culture.

[2] Duquesne was never identified as a charismatic renewal center. This was probably because both Keifer and Storey left the university.

[3] In 1968, charismatic groups began appearing away from college campuses, beginning with a St. Louis prayer group led by Francis McNutt, O.P.

[4] René Laurentin (1977, 14) tabulates the rapid growth in attendance at the early Notre Dame conferences:

1967:	90	1971:	4,500
1968:	100+	1972:	11,000
1969:	450	1973:	25,000
1970:	1,300	1974:	30,000

[5] An example of the early spirit of unity evident among Catholic and Protestant charismatics was the dedication of the entire May 1972 issue of the Catholic charismatic magazine, *New Covenant*, to promoting cooperation among the various pentecostal groups.

[6] The need to address this concern can be seen in O'Connor (1971, 221–62). Kevin and Dorothy Ranaghan (1969, 141–42) take special pains to describe Spirit-baptism within the context of sacramentalism:

> Most truly, most really, the baptism in the Holy Spirit is essentially a part of our Christian initiation, the sacrament of

baptism and its ongoing actualization in our celebration of
eucharist and living the Christian life. . . . To evangelical
pentecostals, baptism in the Holy Spirit is a "new" work of
grace. In the life of a Catholic it is an "old" work, yet practi-
cally "new" because the phrase as used by Catholic pentecostals is a prayer for renewal for everything that Christian
initiation is and is meant to be. In practice it has come to be
an experience of reaffirmation rather than of initiation.
Among Catholic pentecostals this baptism is neither a new
sacrament nor a substitute sacrament. Like the renewal of
baptismal promises, it is a renewal in faith of the desire to
be everything that Christ wants us to be.

[7] For other early statements see McDonnell (1976a).

[8] An early history of the Word of God community was provided by
Charles H. Green and Kevin F. Perotta (1986). For a sociological
evaluation of the community see Roberta Catherine Keane (1974).
See also the personal papers of Thomas Yoder at the Bentley
Historical Library, Ann Arbor, Michigan, for more information.

[9] The Notre Dame prayer group also moved in the direction of
covenant community when Paul DeCelles, Kevin Ranaghan, and
twenty-seven other people formed the People of Praise in 1971.
For a description, see People of Praise Information Service
(1988). Another early covenant community, Mother of God, in
Gaithersburg, Maryland, was formed in the early 1970s under the
leadership of two laypeople, Edith Difato and Judith Tydings.
This community was more informally structured than the others,
with an emphasis on renewal of one's mind, as well as on the
call to individual holiness, prayer, and personal study.

[10] This concern may reflect the fact that the charismatic renewal is
not a typical Catholic movement and the term cannot be comfortably applied to it. This does not mean there have not been
numerous attempts to incarnate the renewal in a way that would
make it recognizable as a movement. I side with those who
believe that the renewal is better understood as the church in
movement rather than as a movement in the church. See Heribert
Muhlen (1978) and Leon Cardinal Suenens (1974).

[11] According to David Barrett (1982, 711) the number of Catholic
pentecostals (U.S.A.) was already at 200,000 by 1970. Their number increased to 1.2 million by 1975.

[12] Ann Arbor became the nexus for the renewal's publishing and
editorial side during the early 1970s. South Bend became the

center for services such as the planning for large conferences and the distribution of tapes, literature, and prayer group directories.

[13] Martin uses the term *secular humanism* several times without explicitly defining it. He portrays secular humanism in terms of an atmospheric change that, in the American context, involves a "whole counter-foundation . . . cloaked in Christian language and rites" (1971, 21). The sense of his argument is that secular humanists attempted to attribute personal achievement and happiness to human effort and that such an attitude diminished the expectancy of divine activity in human life and had come to have a practical ascendancy for many Catholics. See also James Hitchkok (1982).

[14] In his views on a "community of communities," Clark was particularly influenced by Canadian writer Max Delespesse. See Delespesse (1969).

[15] An example of this integration was the 1975 Southern Regional Conference, held at Southern Methodist University in Dallas. In addition to Catholics such as Cardinal Suenens, Ralph Martin, and Fr. Francis McNutt, the speakers included David du Plessis and Rev. Bob Mumford, a nondenominational charismatic. See Louis Bourassa (1975b).

[16] The level of Protestant involvement became clear in December 1973, when fourteen leaders of the international charismatic renewal were named as contributing editors to *New Covenant.* Included were Rev. Larry Christenson (Lutheran), Rev. David du Plessis (Assemblies of God), Dr. Robert Frost (nondenominational charismatic), Rev. Michael Harper (Anglican), Rev. Ken Pagard (Baptist), Rev. Graham Pulkingham (Episcopalian), Dr. Vinson Synan (Pentecostal Holiness), and Dr. J. Rodman Williams (Presbyterian).

[17] The entire September 1974 *New Covenant* is devoted to a vision of total Christian unity. Ralph Martin's keynote address was completely reproduced there.

[18] Martin has been portrayed as a significant prophetic voice in the renewal. His authenticity has been called into question recently, especially by those who see his messages weighted down by "doom and gloom." For his later depiction of the plight of the Catholic Church see R. Martin (1982a).

[19] There were those who held reservations to this dominant view. See, for example, Paul Labeau's (1975) review of Martin's *Fire on Earth.*

[20] Kilian McDonnell (1975) has argued that pentecostals have a tendency to confuse the terms *ecumenical* and *nondenominational*. In nondenominational settings, the issues that divide were not discussed at length, whereas in ecumenical settings they were focused upon. See also Dulles (1976a, 1976b). For a pastoral adaptation, see McKinney (1976).

[21] A discussion of this problem is also found in Edward O'Connor (1974). O'Connor's concern over institutionalization extended to "[leaders] tempted to use authority as a lever for imposing their own will" (1974, 275). This may have hinted at the reason for his resignation from the National Service Committee in 1974.

[22] The controversial incorporation of non-Catholic "heterodoxy" into the practices of the renewal is also discussed in Fichter (1975, 39–57).

[23] A heavy prophetic message came out of the January 1976 National Service Committee meeting.

> Son of man, do you see that city going bankrupt? Are you willing to see all of your cities going bankrupt? Are you willing to see the bankruptcy of the whole economic system you rely on now so that all money is worthless and cannot support you? Are you willing to see no law, no order, no protection for you except that which I myself will give you? . . . Son of man, do you see those Churches which you can go to so easily now?—Are you ready to see them with bars across their doors, with doors nailed shut? . . . Son of man, I call you to be ready for that. That is what I am telling you about. The structures are falling and changing—it is not for you to know the details now . . . but do not rely on them as you have been. I want you to make a deeper commitment to one another. . . . When you see it all shut down, when you see everything removed which has been taken for granted, and when you are prepared to live without these things, then you will know that I am making you ready (National Service Committee 1976b, 3).

[24] The main account of the Kansas City conference is found in David Manuel (1977). See also the extensive article by John Blattner (1977). Both accounts are notable for their glowing assessments of the unity displayed at Kansas City. Even a secular writer was struck by what he saw: "They were Catholic, Baptist, Presbyterian, Episcopalian and Methodist, all praising the Lord and embracing each other in brotherly love. Even for a casual

observor of Christian religious history, such a moment of ecumenical bliss certainly gave the impression that a miracle had, indeed, taken place" (Rifkin and Howard 1979, 178).

[25] Yocum (1978) was "writing more as a prophet than as an interpreter of prophecy" in order to affirm messages he himself had helped deliver. Yocum was known for writing a widely circulated book on prophecy and the measures to test or interpret prophecy. Haughey does not challenge the validity of the prophetic gift per se but questions whether those involved in speaking forth prophecies can also be the ones to interpret their validity.

[26] Steve Clark (1978b) responded to Haughey's challenge in an essay in which he questioned whether—given societal trends—a Christian witness based upon Haughey's inclusivist position was even possible.

[27] Clark also spoke to this theme: "Within the charismatic communities, the heads are commonly chosen as the need arises because of their ability to do the job. They often have not been trained for ordination nor could they be spared for four years at a seminary. That does not mean that they are untrained for pastoral service nor that they are uneducated theologically. They often are capable in building community and caring for people, and they often have as much theological understanding as the normal parish priest" (1975, 78).

[28] As it has in the church in general, the nature of male-female relationships has been seen as problematic for the charismatic renewal. See Judith Bardwick (1970), S. Clark (1980), and R. Martin (1982b). A more moderately worded statement was issued shortly after the report to the bishops.(National Service Committee 1978a).

[29] Ambiguity over how to interpret events was evidenced at the 1979 National Leadership Conference. Some speakers, such as Fr. John Bertolucci, an up-and-coming evangelist, described the movement as "just beginning." Others, such as Fr. John Randall, a National Service Committee member from Providence, Rhode Island, expressed concern about a "revolving door syndrome," meaning that Catholics would be involved with the renewal for a period of two or three years and then leave. Given this uncertainty, the title of the report on the 1979 conference, "Speakers Agree Charismatic Renewal Has 'Only Begun,'" (National Service Committee 1979) seems overly optimistic.

[30] A Christianity Today–Gallup Poll, conducted in early 1980, showed that 18 percent of American adult Catholics considered

themselves charismatic. This would put the membership of the renewal at about nine million. This number was obviously too high, and Kilian McDonnell (1980) observed that many Catholics had begun to equate the term *charismatic* with all manners of spiritual renewal. He estimated that perhaps one-tenth of those who claimed to be charismatic actually spoke in tongues. This would still be a considerable number, something like nine hundred thousand Catholics.

[31] The National Advisory Committee is a large group of approximately sixty persons that assists the service committee in defining problems and reaching decisions. The advisory committee is made up of one or two persons from each of the ecclesiastical provinces in the United States, nine members at large, and six representatives of the Hispanic renewal.

[32] These difference can be seen by comparing two statements. Steve Clark described a prominent function of the Association of Communities as acting as a bulwark against the inevitable collapse of society: "The Benedictine monasteries are a good example of a group of communities that were able to be a bulwark for the church without becoming sectarian. The Benedictine communities strengthened the church in Europe after the barbarian invasions had damaged normal church structures. Many other groups within the church have served as a bulwark without becoming sectarian or falling into a 'faithful remnant' mentality" (1978a, 23).

Clark's position was that his Ann Arbor group was not trying to form an elite church within the church, including its own lay version of a hierarchy. Despite this emphatic disclaimer, charges of exclusivism and excessive manipulation by the Ann Arbor group were frequently voiced in my 1989 visit with the People of Praise in South Bend.

The People of Praise considered their position to be more centrist than Ann Arbor's. This was portrayed in the original statement of purpose of their community publication, *New Heaven, New Earth:* "It is our conviction that as Christians we need to be concerned with human life in all its dimensions. Christianity is meant to pervade all of human culture, and so our vision is for human culture completely renewed in Christ" (People of Praise 1983, 1). Although not as pronounced as John Haughey's inclusivist position, their point of view was portrayed as a type of Christian humanism and contrasted to the fortress mentality of the new Ann Arbor–Steubenville axis.

South Bend's humanist position has led to a reappraisal of the prophecies given in the mid and late 1970s, many of which came from the Ann Arbor–Steubenville camp (Ranaghan 1978).

[33] Bp. Joseph McKinney of Grand Rapids, Michigan, was chairperson of the National Service Committee from 1981 to 1983. Fr. Ken Metz, the original liaison for the archdiocese of Milwaukee, was the chairperson from 1984 to 1987. He has been replaced by Bp. Sam Jacobs, formerly a liaison from Monroe, Louisiana. This may also indicate a growing clerical influence in the renewal.

[34] Another model effort is the Southern California Renewal Center (Farmer 1986).

[35] The next year, conference numbers were back down to nine thousand. The fact that 1982 was the fifteenth anniversary of the renewal may have been a significant factor in the one year increase in attendance that year.

[36] The committee went through a major restructuring following the 1982 Notre Dame Conference. Part of the back-to-the-basics approach was a shift from centralized decision to more personal involvement with regional and local leaders. Some of the practical implications of the new campaign were described by Sr. Ann Shields (1982) and by Bert Ghezzi (1983). S. Clark (1982, 1983) seemed more hesitant to subcribe to any belief that a fresh move of the Holy Spirit had begun; instead he saw evidence to support the claim that the renewal's influence had declined.

[37] The split between Ann Arbor and South Bend became complete in January 1984, when they mutually decided to separate the services they had once provided together. People of Praise (South Bend) continued the Notre Dame national conferences and their book and tape ministry. Word of God (Ann Arbor) retained *New Covenant* and Servant Publications. This was of particular significance, since *New Covenant* remained the central source for information on the renewal.

[38] "I have seen more conversions, more healings, and more genuine repentance at FIRE rallies than I have anywhere else. The simple truth is lives are touched as the gospel is preached in unity with the Holy Father and the Magisterium of the Roman Catholic Church" (Scanlan 1988, 1).

[39] I became exposed to this controversy when I attempted to organize a street evangelism campaign promoting a September 1984 Chicago FIRE rally. The meeting was cosponsored by the archdiocese of Chicago and the Chicago Day of Renewal, the coordinating office for the local charismatic renewal. In the course of this prerally campaign, it became evident that there was a growing level of mistrust toward FIRE. The visiting FIRE team was seen as fundamentally indifferent toward ongoing, locally

based evangelism efforts. The result was that a one-day event did occur, which was much like any other charismatic rally, but there was no follow-up to implement a long-term strategy for evangelizing in the Chicago area.

[40] This proclamation is on the masthead of the group's newsletter, AD 2000. They are not alone in their ambition. See also David Barrett (1987).

Chapter 3

[1] Henry I. Lederle argued that Fr. Peter Hocken was an exception to the dominant Catholic position. He interpreted Hocken as wanting to preserve the classical pentecostal emphases (Lederle 1988, 85–90). In an interview in 1990, Hocken told me that Lederle's book represented an early phase in his thinking on Spirit-baptism, but that he currently supports the Catholic view, although he maintains his concern that the expectation for receiving special pentecostal gifts must not be lost.

[2] These texts have been supplemented by other references, including G. Jones (1983). After reading these primary sources, I found myself in fundamental agreement with Roland H. Wessels' statement that: "[Assemblies of God doctrinal teachers] draw together 'the teaching of Scripture' about the Holy Spirit in proof text fashion. However, their presentations are not the result of independent, even if interdependent, work on the texts of Scripture. Two facts indicate this: first they are extremely similar in constructive content; almost all the same points are made in each. Second, they contain few hints of debates or discussions which reflect a development of view by the writers. What is being offered, it appears, is a tradition whittled down almost to a formula" (1966, 124–25).

There is an apologetic concern in all of the Assemblies writings revolving around the claim of having received a special revelation. An ahistorical inductive and evidential approach to the Scriptures is used to justify pentecostalism's present existence. This lack of appeal to earlier Christian history most probably stems from a belief that the church lost full power soon after the apostolic age. The result has been a tendency to see true advances in spirituality as a series of crisis interventions, in which God attempts to win the church back to faithfulness through extraordinary displays of power.

[3] For example, Rev. Arvid Kingsriter, an Assemblies presbyter, emphasizes an inner witness leading to the assurance of Spirit-

baptism: "In addition to the outward evidence, God has provided an inward evidence at the time of Spirit baptism to authenticate and secure all the assurances the believer receives at salvation. Listen to the apostle Paul as he later wrote to the Ephesians: 'That we who first trusted in Christ should be to the praise of His glory. In Him you also trusted, after you heard the word of truth, the gospel of your salvation; in whom also, after having believed, you were sealed with the Holy Spirit of promise' (Eph. 1.12, 13)" (1983, 158).

[4] See Laurence W. Wood, *Pentecostal Grace* (Wilmore, Kentucky: Francis Asbury Publishing, 1980) for an analysis of Fletcher's use of pentecostal-style language and Wesley's allowance for a special reception of the Holy Spirit as an aid to Christian perfectionism.

[5] John L. Peters described the initial sense as follows: "Among these [Holiness] groups the term 'pentecostal' meant primarily that the organization stressed entire sanctification, of which Pentecost was conceived as the prototype. The name did not indicate any addiction to charismata" (1956, 50).

[6] "This revelation of the purpose of God in Scripture should be sought in its *didactic,* rather than its historical parts. More precisely, we should look for it in the teachings of Jesus, and in the sermons and writings of the apostles, and not in the purely narrative portions of the Acts" (Stott 1964, 8). For a pentecostal rejoinder to Stott, see Stronstad (1984).

[7] Charles Hummel addresses this issue. Hummel's basic argument is that Luke and Paul use the phrase *baptize in the Holy Spirit* in different contexts. "According to Luke's teaching, the baptism in the Spirit for the disciples was an empowerment for Christian witness. According to Paul, the baptism in the Spirit for the Corinthians meant their incorporation into the body of Christ. Luke's context is the unfolding of redemptive history and the mission of the church, while Paul's is the experience of the individual believers once they become members of Christ's body. The distinction—the two meanings of baptize in the Spirit—helps to clarify the significance of Pentecost for the church today" (1978, 182).

James Barr argues that interpreting Luke's Spirit-baptism usages as if they were Pauline was a case of "illegitmate identity transfer" (1961, 222). Lederle believes that Hummel went too far in his distinction between Luke and Paul (1988, 69). Harold D. Hunter asserts that setting up such an opposition between New Testament accounts would not have been the intent of the early witnesses (1983, 67–68).

[8] See Riggs (1949, 79–83). Williams describes Spirit-baptism as "an enduement of power on the cleansed [regenerated] believer" (1953, 3: 46). It is notable that he based his views upon Ephesians 1:13. This attempt to employ a Pauline teaching of Scripture may have demonstrated an awareness of the need to expand upon a Lucan base.

[9] Wessels states: "The system of thought of the Assemblies concerning the Spirit's working does not really need the Spirit baptism to be complete. The simple truth is that the Assemblies believes one receives the Spirit at conversion and so they do not really need to posit some second experience for the same purpose" (1966, 336–37). I find this claim to be unconvincing. I think it is better to say that the Assemblies apologists began with an experience of Spirit-baptism in which, given their previous Christian conversions, subsequence seemed to be a central claim. The point is that they did feel the need to "posit some second experience."

A vital resource for the study of classical pentecostal views on Spirit-baptism is Bruner (1970). Bruner, a Protestant evangelical, disputes the need for a crisis experience (such as Spirit-baptism) as a prerequisite to experiencing fullness of the Spirit. He also asserts that Spirit-baptism should be linked to water baptism and not be viewed as separable from it (1970, 193–94). For his full argument see Frederick Dale Bruner and W. Hordern (1984).

Another significant reflection on Spirit-baptism claims is Dunn (1970). Dunn's book is irenic in its attitude toward pentecostals, but his critique is thoroughgoing. He argues that Christian conversion-initiation should be seen as a seamless event, with Spirit-baptism understood to be the foundation (rather than subsequent to) repentance, faith, water baptism, and all gifts of the Holy Spirit (1970, 21–22).

Dunn's book, in particular, stirs considerable reaction from pentecostals. The two most comprehensive responses are H. Hunter (1983) and a direct refutation by the Baptist charismatic Howard Ervin (1984).

[10] "The question [of Spirit-baptism having a definitive biblical pattern] cannot be decided from the four gospels, because they contain the prophecies of the coming of the Spirit, and a prophecy is made perfectly clear only by fulfillment; neither can it be settled by the Epistles, for they are largely pastoral instructions addressed to established churches where the power of the Spirit with outward manifestations was considered the normal experience of every Christian. It is therefore evident that the matter must be settled by the book of Acts" (Pearlman 1935a, 313).

[11] Riggs's distinction between the Spirit of the Son and the Holy Spirit is extremely problematic and could lead to charges of promoting a quadernity. Ernest S. Williams obliquely acknowledged this: "From time to time persons arise teaching that the Spirit of Christ and the Holy Spirit are two different persons. Some have taught that at conversion a person receives the Spirit of Christ: at sanctification or the baptism with the Spirit, he receives the Holy Spirit. This teaching would make operative two Spirits from God" (1953, 3: 13).

Williams's solution is that the Holy Spirit and the Spirit of Christ were two names for the same divine executor. The potential for confusion over whether two spirits are being claimed led Wessels to write: "One is forced [by such remarks] to the conclusion that there must be a fourth in the Godhead, a Spirit who is acting here on earth under the name 'Christ'" (1966, 214). Such problems suggest the lack of linguistic precision in much of pentecostal theology.

[12] James G. Dunn counters by claiming that the basic Christian commitment of the Samaritans must have been in some way defective (Dunn 1970, 54).

[13] Assemblies writers have usually held that Cornelius was a righteous pagan and not a Christian prior to Peter's visit (D. V. Hurst and T. J. Jones 1959, 111).

[14] Williams (1953) also argues that the event was a unique act of the Holy Spirit.

[15] Again, Dunn questioned whether the Ephesians had truly been converted. "The twelve Ephesians are therefore further examples of men who were not far short of Christianity, but were not yet Christians because they lacked the vital factor—the Holy Spirit" (1970, 88). The issue centers around the use of the term *disciples* in this context. Luke used an indefinite pronoun, which has caused critics like Dunn to see it as an instance where the author is making a distinction between the Ephesian group and the regular disciples. Contra Dunn see Stronstad (1984, 90).

[16] It is disputable whether disciples baptized only into the baptism of John can be viewed as fully Christian, since John's baptism was unto repentance while Christian baptism was unto salvation.

[17] "The freedom to say that Jesus exercised gifts of the Spirit is consistent with the insistence that Jesus was dependent upon the anointing of the Spirit to perform His ministry, and with [Assemblies writer] Frank Boyd's teaching that Christ emptied

Himself of His 'divine powers' to become man" (Wessels 1966, 181). There is, of course, no evidence that Jesus spoke in tongues at his water baptism to manifest his Spirit-baptism.

[18] Bruner's observation is pertinent: "It will sometimes be admitted [by pentecostals] that while Holy Scripture may nowhere explicitly say that speaking in tongues is the initial evidence of the Baptism in the Holy Spirit, nevertheless the weight of events in Acts where tongues-speaking does in fact occur upon the receipt of the Spirit compels the doctrine implicitly" (Bruner 1970, 78).

[19] Buntain describes the unsurpassable "cleanness of heart and spirit" that the experience of the tongues of fire engendered on that day (1954, 14). Horton writes: "The Appearance of fire came over the whole group to indicate God's acceptance of the whole Body as a temple. Then it broke up with the single tongue on the head of each to show God's acceptance of the body of each as a temple of the Spirit" (1976, 141).

[20] "It is probably fair—and important—to note that in general the Pentecostals' experience has preceded their hermeneutics. In a sense, the Pentecostal tends to exegete his experience. For example, the doctrine of Spirit-baptism as distinct from and subsequent to conversion did not flow naturally out of his reading of Scripture. . . . When he did have a dynamic experience in the Holy Spirit, he said with Peter, 'This is that.' The fact that it happened after his conversion helped him to see this very pattern in Scripture: he saw the analogy with Jesus and the apostles, and the precedent in Samaria (Acts 8) and Paul (Acts 9). What followed was perfectly natural. He took the scriptural pattern he had now found, supported by his own personal experience and that of thousands of others, and made it normative for all Christians" (Fee and Stuart 1982, 122).

[21] Since 1959, all ordained Assemblies of God ministers have been required to adhere to all tenets of the Statement of Fundamental Truths (Wessels 1966, 114–16).

For a moderate rebuttal of Fee, see Menzies (1983, 62–69). A good introduction to the creation of a new pentecostal hermeneutic is contained in Ervin (1981, 11–25).

[22] "On the active side there appears to be an advocacy of the seemingly superhuman feat of sinlessness. . . . On the passive side there appears to be a proposal for an almost equally superhuman self-emptying. . . . We may say that the two classic poles of reli-

gious ardor express themselves in the Pentecostal conditions of active and passive obedience: an extremely optimistic self-assertion (sinlessness), and an extremely pessimistic self-negation (nothingness)—what are sometimes called the distinctively Western and Eastern varieties of religious expression" (Bruner 1970, 103).

[23] In the winter of 1978, I participated in such a "tarrying meeting." The group prayed intensely with a woman for about an hour. She did not experience Spirit-baptism at that point. But after repeated tarryings, over several nights, she broke out in tongues. The issue of timing for Spirit-baptism was broached in Brumback: "Hence, the tarrying of the disciples [until the day of Pentecost] was primarily imposed upon them so that all things could fit into the divinely arranged plan" (1949, 192).

Wheelock notes that pentecostals ardently desire to be obedient to this timing of divine initiatives: "More broadly speaking, the tarrying [among pentecostals] called upon the virtues of obedience, patience, and faith, and it underscores the belief that the power to carry out the mandate of the Great Commission comes only from God" (1983, 186).

[24] Williams describes evangelical thinkers such as A. J. Gordon and Andrew Murray as supporting the idea that there is an ongoing operation of the Holy Spirit subsequent to regeneration (1953, 3: 59–61). This appeal to prominent evangelicals probably represents an attempt to make the pentecostal argument for a dual approach to faith more palatable to conservative evangelicals.

[25] Pearlman argues that there are, in fact, two moments of faith: initially faith toward Christ in conversion and subsequently faith toward the Holy Spirit in Spirit-baptism (1935a, 236).

[26] Bruner argues—from a Reformed perspective—that classical pentecostals are straying from the pure gospel and embracing a form of legalism by stressing spiritual works as essential to obtaining Spirit-baptism: "The reversal of the apostolic sequence of grace-then-obedience lies at the bottom of the Pentecostal error" (1970, 233).

[27] Bruner cited Cantelon's remark as a primary example of pentecostals finally seeing the *sola fide* position as untenable (1970, 102). See also Pearlman (1935a, 318) and Riggs (1949, 112) for a description of activist faith.

[28] "Since Pentecostals see that the spiritual baptism in the New Testament was a veritable *experience,* they fear to make this event a matter of faith *alone*" (Bruner 1970, 109–10).

[29] Pearlman writes about a continuous walk in the Spirit: "But after all is said concerning the correct mode of receiving the power of the Spirit, it must be remembered that it is even more important to *remain* filled with the Spirit. . . . First, there is the *initial filling* when a person is for the first time baptized in the Holy Spirit. Second, there is the *habitual condition* referred to in the words, 'full of the Holy Ghost' (Acts 6:3; 7:55; 11:24), which words describe the daily life of a spiritual person . . . third, there are fillings or *anointings for special occasions*" (Pearlman 1935b, 64). See also Holdcroft (1962, 83) and Williams (1953, 3: 57–59).

[30] See Bruner (1970, 108) for examples of heedlessness to the personal cost involved in pentecostal discipleship. Holdcroft summarized the dominant attitude when he observed that the cost was more apparent than real, being so only from the human point of view (1962, 116).

[31] "The ordinance of Baptism by a burial with Christ should be observed as commanded in the Scriptures, by all who have really repented and in their hearts have truly believed on Christ as Savior and Lord. In so doing, they have the body washed in pure water as an outward symbol of cleansing, while the heart has already been sprinkled with the blood of Christ as an inner cleansing" (Winehouse 1959, 17). This viewpoint distances water baptism from any integral connection with Spirit-baptism.

[32] "For the New Testament and for the early Church, all that the Pentecostals understand by 'baptism in the Spirit' is referred, quite strictly and simply, to what it means to be a Christian at all. The experience of the Spirit is not subsequent to that of conversion and faith; the experience of Pentecost is identical with the baptismal confession that 'Jesus is Lord'" (Tugwell 1971, 272). The most extensive study yet on this subject is Kilian McDonnell and George Montague (1991a).

[33] "Without commenting on the theological meaning of such a doctrine [as subsequence], one would have to say that the Catholic doctrine of sanctification is conceived in quite different terms, though a different kind of two-level doctrine is not absent from the Catholic theological tradition. These precise distinctions are, however, generally foreign to the Catholic culture. Receiving the fullness of the Spirit does not belong to a later stage of Christian life, but theologically belongs to its beginnings" (K. McDonnell 1980, 3: 38–39).

[34] "Experience is knowledge at the personal level and has in it some elements of the non-conceptual. This non-conceptual apprehen-

sion of God is part of the experience. One must not, without qualification, oppose thought to experience, as though the reflective process cannot also be involved in experience. In the same way, faith is not to be placed in opposition to experience. While the conceptual is not entirely absent from experience, experience is the acknowledgment at the personal level of the reality and presence of God who approaches man. It is the realization at the personal level of God's claim" (ibid., 3: 32).

[35] The essence of the argument is in McDonnell (1989, ix–xxvii). McDonnell indicates that there are patristic evidences to support the idea of the imparting of Spirit-baptism at the time of the sacraments of initiation. During a September 29, 1989, phone conversation with me, he discussed current research that pointed to Spirit-baptism as being originally a matter of public liturgy and not merely of private piety.

[36] McDonnell believes that Spirit-baptism's manifestations within the sacraments of initiation ceased because of increased formalism in religion, especially resulting from a reaction against Montanism (a second-century burst of charismatic enthusiasm that was condemned as excessive and even heretical) (Kilian McDonnell and Arnold Bittlinger 1972, 44).

[37] It is noteworthy that Gelpi portrayed Spirit-baptism as a prayer of petition for greater grace rather than as an experience of empowerment (Gelpi 1971, 223–26).

[38] "The mere fact that the gifts of the Spirit can in fact be given outside the sacramental system is of itself no proof that such is their normative mode of reception. There is in fact solid evidence in Scripture that anyone who is truly open to the charismatic anointing of the Spirit is summoned by God to full participation in the sacramental life of the eucharistic community" (Gelpi 1976, 252).

[39] The sense of Gelpi's comment is that the neophyte and God are cooperating in this transformation. In using such terminology, care should be given to avoid a tendency toward pelagianism, the belief that one can effect one's own salvation. Baptism must be seen as a gift of faith before it is seen as an act of faith (ibid., 141).

[40] Gelpi wrote that alternative phrases such as "an experience of Spirit-baptism" and "a fuller release of the gifts of the Spirit" are legitimate expressions for Spirit-baptism, provided they do not imply that a type of delayed detonator is implanted at baptism (ibid., 150–51).

[41] "Unfortunately there is no English word which fully expresses the meaning of Saint Thomas' innovatio; "renewal" is about as close as we can come, but it does not have the same sense of 'going forward into something new'" (Sullivan 1974, 66).

[42] Sullivan's argument is largely built upon *Summa Theologiae:* "Accordingly in the destinary [recipient] of a mission we should take into account both the indwelling by grace and a quality of newness brought about by grace. There is, then, an unseen mission to all in whom these two occur. . . . Still there is a special instance of an invisible mission based on an increase in grace when someone advances to a new act or new stage of grace, e.g., to the grace of miracles or prophecy or to delivering himself in the fervor of his charity to martyrdom or to renunciation of all he possesses or to taking up any sort of heroic task" (I, q. 43, a. 6).

[43] "The solutions which had been most commonly adopted in the literature of the Catholic charismatic renewal is to see the 'giving' or 'imparting' of the Holy Spirit as taking place exclusively in the sacraments. There is an evident reluctance to speak of a new imparting of the Spirit except through the reception of a sacrament, as though this would be incompatible with Catholic theology" (Sullivan 1982, 62).

[44] Sullivan argues that Aquinas was not alone nor on the margins in asserting that there were subsequent sendings. "We know from a previous work of St. Thomas that he was aware that some medieval theologians held that there was a new sending of the Spirit whenever there was an increase of grace or virtue in the soul. St. Thomas did not reject this view outright, but he prefers to speak of such a new sending of the Divine Person where it is a question of a decisively new work of grace, such as can be described as 'moving into a new act or new state of grace [quotation from I Sent. d.15, q.5, a.1, sol.2]'" (1982, 71).

[45] "The fact that the Pentecostal experience can be fruitfully interpreted in the light of other Christian traditions—a fact which I believe is becoming more and more clear—suggests that it is basically a Christian experience, and not something Evangelical Protestant" (Sullivan 1978, 91). In this remark, Sullivan seems to be saying that classical pentecostals, despite their claims, are not the sole interpreters of the pentecostal experience. He implies that the pentecostal surge should be interpreted in a larger context than a single Christian tradition.

[46] Sullivan spoke of sovereign new actions of the Holy Spirit: "To speak of praying for a 'new outpouring of the Spirit' would also

help correct the impression that 'baptism in the Spirit' is a once-in-a-lifetime event. I am convinced that there will never be a time during our pilgrimage on earth when the Lord could not give us a powerful new gift of his Spirit that would really move us into some new act or new state of grace" (1982, 75).

Chapter 4

[1] The following is a list of those I interviewed and the date and location of interview.

ASSEMBLIES OF GOD

Dick Champion, editor of *Pentecostal Evangel*, 20 February 1990, Springfield, Mo.

Gary McGee, Associate Professor of Church History, Assemblies of God Theological Seminary, 21 February 1990, Springfield, Mo.

Jerry Sandidge, pentecostal leader in the international Roman Catholic–pentecostal dialogue and Senior Pastor, Evangel Temple Christian Center, 21 February 1990, Springfield, Mo.

Cecil M. Robeck, Jr., Associate Professor of Church History and Assistant Dean of Academic Programs, Fuller Theological Seminary, 4 April 1990, Pasedena, Calif.

Russell Spittler, Professor of New Testament and Director of the David J. Du Plessis Center for Christian Spirituality, Fuller Theological Seminary, 4 April 1990, Pasedena, Calif.

OTHER CLASSICAL PENTECOSTALS

H. Vinson Synan, Chairman, North American Renewal Service Committee, 23 February 1990, Oklahoma City, Okla.

CATHOLIC CHARISMATICS

Kevin Ranaghan, author and head coordinator of People of Praise covenant community, 19 February 1990, South Bend, Ind.

Walter Matthews, Assistant Director of Chariscenter, the information arm of the National Service Committee, and member of the National Service Committee, 28 February, 1990, South Bend, Ind.

Fr. Peter Hocken, ecumenist, historian, and theologian, Mother of God covenant community, 2 March 1990, Gaithersburg, Md.

Abbot David Gareats, Pecos Benedictine Monastery, 8 April 1990, Pecos, N. Mex.

Ralph Martin, author, member of the FIRE evangelistic team, and leader of the Word of God covenant community, 30 March 1990, Ann Arbor, Mich.

Keith Fournier, Director, Catholic Evangelization Center, University of Steubenville, 30 March 1990, Steubenville, Ohio.

David Thorp, Director of Evangelization Office, Archdiocese of Boston, and member of the National Service Committee, 1 May 1990, Boston, Mass.

Sr. Josephe Marie Flynn, liaison for the charismatic renewal, Archdiocese of Milwaukee, and member of the National Advisory Committee, 11 July 1990, White Plains, N. Y.

Sr. Nancy Kellar, evangelist, leader of the Elizabeth Ann Seton Retreat House, and member of the National Service Committee, 11 July 1990, White Plains, N. Y.

OTHER CATHOLICS

Kilian McDonnell, O.S.B., theologian and prominent ecumenist, 27 February 1990, Collegeville, Minn..

Bp. Joseph Leibrecht, Springfield–Cape Girardeau diocese, 22 February 1990, Springfield, Mo.

Fr. Ed Eftink, special representative to the Springfield Roman Catholic–Assemblies of God dialogue, 22 February 1990, Springfield, Mo.

I have the transcripts of all of these interviews.

[2] I mainly chose the people I interviewed from the Catholic charismatic renewal or from the Assemblies of God. There were four exceptions. Vinson Synan, a leader from the Pentecostal Holiness Church, was chosen because of his role as chair of the North American Renewal Service Committee and because of his ongoing prominence as a bridge person between various pentecostal and charismatic groups. Fr. Kilian McDonnell was chosen because of his vast understanding of both pentecostalism and ecumenism. Neither Bp. Joseph Leibrecht, of the Springfield–Cape Girardeau diocese, nor Fr. Ed Eftink, his special representative to the Springfield Assemblies of God–Roman Catholic dialogue, are pentecostal Catholics, but they were chosen because of their leadership in the only ongoing Roman Catholic–classical pentecostal dialogue in the United States.

[3] Such a concern was voiced by Charles Whitehead, the new chair for the International Catholic Charismatic Office in Rome: "Is it all over for the charismatic renewal? Are the charismatics about to

disappear again? It's surprising that after only twenty or so years of charismatic renewal I have to ask such a question, but the warning signs are there. Many of us are tired. We are finding it harder to step out in faith, so we rely on techniques and not the Holy Spirit. . . . The old human problems remain. Have we started to build a theology around our unbelief, explaining why God probably won't act?" (R. Martin 1990a, 12).

[4] To the best of my knowledge, the Assemblies of God is the only Pentecostal denomination to have *officially* positioned itself against ecumenical relations with non-pentecostal, nonevangelical Christians.

[5] Hocken has held this perspective for some time. See Hocken (1979, 310–21).

[6] In 1961, the Assemblies of God strengthened their Reformed influence and weakened Wesleyan influences when they removed the word *entire* from their denominational statement on sanctification because it was considered ambiguous. Dieter et al. (1987, 112).

[7] The subject matter for the Vatican's 1993 Catholic-pentecostal dialogue will be common witness and evangelization.

Chapter 5

[1] The General Council produced a document, *Strategy for the 1990s*, which announced three goals for Decade of Harvest: (1) "winning five million persons to Christ in America"; (2) "disciple and train 20,000 persons for the ministry"; and (3) "establish 5,000 churches in a decade" (Assemblies of God, Executive Presbytery 1989, 2). Such campaigns usually promote lofty goals, but this one especially so.

[2] On November 13, 1989, I attended Peter C. Wagner's Fuller Seminary course on church growth. In evangelical-pentecostal circles, Wagner promotes targeting the "felt needs" of subgroups in the general population in order to build a congregation quickly. This audience segmentation approach has led to the establishment of fast-track churches servicing very specific populations (Wagner 1987).

[3] Mel Robeck told me he gave full reports on his ecumenical involvements to his denominational superiors: "I keep my ecumenical stuff ever before them [the Assemblies leadership]."

Robeck felt that some of the leaders believed that the denomination acted precipitously in its 1961 bylaw, which prohibited large-scale ecumenical activity (interview by author, 4 April 1990).

[4] Self-described third-wave evangelicals distinguish themselves from first-wave pentecostals and second-wave charismatics, especially by distancing themselves from traditional pentecostal terminology. They are also reluctant to accept or trust the open use of the so-called word gifts such as tongues, the interpretation of tongues, and prophecy. A major emphasis of the third wave remains public prayer for healing.

[5] Margaret M. Poloma observes: "Although verbally supportive of the charismatic movement . . . in fact the national organization demonstrates little support. This lack of support may be illustrated by the national organization's most recent failure to be formally represented at either the 1986 North American Leaders Conference in New Orleans, attended by some 7,000 charismatic leaders, or the July 1987 North American Congress on the Holy Spirit & World Evangelism, also in New Orleans, attended by 35,000 charismatics" (1989, 181).

In representing the most established part of classical pentecostalism, Assemblies leaders have felt compelled to respond somewhat to the recent initiatives. But customarily the denomination has been unwilling to join in an effort it does not sponsor. Poloma's use of the term *failure* may be a bit strong in describing this cautious style of response.

[6] Articles 3 and 4 of the *Decree on Ecumenism* reads as follows:

> It follows that the separated Churches and Communities as such, though we believe them to be deficient in some respects, have been by no means deprived of significance and importance in the mystery of salvation. . . . For men who believe in Christ and have been truly baptized are in communion with the Catholic Church even though this communion is imperfect. . . .
>
> Moreover, some and even very many of the significant elements and endowments which together go to build and give life to the Church itself, can exist outside the visible boundaries of the Catholic Church: the written word of God; the life of grace; faith, hope, and charity, with the other interior gifts of the Holy Spirit, and visible elements too. All of these, which come from Christ and lead back to Christ, belong by right to the one Church of Christ (Gonzalez 1967, 197–99).

The council used the imagery of the "people of God," partly to extend an ecumenical bridge to non-Catholic Christians. It is through this metaphor that the *Degree on Ecumenism* should be read.

Francis Sullivan, S.J. agreed with commentators who said that changing the text of the Vatican II's Constitution on the Church from saying the Church of Christ is (*est*) the Catholic Church to saying that it subsists in (*subsistit*) the Catholic Church was a step toward a fuller recognition of non-Catholic Christians. Sullivan concludes: "I believe that one can think of the universal Church as a communion, at various levels of fullness, of bodies that are more or less fully Churches. . . . The Church of Christ is certainly something more than any 'collection' (summa); it is a real communion, realized at various degrees of density or fullness, of bodies, all of which, though some more fully than others, have a truly ecclesial character" (1986, 123).

[7] Dietrich Bonhoeffer has a pertinent insight: "A community life under the auspices of the Word will remain healthy only where . . . it is understood as an element of the one, holy, universal Church. . . . Any principle of selection and any consequent separation that are not conditioned by complete objectivity . . . are of the greatest danger for a Christian community. On this path of spiritual selectivity, psychological factors always creep in . . . and lead to a sectarian spirit" (1958, 2).

[8] Fr. Hocken remarked to me: "One of the problems is that people have an emotional way of handling prophecy. They get all excited, but they're not used to going home and praying about it and wrestling with it. The most important prophecies at Kansas City were not heeded and obeyed" (interview by author, 2 March 1990).

[9] I had a phone conversation with Sr. Linda Koontz, a leading renewal evangelist. During our talk, she indicated her belief that the renewal had experienced "a clear pattern of decline." She believed this was because most Catholic charismatics were not harboring a vision for evangelization: "If we don't evangelize, we'll fossilize and vaporize." She agreed that many charismatics had turned inward and that they were less open to sharing charismatic experiences (9 January 1990).

[10] A sign of reconciliation between rivals occurred August 18, 1990, at the Indianapolis Evangelization Conference. During an afternoon session Bill Beatty, at that time a leader in the South Bend People of Praise community, publicly asked forgiveness for past

offenses from Ralph Martin, then a leader of the Ann Arbor's Word of God community. Beatty went so far as to wash Martin's feet as a sign of his desire for restored fellowship (Beatty 1990, cassette tape #82).

[11] Ralph Martin, one of the principals in the battles of the late 1970s and early 1980s, admits as much in a published appeal for forgiveness (1990b, 6, 33). What is now needed is to move from general pleas to active reconciliation.

[12] Personal correspondence from Helen Hoffman to author January 15, 1990.

[13] Bernard Lonergan, S.J., rightly asserts that meaningful learning is such a "a self-correcting process" (1979, 209).

[14] McDonnell states that there is a new self-awareness in the Roman Catholic Church and that familial images are being used to portray it. Christians are called to reconciliation, much as estranged family members are called to forgive each other. What results from such reconciliation is recognition of the ties that bind: "In the family reconciliation model no one member is unrepentant; no member stands still; all are on their knees. Typical of reconciliation is a new openness, a willingness to take the initiative, to dare the first step, a readiness to distinguish between the substance of the faith and the variable forms it took in history, a reluctance to identify over-hastily beliefs particular to the Roman church as belonging to the substance of the gospel" (1978, 61).

[15] Hocken's book is an exploratory statement on Spirit-baptism as the Holy Spirit's own ecumenical initiative. He argues that, because Spirit-baptism is divine ordained, its special graces can surmount historic barriers. Hocken does not describe shared pentecostal experience as superceding church traditions, and a mature renewal movement will maintain an openness to insights from all the traditions.

[16] "This [intratextual catechesis, that is, speaking from within the biblical language structure] has been the primary way of transmitting the faith and winning converts. . . . In the early days of the Christian church, for example, it was the gnostics, not the catholics, who were most inclined to redescribe the biblical materials in a new framework. Pagan converts to the catholic mainstream did not, for the most part, first understand the faith and then decide to become Christians; rather, the process was reversed: they first decided and then they understood. More precisely, they were first attracted by the Christian community and form of life" (Lindbeck 1984, 132).

[17] Cullmann purposely distances himself from views set forth by Heinrich Fries and Karl Rahner. They stress the present reality of diversity but, unlike Cullmann, seem to believe that diversity is an interim situation: "This [issue of confessional status] is left to a broader consensus in the future" (1985, 25). Cullmann also separates himself from Yves Congar's (1984) desire for a fusion of Christian churches based upon reconciled diversity.

[18] Cardinal Joseph Ratzinger argues that unity through diversity can be a *felix culpa* and signpost to a more complete unity. "Following the path indicated by Cullmann we should therefore first try to find unity through diversity. That means to accept what is useful in these divisions, to take the poison out of it and to receive precisely the positive element from this diversity—naturally in hope that finally the division will cease to be a division at all and is merely a polarity without opposition" (1988, 139).

[19] In the literature leading up to the event, promoters of the Indianapolis Congress on the Holy Spirit and Evangelization described it as, "probably the most important gathering of Christians ever to assemble in North America" (North American Renewal Service Committee 1989, 3).

[20] In a conversation with Jerry Sandidge, I was introduced to some of the hard questions proposed for deliberation at the 1990–94 Roman Catholic–pentecostal international dialogue. These included (1) views of world mission; (2) different assessments of non-Christian religions; (3) common witness and shared ministry; and (4) proselytism (interview by author, 2 November 1989).

[21] Abraham (1989) contends that an attempt to gain popular acceptance by "flattening out" the gospel message (that is, accommodating gospel salvation to the contemporary climate so much that it loses its ability to challenge) has made the traditional themes of evangelism seem eccentric or obsolete to many.

[22] I guardedly agree with Phillip E. Hammond's (1969) critique of Berger's fixation on the church as a social institution. Hammond, though sympathetic, sees Berger as too committed to the "churchly element" in religion. Berger's inclination as a sociologist is toward the social functions of religion, often at the cost of emphasising its prophetic role. See also Hammond (1986).

[23] Berger describes "symbolic universes" in *The Sacred Canopy*. These provide a way to integrate experience at the highest level, a function necessitated by day-to-day reality's inability to perform such a task. Religion is the archetypical symbolic universe, "the establishment . . . of an all-embracing sacred order, that is, of a

sacred cosmos that will be capable of maintaining itself in the
ever present face of chaos" (1967, 51).

[24] For a classic depiction of the demonic abuse ("the invasion and
possession of the self by spirit which is not Holy Spirit") of political power see Niebuhr (1943, 2: 110–14).

[25] "After an appearance of rationality, coupled with an obvious
indifference to Christianity . . . we have witnessed for a half century now a prodigious resurgence of religions. But they are no
longer the same" (Ellul 1975, 129). For a fuller exposition of "secular religions" (the expression is Raymond Aron's) see Ellul (1975,
122–65).

[26] "Most of our [Christian theologians'] energy has been given to
questions of fundamental viability, to considerations of method,
and to the problem of translating or adapting traditional material
to the modern world. Many of those who were nurtured in the
Barthian tradition—Paul van Buren comes to mind—embraced a
version of secularism that left little space for anything remotely
akin to evangelism in the traditional sense" (Abraham 1989, 140).

How do you interpret a Christian message to a contemporary
audience who may not comprehend traditional categories? For an
introduction to this complex issue, see Anthony C. Thiselton
(1980).

Despite their differences, both Catholic and classical pentecostals share the belief that there is a special spiritual hermeneutic that is gained through Spirit-baptism. This view is based in the
belief that they have personally experienced the mighty acts of
God *pro nobis* and can apply the Scriptures existentially. For an
exploration of the potential for developing this pentecostal
hermeneutic, see Mark D. McLean (1984).

Bibliography

Abbott, Walter M., S.J., ed. 1989. *The Documents of Vatican II.* New York: Crossroad Publishing.

Abraham, William J. 1989. *The Logic of Evangelism.* Grand Rapids, Mich.: William Eerdmans Publishing.

"Advisory Committee Meets." 1971. *New Covenant* 1, no. 1 (July): 7–8.

Ahlstrom, Sydney E. 1972. *A Religious History of the American People.* New Haven, Conn.: Yale University Press.

Alexander, Patrick H. 1988. "Gordon Donald Fee." In *Dictionary of Pentecostal and Charismatic Movements,* ed. Stanley Burgess and Garry McGee, 305. Grand Rapids, Mich.: Zondervan Books.

Allen, A. A. N.d. *The Fatal Word That Will Jam Hell to the Doors.* Dallas: A. A. Allen Publications.

Anderson, Gerald A., and Thomas F. Stransky, eds. 1975. *Mission Trends #2 : Evangelization.* New York: Paulist Press.

Anderson, Robert Mapes. 1979. *Vision of the Disinherited: The Making of American Pentecostalism.* New York: Oxford University Press.

Aridas, Chris. 1977. "Charismatic Renewal on Long Island: A Parochial Approach." *Catholic Charismatic* 2, no. 3 (August/September): 4–7.

———. 1987. "Charismatic Renewal's Growth Continues." *Long Island Catholic* (19 February): 2.

Assemblies of God, Executive Presbytery. 1949. *Latter Rain.* White paper. Springfield, Mo.: Gospel Publishing. Available at the Archives, Assemblies of God Headquarters, Springfield, Mo.

———. 1976. *The Discipleship and Submission Movement.* White paper. Springfield, Mo.: Gospel Publishing.

———. 1980. *The Life of Faith.* White paper. Springfield, Mo.: Gospel Publishing.

———. 1989. *Strategy for the 1990s.* Springfield, Mo.: Gospel Publishing.

Assemblies of God, General Council. 1914. Minutes. Available at the Archives, Assemblies of God Headquarters, Springfield, Mo.

———. 1915. Minutes. Available at the Archives, Assemblies of God Headquarters, Springfield, Mo.

———. 1916. Minutes. Available at the Archives, Assemblies of God Headquarters, Springfield, Mo.

———. 1919. Minutes. Available at the Archives, Assemblies of God Headquarters, Springfield, Mo.

———. 1921. Minutes. Available at the Archives, Assemblies of God Headquarters, Springfield, Mo.

———. 1941. Minutes. Available at the Archives, Assemblies of God Headquarters, Springfield, Mo.

———. 1963. Minutes. Available at the Archives, Assemblies of God Headquarters, Springfield, Mo.

Assemblies of God, General Presbytery. 1952. Minutes. Available at the Archives, Assemblies of God Headquarters, Springfield, Mo.

———. 1956. Minutes. Available at the Archives, Assemblies of God Headquarters, Springfield, Mo.

———. 1976. *The Discipleship and Submission Movement.* Springfield, Mo.: Gospel Publishing.

———. 1987. *A Summary of Some Kingdom Now Doctrines Which Differ from the Teaching of the Assemblies of God.* White paper.

Available at the Archives, Assemblies of God Headquarters, Springfield, Mo.

————. 1988. *The Initial Evidence of the Baptism in the Holy Spirit.* Springfield, Mo.: Gospel Publishing.

Bahnsen, Greg L. 1984. *Theonomy in Christian Ethics.* Phillipsburg, N.J.: Presbyterian and Reformed Publishing.

Bardwick, Judith. 1970. *The Psychology of Women.* New York: Harper and Row.

Barr, James. 1961. *The Semantics of Biblical Language.* London: Oxford University Press.

Barrett, David, ed. 1982. *World Christian Encyclopedia.* New York: Oxford University Press.

————. 1987. *700 Plans to Evangelize the World.* Altamonte, Fla.: Creation House.

————. 1988. "The 20th Century Pentecostal/Charismatic Renewal in the Holy Spirit, with Its Goal of World Evangelization." *AD 2000 Together* 2, no. 5 (Fall): 11–22.

Bartleman, Frank. 1925. *How Pentecost Came to Los Angeles.* Los Angeles: privately printed. Reprinted as *Azusa Street.* Plainfield, N.J.: Logos International Press, 1980.

Beatty, Bill. 1990. *Who Can Stop the Spring?* Cassette #82. Albuquerque, N.M.: Hosanna Tapes.

Bell, Bob. 1973. "Charismatic Communities: Questions and Cautions." *New Covenant* 3, no. 1 (July): 4–5.

Bell, Eudorus. 1913. "A Proposal." *Word and Witness* (20 December): 1. Available at the Archives, Assemblies of God Headquarters, Springfield, Mo.

————. 1915. *Word and Witness.* (19 December): 5.

Berger, Peter. 1967. *The Sacred Canopy.* Garden City, N.J: Doubleday.

————. 1969. *A Rumor of Angels: Modern Society and the Rediscovery of the Supernatural.* Garden City, N.J.: Doubleday.

————. 1973. *The Homeless Mind.* New York: Random House.

————. 1977. "Secular Theology and the Supernatural." *Theological Studies* 38: 39–56.

Berger, Peter, and Thomas Luckman. 1966. *The Social Construction of Reality.* Garden City, N.J.: Anchor Books.

Bess, Donovan, 1963. "Speaking in Tongues: The High Church Heresy." *Nation* 197, no. 9 (28 September): 173–77.

Beuther, Walter. 1952. "Some 'Weightier Matters.'" *Pentecostal Evangel* 39 (30 March): 11.

Bittlinger, Arnold. 1978. *Papst und Pfingstler: Der romisch Katholisch-pfingstliche Dialog und seine okumenische Relevanz.* Frankfurt am Main: Verlag Peter Lang.

Blattner, John. 1977. "A Living Prophecy." *New Covenant* 7, no. 4 (October): 4–10.

Bloch-Hoell, Nils. 1964. *The Pentecostal Movement.* New York: Humanities Press.

Blumhofer, Edith Walvogel. 1983. "The Finished Work of Calvary: William Durham and a Doctrinal Controversy." *Assemblies of God Heritage* 3, no. 3 (Fall): 9–11.

———. 1985. *The Assemblies of God: A Popular History.* Springfield, Mo.: Radiant Books.

———. 1987. "Divided Pentecostals: Bakker vs. Swaggart." *Christian Century* 104, no. 15 (May): 430–31.

———. 1988. "Assemblies of God." In *Dictionary of Pentecostal and Charismatic Movements,* ed. Stanley Burgess and Garry McGee, 23–28. Grand Rapids, Mich.: Zondervan Books.

———. 1990. *The Assemblies of God: A Chapter in the History of American Pentecostalism,* 2 vols. Springfield, Mo.: Gospel Publishing.

Blumhofer, Edith W., and Paul B. Tinlin. 1991a. "Charismatics Converge, Diverge." *Christian Century* 108, no. 29 (September): 814–16.

———. 1991b. "Decade of Decline or Harvest? Dilemmas of the Assemblies of God." *Christian Century* 108, no. 21 (July): 684–87.

Boardman, William E. 1858. *The Higher Christian Life.* Boston: Henry Hoyt Publishing.

Boddy, A. A. 1912. "They Two Went On." *Latter Rain Evangel* (October): 6.

Bonhoeffer, Dietrich. 1958. *Gemeinsames Leben,* 9th ed. Munich: C. Kaiser.

Bord, Richard, and Joseph E. Faulkner. 1983. *The Catholic Charismatics: The Anatomy of a Modern Religious Movement.* University Park, Pa.: Penn State Press.

Bosworth, Fred F. 1918. *Do All Speak with Tongues?* (25 May) Available at Central Bible College Archives, Springfield, Mo.

Boucher, John. 1988. "CHARISM: Charismatic Institute of Spirituality and Ministry." *Living Light* 25, no. 1 (October): 3–5.

Bourassa, Louis. 1975a. "It's Time to Build." *New Covenant* 4, no. 7 (January): 14–17.

———. 1975b. "Jesus Renews the Hearts of Men." *New Covenant* 4, no. 11 (May): 24–25.

Brumback, Carl. 1949. *What Meaneth This? A Pentecostal Answer to a Pentecostal Question.* Springfield, Mo.: Gospel Publishing.

———. 1961. *Suddenly . . . From Heaven: A History of the Assemblies of God.* Springfield, Mo.: Gospel Publishing.

Bruner, Frederick Dale. 1970. *A Theology of the Holy Spirit.* Grand Rapids, Mich.: William E. Eerdmans Publishing.

Bruner, Frederick Dale, and W. Holdern. 1984. *The Holy Spirit: Shy Member of the Trinity.* Minneapolis: Augsburg Press.

Buckingham, Jamie. 1975. "Shepherding." *New Wine* 8, no. 2 (February): 8–12.

Buntain, D. N. 1954. *The Holy Ghost and Fire.* Springfield, Mo.: Gospel Publishing.

Burgess, Stanley, and Gary McGee, eds. 1988. *Dictionary of Pentecostal and Charismatic Movements.* Grand Rapids, Mich.: Zondervan Publishing.

Burnham, Frederic, ed. 1984. *Postmodern Theology: Christian Faith in a Pluralistic Age.* Philadelphia: Westminster Press.

Byrne, Jim. 1972. "Conversion and the Church Today." *New Covenant* 1, no. 7 (February): 9.

Campbell, Joseph. 1951. *The Pentecostal Holiness Church.* Franklin Springs, Ga.: The Publishing House of the Pentecostal Holiness Church.

Cantalamessa, Raniero, O.F.M. 1991. "That They May All Be One So That the World May Believe." *One in Christ* 27, no. 3: 201–8.

Cantelon, Willard. 1951. *The Baptism in the Holy Spirit.* Springfield, Mo.: Gospel Publishing.

Carlson, G. Raymond. 1976. *Spiritual Dynamics: The Holy Spirit in Human Experience.* Springfield, Mo.: Gospel Publishing.

———. 1977. *Our Faith and Fellowship.* Springfield, Mo.: Gospel Publishing.

"Catholic Bishops to Issue Guidelines on the Renewal." 1975. *New Covenant* 4, no. 8 (February): 26.

"Catholic Charismatic Renewal: Giving Vigorous Response to God's Word." 1976. *New Covenant* 6, no. 6 (December): 22–23.

Cavnar, Jim. 1973. "Types of Prayer Meetings." *New Covenant* 2, no. 10 (April): 20–21.

———. 1983. "A Baptism of Fire." *New Covenant* 13, no. 2 (September): 13–15.

"CHARISM." 1987. *New Covenant* 16, no. 9 (April): 30.

Charismatic Leaders Conference Report on the Shepherding Issue. 1976. Available in Shepherding-Discipleship file, Holy Spirit Research Center, Oral Roberts University, Tulsa, Okla.

"The Charismatics Among Us: Christianity Today–Gallup Poll." 1980. *Christianity Today* 24, no. 4 (22 February): 25–29.

Chilton, David. 1985. *Paradise Restored: An Eschatology of Dominion.* Tyler, Tex.: Reconstruction Press.

Christians, Christian G., and Jay M. Van Hook, eds. 1981. *Jacques Ellul: Interpretative Essays.* Urbana, Ill.: University of Illinois Press.

Clark, Elmer T. 1949. *Small Sects in America.* New York: Abingdon Press.

Clark, Stephen B. 1970. *The Work of the Cursillo and the Work of the Renewal.* Phoenix: Ultreya Press.

———. 1972. *Building Christian Communities: Strategy for Renewing the Church.* Notre Dame, Ind.: Ave Maria Press.

———. 1975. *Unordained Elders and Renewal Communities.* New York: Paulist Press.

———. 1976. *Baptized in the Spirit and Spiritual Gifts.* Pecos, N.M.: Dove Publications.

———. 1978. *The Life in the Spirit Seminars Team Manual, Catholic Edition.* Ann Arbor, Mich.: Servant Publications.

———. 1980. *Man and Woman in Christ.* Ann Arbor, Mich.: Servant Publications.

Clark, Steve. 1974. "What is Christian Community?" *New Covenant* 4, no. 5 (November): 4–5.

———. 1978a. "Association of Communities." *New Covenant* 7, no. 10 (April): 22–23.

———. 1978b. "The Christian and the World." *New Covenant* 7, no. 12 (June): 18–20.

———. 1982. "Renewing the Renewal." *New Covenant* 12, no. 4 (November): 20–21.

———. 1983. "Are We Charismatic?" *New Covenant* 12, no. 7 (February): 24–25.

Commager, Henry Steele. 1959. *The American Mind.* New Haven, Conn.: Yale University Press.

Congar, Yves, O.P. 1965. *Lay People in the Church: A Study for a Theology of Laity.* Trans. D. Atwater. Westminster, Md.: The Newman Press.

———. 1966. *Tradition and Traditions.* Trans. Michael Naseby. London: Burns and Oates.

———. 1967. *Ecumenism and the Future of the Church.* Chicago: The Priory Press.

———. 1981. "Trials and Promises of Ecumenism." In *Voices of Unity,* ed. Ans J. Van der Bent. Geneva: World Council of Churches.

———. 1984. *Diversity and Communion.* Trans. John Bowden. London: SCM Press.

Connelly, James, C.S.C. 1971. "The Charismatic Movement: 1967–1970." In *As the Spirit Leads Us,* ed. Kevin Ranaghan and Dorothy Ranaghan, 211–32. New York: Paulist Press.

Connor, John, C.S.C. 1972. "Covenant Communities: A New Sign of Hope." *New Covenant* 1, no. 10 (April): 2–8.

Copeland, Kenneth. 1979. "Interview with Kenneth Copeland." *Charisma* 4 (June): 21–25.

Council on Evangelism. 1968. "Pentecost in Other Churches." *Our Mission in Today's Worlds, August 26–29, 1968, St. Louis.* Springfield, Mo.: Gospel Publishing.

Cullmann, Oscar. 1988. *Unity through Diversity.* Trans. M. Eugene Boring. Philadelphia: Fortress Press.

Cully, Kendig Brubaker, ed. 1962. *Confirmation: History, Doctrine, and Practice.* Greenwich, Conn.: Seabury Press.

Cunningham, Robert C. 1972. *Filled with the Spirit.* Springfield, Mo.: Gospel Publishing.

Dayton, Donald. 1975. "From 'Christian Perfection' to the 'Baptism in the Holy Ghost.'" In *Aspects of Pentecostal-Charismatic Origins,* ed. Vinson Synan, 39–54. Plainfield, N.J.: Logos Press.

———. 1979. "The Evolution of Pentecostalism." *Covenant Quarterly* 32, no. 8 (August): 28–40.

———, ed. 1985. *Three Early Pentecostal Tracts.* New York: Garland Press.

———. 1987. *The Theological Roots of Pentecostalism.* Metuchen, N.J.: Scarecrow Press.

DeCelles, Paul. 1973. "Reflections on the 1973 Conference." *New Covenant* 3, no. 1 (August): 24–25.

Delespesse, Max. 1969. *The Church Community: Leaven and Life-Style.* Trans. Kenneth Russell. Ottawa: Novalis Press.

Dieter, Melvin E. 1980. *The Holiness Revival in the Nineteenth Century.* Metuchen, N.J.: Scarecrow Press.

Dieter, Melvin E., et al. 1987. *Five Views of Sanctification.* Grand Rapids, Mich.: Zondervan Publishing.

Dolan, Jay. 1985. *The American Catholic Experience.* New York: Doubleday.

Duin, Julia. 1987. "New Orleans: Preparing for World Evangelism." *New Covenant* 17, no. 2 (September): 22–24.

———. 1992. "At 25, Charismatics Hope They Can Renew Their Renewal." *National Catholic Reporter* (29 May): 6.

Dulles, Avery, S.J. 1976a. "Ten Principles of Ecumenism." *New Covenant* 5, no. 12 (June): 29–33.

———. 1976b. "Ten Principles of Ecumenism: Part Two." *New Covenant* 6, no. 1 (July): 26–29.

Dunn, James D. G. 1970. *Baptism in the Holy Spirit.* Naperville, Ill: A. R. Allenson.

———. 1977. *Unity and Diversity in the New Testament: An Inquiry into the Character of Earliest Christianity.* Philadelphia: Westminster Press.

du Plessis, David. 1979. "Du Plessis Interview." Interview by Russell Spittler. *Agora* 2, no. 1: 8–13.

Durasoff, Steve. 1974. *Bright Wind of the Spirit: Pentecostalism Today.* Englewood Cliffs, N.J.: Prentice-Hall Publishing.

Durham, William. 1912. "God's Finished Work." *Pentecostal Testimony* (August): 4–7.

"The Easy Way." 1967. *Our Sunday Visitor* (30 April): 4.

Ecumenical Trends. 1992. 21, no. 3 (March).

"Editorial." 1912. *Apostolic Faith.* (July): n.p. Available at the Archives, Assemblies of God Headquarters, Springfield, Mo.

Editorial on the Indianapolis rally. 1989. *AD 2000 Together* 3, no. 4 (June): 3.

Ellul, Jacques. 1964. *The Technological Society.* Trans. John Wilkerson. New York: Knopf Press.

———. 1967a. *The Political Illusion.* Trans. Konrad Kellen. New York: Random House.

———. 1967b. *The Presence of the Kingdom.* Trans. Olive Wigon. New York: Seabury Press.

———. 1975. *The New Demons.* Trans. C. Edward Hopkin. New York: Seabury Press.

———. 1980. *The Technological System.* Trans. John Wilkerson. New York: Seabury Press.

———. 1986. *The Subversion of Christianity.* Trans. Geoffrey W. Bromiley. Grand Rapids, Mich.: William Eerdmans Publishing.

Emmett, Dorothy. 1958. *Function, Purpose and Powers.* Philadelphia: The Temple University Press.

Engel, James. 1977. *How Can I Get Them to Listen?* Grand Rapids, Mich.: Zondervan Publishing.

Ervin, Howard M. 1981. "Hermeneutics: A Pentecostal Option." *Pneuma* 3, no. 2 (Fall): 11–25.

———. 1984. *Conversion-Initiation and the Baptism in the Holy Spirit.* Peabody, Mass.: Hendrickson Publishers.

Etter, Maria B. Woodworth. 1916. *Marvels and Miracles; Signs and Wonders.* Chicago: Hammond Press.

Ewart, Frank J. 1947. *The Phenomenon of Pentecost: A History of the Latter Rain.* St. Louis: Pentecostal Publishing House.

Fahey, Sheila. 1977. *Charismatic Social Action.* New York: Paulist Press.

Farah, Charles. 1975. "A Modest Proposal for Unity." Paper given to the Charismatic Leaders Conference. Available in the Shepherding-Discipleship files, Holy Spirit Research Center, Oral Roberts University, Tulsa, Okla.

Farmer, David. 1986. "The Rise of Renewal Centers." *New Covenant* 15, no. 7 (February): 12–13.

Fasching, Darrell J. 1981. *The Thought of Jacques Ellul: A Systematic Exposition.* Toronto: The Edwin Mellen Press.

Faupel, David W. 1973. *The American Pentecostal Movement: A Bibliographical Essay.* Wilmore, Ky.: G. L. Fisher Library.

Fee, Gordon D. 1985. "The Issue of Separability and Subsequence." *Pneuma* 7, no. 2 (Fall): 87–99.

———. 1987. *The First Epistle to the Corinthians.* Grand Rapids, Mich.: Eerdmans Publishing.

Fee, Gordon D., and Douglas Stuart. 1982. *How to Read the Bible for All It's Worth: A Guide to Understanding the Bible.* Grand Rapids, Mich.: Zondervan Publishing.

Fichter, Joseph, S.J. 1975. *The Catholic Cult of the Paraclete.* New York: Sheed and Ward.

Finney, Charles Grandison. 1872. *Power from on High: Who May Expect the Enduement.* Boston: Willard Tract Depository.

———. 1908. *Memoirs of Reverend Charles G. Finney Written by Himself.* New York: Fleming H. Revell.

Flower, J. Roswell. 1920. "The Evidence of the Baptism." *Pentecostal Evangel* (17 April): 2.

———. 1953. Personal Letter to Jack Coe from J. Roswell Flower. *Herald of Healing* (April–May): 26.

———. N.d. "The Early History of the Assemblies of God." Privately published essay for Central Bible College classes. Central Bible College Archives, Springfield, Mo.

Ford, John T. 1983. "Ecumenical Commitment as the Broadening of Horizons." *Midstream* 22 (April): 199–206.

———. 1986. "Bilateral Conversations and Denominational Horizons." *Journal of Ecumenical Studies* 23, no. 3 (Summer): 518–28.

Ford, Josephine M. 1970. *The Pentecostal Experience.* New York: Paulist Press.

———. 1975. *Which Way for Catholic Pentecostals?* New York: Harper and Row.

———. 1976. "Discord at South Bend." *Sign* 55, no. 5 (February): 11–14.

Foster, Fred J. 1965. *Think It Not Strange.* St. Louis: Pentecostal Publishing House.

Fries, Heinrich, and Karl Rahner, S.J. 1985. *Unity of the Churches: An Actual Possibility.* Trans. Ruth L. Gutsch and Eric W. Gutsch. New York: Paulist Press.

Frodsham, Stanley. 1928. "Disfellowshipped." *Pentecostal Evangel* (18 August): 7.

———. 1946. *With Signs Following: The Story of the Pentecostal Revival in the Twentieth Century.* Springfield, Mo.: Gospel Publishing.

Gee, Donald. 1949. *The Pentecostal Movement: Including the Story of the War Years, 1940–47.* London: Elim Publishing.

———. 1960. "Contact Is Not Compromise." *Pentecost* 53 (November): 3–4.

Gelpi, Donald., S.J. 1971. *Pentecostalism: A Theological Viewpoint.* New York: Paulist Press.

———. 1976. *Charism and Sacrament: A Theology of Christian Conversion.* New York: Paulist Press.

———. 1978. *Experiencing God: A Theology of Human Experience.* New York: Paulist Press.

———. 1987. "The Church Sacramental and Charismatic." *Church* 3, no. 1 (Spring): 19–24.

Ghezzi, Bert. 1973. "Building on Rock." *New Covenant* 3, no. 3 (September): 3–6.

———. 1975. "A Joyful Pilgrimage." *New Covenant* 5, no. 1 (July): 14–19.

———. 1983. "Who's Building the House?" *New Covenant* 12, no. 8 (March): 16–18.

Gilkey, Langdon. 1969. *Naming the Whirlwind: The Renewal of God-Language.* Indianapolis: Bobbs Merrill Publishing.

———. 1976. *Reaping the Whirlwind: A Christian Interpretation of History.* New York: Seabury Press.

Goff, James R., Jr. 1988a. "Charles Fox Parham." In *Dictionary of Pentecostal and Charismatic Movements,* ed. Stanley Burgess and Garry McGee, 660–61. Grand Rapids, Mich.: Zondervan Books.

———. 1988b. *Fields White unto Harvest: Charles F. Parham and the Missionary Origins of Pentecostalism.* Fayetteville, Ark.: University of Arkansas Press.

Gonzalez, Rev. J. J., ed. 1967. *The Sixteen Documents of Vatican II.* Boston: The Daughters of Saint Paul.

Goss, Ethel A. 1958. *The Winds of God.* New York: Comet Press.

Greeley, Andrew. 1989. *Religious Change in America.* Cambridge, Mass.: Harvard University Press.

Green, Charles H., and Kevin F. Perotta. 1986. "A Pioneering Covenant Community." *Pastoral Renewal* 11, no. 5 (July–August): 1, 14–20.

Griffin, William A. 1987. "Kingdom Now: New Hope or New Heresy?" Paper given to the Seventeenth Annual Society for Pentecostal Studies Meeting. Holy Spirit Research Center, Oral Roberts University, Tulsa, Okla.

Gros, Jeffrey, F.S.C. 1987. "Confessing the Apostolic Faith from the Perspective of the Pentecostal Churches." *Pneuma* 9, no. 1 (Spring): 5–16.

Hagin, Kenneth. 1978. *Thresholds of Faith.* Tulsa, Okla.: Kenneth Hagin Ministries.

———. 1979a. *How to Turn Your Faith Loose.* Tulsa, Okla.: Kenneth Hagin Ministries.

———. 1979b. *How to Write Your Own Ticket with God.* Tulsa, Okla.: Kenneth Hagin Ministries.

———. 1979c. *Words.* Tulsa, Okla.: Kenneth Hagin Ministries.

Hammond, Philip E. 1969. "Peter Berger's Sociology of Religion: An Appraisal." *Soundings* 52, no. 4 (Winter): 415–24.

———. 1986. "Religion in the Modern World." In *Making Sense of Modern Times: Peter L. Berger and the Vision of Interpretative Sociology,* ed. James D. Hunter and Stephen C. Ainsley, 415–24. London: Routledge and Kegan Paul.

Harrell, David Edwin, Jr. 1976. *All Things Are Possible: The Healing and Charismatic Renewals.* Bloomington, Ind.: Indiana University Press.

Harrison, Irvine J. 1954. "A History of the Assemblies of God." Th.D. diss., Berkeley Baptist Divinity School, Berkeley, Calif.

Haughey, John, S.J. 1976. "The Domestication of the Holy Spirit." *Catholic Charismatic* 1, no. 1 (April–May): 10.

———. 1978. "Salt or Leaven?" *New Covenant* 7, no. 12 (June): 14–17.

Hawtin, Ern. 1949. "How This Revival Began." *Sharon Star* 1 (August): 3–4.

Hitchkok, James. 1982. *What Is Secular Humanism? Why Humanism Became Secular and How It Is Changing the World.* Ann Arbor, Mich.: Servant Publications.

Hocken, Peter. 1974. "Catholic Pentecostalism: Some Key Questions." *Heythrop Journal* 15, no. 2 (April): 131–43.

———. 1979. "Charismatic Renewal, the Churches and Unity." *One in Christ* 15, no. 4 (Winter): 310–21.

———. 1980. "Come Holy Spirit I: Life in the Spirit Seminars." *Clergy Review* 65, no. 11 (November): 404–8.

———. 1987. *One Lord, One Spirit, One Body.* Gaithersburg, Md.: Word Among Us Press.

———. 1988a. "Charismatic Communities." In *Dictionary of Pentecostal and Charismatic Movements,* ed. Stanley Burgess and Garry McGee, 127–30. Grand Rapids, Mich.: Zondervan Books.

———. 1988b. "Charismatic Movement." In *Dictionary of Pentecostal and Charismatic Movements,* ed. Stanley Burgess and Garry McGee, 130–60. Grand Rapids, Mich.: Zondervan Books.

———. 1989. "Signs and Evidence: The Need for Catholic-Pentecostal Dialogue on the Relationship between the Physical and the Spiritual." *Pneuma* 11, no. 2 (Fall): 123–33.

Holdcroft, L. Thomas. 1962. *The Holy Spirit: A Pentecostal Interpetation.* Springfield, Mo.: Gospel Publishing.

———. 1980. "The New Order of the Latter Rain." *Pneuma* 2, no. 3 (Fall): 46–60.

Hollenweger, Walter. 1965. "Handbuch der Pfingstbewegung." Ph.D. diss., University of Zurich.

———. 1966. "The Pentecostal Movement and the World Council of Churches." *Ecumenical Trends* 3, no. 18: 310–20.

————. 1972. *The Pentecostals: The Charismatic Movement in the Churches.* Minneapolis: Augsburg Publishing.

Holloway, James Y., ed. 1970. *Introducing Jacques Ellul.* Grand Rapids, Mich.: William B. Eerdmans Publishing.

Horton, Stanley. 1976. *What the Bible Says About the Holy Spirit.* Springfield, Mo.: Gospel Publishing.

Hummel, Charles. 1978. *Fire in the Fireplace.* Downers Grove, Ill.: Inter-Varsity Press.

Hunter, Harold D. 1983. *Spirit-Baptism: A Pentecostal Alternative.* Lanham, Md.: University Press of America.

————. 1992. "Brighton 91: A Pentecostal Perspective." *Ecumenical Trends* 21, no. 4 (April): 51–54.

Hunter, J. H. 1964. *Besides All Waters.* Harrisburg, Penn.: Christian Publications.

Hunter, James D. 1991. *Culture Wars: The Struggle to Define America.* New York: Basic Books.

Hurst, D. V., and T. J. Jones. 1959. *The Church Begins: A Study Manual of the First Twelve Chapters of Acts.* Springfield, Mo.: Gospel Publishing.

"Intercommunion: A Local Situation." 1973. *New Covenant* 2, no. 9 (March): 14–17.

Jahr, Mary Ann. 1979. "The College of Steubenville: An Environment of Faith." *New Covenant* 8, no. 10 (April): 16–19.

————. 1982. "Renew the Face of the Earth." *New Covenant* 12, no. 1 (July/August): 36–40.

Jones, Charles Edwin. 1968. "Perfectionist Persuasion: A Social Profile of the National Holiness Movement within American Methodism, 1867–1936." Ph.D diss., University of Wisconsin, Madison.

Jones, Gwen, ed. 1983. *Conference on the Holy Spirit Digest: A Condensation of Plenary Sessions and Seminars Held in Springfield, Missouri, 16–18 August 1982,* vol. 1. Springfield, Mo.: Gospel Publishing.

Keane, Roberta Catherine. 1974. "Formal Organization and Charisma in a Catholic Pentecostal Community." Ph.D. diss., University of Michigan, Ann Arbor.

Keifer, Ralph. 1972. "Confirmation and Christian Maturity: The Deeper Issue." *Worship* 46, no. 10 (December): 601–8.

Kelsey, David H. 1975. *The Uses of Scripture in Recent Theology.* Philadelphia: Fortress Press.

Kendrick, Klaude. 1961. *The Promise Fulfilled: A History of the Modern Pentecostal Movement.* Springfield, Mo.: Gospel Publishing.

Kenyon, E. W., and D. Gossett. 1981. *The Positive Confession of the Word of God.* Tulsa, Okla.: Custom Graphics.

Kerr, D. W. 1931. *Phenomena of Pentecost.* Springfield, Mo.: Gospel Publishing.

Kingsriter, Arvid. 1983. "Baptism in the Holy Spirit—An Experience Subsequent to Regeneration." In *Conference on the Holy Spirit Digest: A Condensation of Plenary Sessions and Seminars Held in Springfield, Missouri, 16–18 August 1982,* vol. 1, ed. Gwen Jones. Springfield, Mo.: Gospel Publishing.

Kinnamon, Michael. 1988. *Truth and Community: Diversity and Its Limits in the Ecumenical Movement.* Grand Rapids, Mich.: William B. Eerdmans Publishing.

Knight, John Allan. 1966. "John William Fletcher and the Early Methodist Tradition." Ph.D. diss., Vanderbilt University, Nashville.

Koller, Kerry. 1974. "A Right Strategy for the Kingdom." *New Covenant* 4, no. 5 (November): 12–14.

Kortkamp, A. W. N.d. *What the Bible Says about the Baptism of the Spirit* Tract #4285. Springfield, Mo.: Gospel Publishing.

Labeau, Paul. 1975. Review of *Fire on the Earth* by Ralph Martin. *New Covenant* 5, no. 5 (November): 27.

Lange, Joseph, O.S.F.S. 1976. Editorial. *Catholic Charismatic* 1, no. 1 (March/April): 2.

———. 1980. Editorial. *Catholic Charismatic* 4, no. 5 (December/January): 2.

Lattin, Don. 1984. "The Shepherding Movement: A Former Berkeley Marxist and His Meeting with Jesus." *San Francisco Chronicle* (19 February): 1.

Laurentin, René. 1977. *Catholic Pentecostalism.* Trans. Matthew J. O'Connell. New York: Doubleday.

———. 1982. *Miracles in El Paso?* Ann Arbor, Mich.: Servant Publications.

Lawrence, B. F. 1916. *The Apostolic Faith Restored.* St. Louis: Gospel Publishing House.

Lawson, S. 1986. "Leaders Unite in New Orleans." *Charisma* 11 (December): 58–59.

———. 1987. "The Big Charismatic Get-Together." *Charisma* 12 (September): 56–58.

Lederle, Henry I. 1988. *Treasures Old and New: Interpretations of "Spirit-Baptism" in the Charismatic Renewal.* Peabody, Mass.: Hendrickson Publishers.

Lilly, Fred. 1984. "Following the FIRE." *New Covenant* 14, no. 1 (July–August): 36–38.

———. 1986. "Unity in Christ." *New Covenant* 16, no. 5 (December): 12–14.

Lindbeck, George A. 1984. *The Nature of Doctrine: Religion and Theology in a Postliberal Age.* Philadelphia: Westminster Press.

Lindsay, Gordon. 1950. *William Branham: A Man Sent From God.* Dallas: Voice of Healing.

———. 1951. *The Life of John Alexander Dowie.* Dallas: Voice of Healing.

Link, Hans-Georg, ed. 1985. *Apostolic Faith Today. Faith and Order Paper #124.* Geneva: World Council of Churches.

Lonergan, Bernard., S.J. 1979. *Method in Theology.* New York: Seabury Press.

Lummis, Trevor. 1987. *Listening to History: The Authenticity of Oral Testimony.* London: Hutchinson Education.

MacDonald, William. 1964. *Glossololia in the New Testament.* Springfield, Mo.: Gospel Publishing.

McDonald, William, and John E. Searles. 1885. *The Life of Reverend John S. Inskip, President of the National Association for the Promotion of Holiness.* Chicago: The Christian Witness Company.

McDonnell, John T. 1985. *The World Council of Churches and the Catholic Church.* Toronto: The Edwin Mellen Press.

McDonnell, Kilian, O.S.B. 1968a. "The Holy Spirit and Pentecostalism." *Commonweal* (8 November): 198–204.

———. 1968b. "The Ideology of Pentecostal Conversion." *Journal of Ecumenical Studies* 5, no. 1 (Winter): 105–26.

———. 1970. "Catholic Pentecostalism: Problems in Evaluation." *Dialog* 9 (December): 35–54.

————. 1974a. "The Distinguishing Characteristics of the Charismatic-Pentecostal Spirituality." *One in Christ* 10, no. 2 (April): 117–28.

————. 1974b. *Theological and Pastoral Orientations on the Catholic Charismatic Renewal: Malines Document I.* Ann Arbor, Mich.: Word of Life Books.

————. 1976a. *Charismatic Renewal and the Churches.* New York: Seabury Press.

————. 1976b. "The Vaporization of the Church." *New Covenant* 5, no. 9 (March): 26–30.

————. 1978. *The Charismatic Renewal and Ecumenism.* New York: Paulist Press.

————, ed. 1980. *Presence, Power, Praise: Documents on the Charismatic Renewal.* 3 vols. Collegeville, Minn.: The Liturgical Press.

————, ed. 1989. *Open the Windows: The Popes and the Charismatic Renewal.* South Bend, Ind.: Greenlawn Press.

————. 1989. Telephone interview with author (29 September). Personal notes.

McDonnell, Kilian, O.S.B., and Arthur Bittlinger, eds. 1972. *The Baptism in the Holy Spirit as an Ecumenical Problem.* Notre Dame, Ind.: Charismatic Renewal Services.

McDonnell, Kilian, O.S.B., and George Montague. 1991a. *Christian Initiation and Baptism in the Holy Spirit.* Collegeville, Minn.: Liturgical Press.

————. 1991b. *Fanning the Flame: What Does Baptism in the Holy Spirit Have to Do with Christian Initiation?* Collegeville, Minn.: Liturgical Press.

McGee, Gary B. 1986. *This Gospel . . . Shall Be Preached.* Springfield, Mo.: Gospel Publishing.

McGuire, Meredith B. 1982. *Pentecostal Catholics.* Philadelphia: Temple University Press.

McIntire, Carl. Editorial on pentecostalism. 1944. *Christian Beacon* (27 April): 8. Available at the Archives, Assemblies of God Headquarters, Springfield, Mo.

McKinney, Bishop Joseph. 1972. "A Bishop's Perspective." *New Covenant* 1, no. 4 (October): 2–3.

————. 1976. "Our Part in Ecumenism." *New Covenant* 5, no. 7 (January): 28–29.

McLean, Mark D. 1984. "Toward a Pentecostal Hermeneutic." *Pneuma* 6, no. 2 (Fall): 35–56.

Macquarrie, John. 1975. *Christian Unity and Christian Diversity.* Philadelphia: Westminster Press.

Mahan, Asa. 1870. *The Baptism of the Holy Ghost.* New York: W. C. Palmer.

Maki, Roy H. 1961. "Paganism in Christianity." *Pentecostal Herald* (July): 5, 11 Available in Oneness file at the Holy Spirit Archives, Oral Roberts University, Tulsa, Okla.

Manney, Jim. 1973. "Before Duquesne: Sources of the Renewal." *New Covenant* 2, no. 8 (February): 12–17.

———. 1985. "Father Michael Scanlan and the University of Steubenville." *New Covenant* 15, no. 2 (September): 10–12.

Manuel, David. 1977. *Like a Mighty River.* Orleans, Mass.: Rock Harbor Press.

Marsden, George. 1980. *Fundamentalism and American Culture: The Shaping of Twentieth Century Evangelicalism, 1870–1925.* New York: Oxford University Press.

Martin, Francis. 1975. "Be Wise and Gentle." *New Covenant* 5, no. 4 (October): 4–6.

———. 1986. *Baptism in the Holy Spirit: A Spiritual Foundation.* Steubenville, Ohio: Franciscan University Press.

———. 1987. "The Gold of a Precious Repentance." *New Covenant* 17, no. 2 (September): 23.

Martin, George. 1976. *Parish Renewal: A Charismatic Approach.* Ann Arbor, Mich.: Word of Life Press.

Martin, Ralph. 1971. *Unless the Lord Build the House . . . The Church and the New Pentecost.* Notre Dame, Ind.: Ave Maria Press.

———. 1972. "The Intercommunion Incident." *New Covenant* 2, no. 2 (August): 1.

———. 1974a. "David Wilkerson's Vision." *New Covenant* 3, no. 6 (January): 11–12.

———. 1974b. "God is Restoring His People." *New Covenant* 4, no. 3 (September): 4–6.

———. 1975. *Fire on the Earth.* Ann Arbor, Mich.: Word of Life Press.

————. 1982a. *A Crisis of Truth: The Attack on Faith, Morality, and Mission in the Catholic Church.* Ann Arbor, Mich.: Servant Books.

————. 1982b. *Husbands, Wives, Parents, Children.* Ann Arbor, Mich.: Servant Publications.

————. 1990a. "Is It All Over for the Charismatic Renewal?" *New Covenant* 20, no. 4 (November): 12.

————. 1990b. "Renewal and Repentance." *New Covenant* 20, no. 5 (December): 6, 33.

Marty, Martin. 1975. "Pentecostalism in American Piety and Practice." In *Aspects of Pentecostal-Charismatic Origins,* ed. Vinson Synan, 193–233. Plainfield, N.J.: Logos Press.

————. 1987. "Intercommunion." *Ecumenical Trends* 16, no. 1 (January): 9–10.

Mason, M. E. 1934. *The History and Life Work of Elder C. H. Mason and His Co-laborers.* Privately printed.

Matthews, Walter. 1992. "Through the Basement Window: A History of the National Service Committee." *Chariscenter USA* 17, no. 2 (March): 3, 15.

Menzies, William W. 1971. *Anointed to Serve: The Story of the Assemblies of God.* Springfield, Mo.: Gospel Publishing.

————. 1975. "The Non-Wesleyan Origins of the Pentecostal Movement." In *Aspects of Pentecostal-Charismatic Origins,* ed. Vinson Synan, 81–98. Plainfield, N.J.: Logos Press.

————. 1983. "Biblical Hermeneutics." In *Conference on the Holy Spirit Digest: A Condensation of Plenary Sessions and Seminars Held in Springfield, Missouri, 16–18 August 1982,* vol. 1, ed. Gwen Jones. Springfield, Mo.: Gospel Publishing.

Merrill, Dean. 1983. "The Fastest Growing American Denomination." *Christianity Today* 27 (January): 28, 34.

Methodist Episcopal Church, South. 1894. *Journal, General Conference, Methodist Episcopal Church, South.*

Mills, Watson E. 1985. *Glossolalia: A Bibliography.* Lewiston, N.Y.: Mellen Press.

Milner, Austin P. 1970. *Theology of Confirmation.* Notre Dame, Ind.: Fides Press.

Moberg, David O. 1984. *The Church as a Social Institution.* 2nd ed. Grand Rapids, Mich.: Baker Book House.

Moon, Jesse K. N.d. "A Critical Review: How to Read the Bible for All It's Worth." Privately published essay for Central Bible College classes. Available at the Archives, Pearlman Library, Central Bible College, Springfield, Mo.

Moore, Carey, and Dave Wimbish. 1978. "Catholic Renewal at Crossroads." *Logos Journal* 8, no. 1 (January/February): 62–64.

Muhlen, Heribert. 1978. "A Church in Movement—Not a Movement in the Church." *Theological Renewal* 4 (July): 25–34.

Mumford, Bob. 1975a. "A Defense of Shepherding." *Plumbline Newsletter* (November): 1–2. Available at the Holy Spirit Research Center, Oral Roberts University, Tulsa, Okla.

———. 1975b. Editorial. *Plumbline Newsletter* (November): 3. Available at the Holy Spirit Research Center, Oral Roberts University, Tulsa, Okla.

Myland, D. Wesley. 1910. *The Latter Rain Covenant and Pentecostal Power.* Chicago: Evangel Publishing House.

National Communications Office. 1980. "Editorial." *National Communications Office Newsletter* 5, no. 3 (April–May): 3.

National Conference of Catholic Bishops. 1971. *Report of the Committee on Doctrine of the National Conference of Catholic Bishops, 14 November 1969.* Reprinted in *The Pentecostal Movement in the Catholic Church,* Edward D. O'Connor, C.S.C., 291–93. Notre Dame, Ind.: Ave Maria Press.

National Service Committee. 1972. "A Report on the January 1972 National Service Committee Meeting." *New Covenant* 1, no. 8 (February): 7–9.

———. 1974. "A Statement of the Theological Basis of the Catholic Charismatic Renewal." *New Covenant* 3, no. 6 (January): 21–23.

———. 1975. "A Statement concerning a Recent Controversy." *New Covenant* 5, no. 5 (November): 22–23.

———. 1976a. "A Report on the 1976 National Service Committee Meeting." *National Communications Office Newsletter* 1, no. 3 (February): 1.

———. 1976b. Unsigned prophecy. *National Communications Office Newsletter* 1, no. 3 (February): 3.

———. 1978a. "The Roles of Men and Women in the Catholic Charismatic Renewal." *New Covenant* 7, no. 9 (March): 18–19.

————. 1978b. "The State of the Catholic Church." *New Covenant* 7, no. 7 (January): 4–8.

————. 1979. "Speakers Agree Charismatic Renewal Has Only Begun." *National Communications Office Newsletter* 4, no. 5 (Fall): 1.

————. 1982. "13,000 at Notre Dame Urged to Renew the Face of the Earth." *National Service Committee Newsletter* 7, no. 7 (August): 1.

————. 1983a. "NSC Restructured: Back to the Basics." *National Service Committee Newsletter* 8, no. 2 (February): 1.

————. 1983b. "A Report on the 1982 National Conference." *National Service Committee Newsletter* 8, no. 2 (February): 1–2.

Nelson, Douglas J. 1981. "For Such a Time as This: The Story of Bishop William J. Seymour and the Azusa Street Revival." Ph.D. diss., University of Birmingham, England.

————. 1984. *A Brief History of the Church of God in Christ.* Privately published.

Nelson, John Oliver. 1935. "The Rise of the Princeton Theology." Ph.D. diss., Yale University, New Haven, Conn.

Newman, John Henry. 1894. *An Essay on the Development of Christian Doctrine.* London: Longmans and Green.

Nichol, John Thomas. 1966. *Pentecostalism.* New York: Harper and Row.

Niebuhr, Reinhold. 1943. *The Nature and Destiny of Man.* 2 vols. New York: Charles Scribner's Sons.

Nienkirchen, Charles. 1988. "Christian and Missionary Alliance." In *Dictionary of Pentecostal and Charismatic Movements,* ed. Stanley Burgess and Garry McGee, 163–66. Grand Rapids, Mich.: Zondervan Books.

Noll, Mark A., ed. 1983. *The Princeton Theology, 1812–1921: Scripture, Science and Theological Method from Archibald Alexander to Benjamin Breckenridge Warfield.* Grand Rapids, Mich.: Baker Book House.

————. 1986. *Between Faith and Criticism: Evangelicals, Scholarship, and the Bible in America.* San Francisco: Harper and Row.

North American Renewal Service Committee. 1987a. Editorial. *AD 2000* 1, no. 7 (Fall): 1.

————. 1987b. "Report on New Orleans 1987." *AD 2000* 1, no. 7 (Fall): 1.

————. 1987c. "Statement of Policy Provides a Pattern for Working Together." *AD 2000* 1, no. 1 (February): 3.

————. 1989. "Report on Indianapolis Congress." *AD 2000 Together* 3, no. 4 (1989): 3.

North, Gary. 1987. *Liberating Planet Earth*. Fort Worth, Tex.: Dominion Press.

"Notre Dame Priests and Students Hold Pentecostal Prayer Meetings." 1967. *National Catholic Reporter* (19 April): 3.

O'Connor, Edward D., C.S.C. 1971. *The Pentecostal Movement in the Catholic Church*. Notre Dame, Ind.: Ave Maria Press.

————. 1974. "When the Cloud of Glory Dissipates." *New Catholic World* 217, no. 1301 (November–December): 271–75.

————. 1975. "The Hidden Roots of the Charismatic Renewal in the Catholic Church." In *Aspects of Pentecostal-Charismatic Origins,* ed. Vinson Synan. Plainfield, N.J.: Logos Press.

O'Dea, Thomas. 1961. "Five Dilemmas in Institutionalization of Religion." *Journal for the Scientific Study of Religion* 1, no. 1 (October): 30–39.

Osterberg, Arthur. 1956. Interview. *Los Angeles Times* (9 September): 1, 12.

Papa, Mary. 1967. "People Having a Good Time Praying." *National Catholic Reporter* (17 May): 1, 10.

Pardington, George A. N.d. *Twenty-Five Wonderful Years: A Popular Sketch of the Christian and Missionary Alliance*. Privately published.

Parham, Charles. 1926. "The Latter Rain." *Apostolic Faith* (July): 3. Available at the Archives, Assemblies of God Headquarters, Springfield, Mo.

Parham, Sarah E. 1930. *The Life of Charles F. Parham: Founder of the Apostolic Faith Movement*. Joplin, Mo.: Tri-State Printing.

Paulk, Earl, Jr. 1984. *Satan Unmasked*. Atlanta: Kingdom Publishers.

————. 1985. *Life in the Eternal Kingdom*. Decatur, Ga.: K-Dimension Publishers.

Pearlman, Myer. 1935a. *Knowing the Doctrines of the Bible.* Springfield, Mo.: Gospel Publishing.

———. 1935b. *Let's Meet the Holy Spirit.* Springfield, Mo.: Gospel Publishing.

People of Praise Information Service. Statement of Purpose. 1983. *New Heaven, New Earth* 1, no. 1 (January): 1.

———. 1988. *The People of Praise Fact Sheet.* South Bend, Ind.: Greenlawn Press.

Perkins, E. M. 1927. *Fred Francis Bosworth: His Life Story.* Detroit: Privately published.

Perrotta, Kevin. 1976. "Lord: The Kingdom, the Power, and the Glory Are Yours." *New Covenant* 6, no. 2 (August): 12–19.

Peters, John L. 1956. *Christian Perfection and American Methodism.* Nashville: Abingdon Press.

Piper, William H. 1908. "Go Forward." *Latter Rain Evangel* (October): 9–13. Available at the Archives, Assemblies of God Headquarters, Springfield, Mo.

Plowman, Edward E. 1975. "The Deepening Rift in the Charismatic Movement." *Christianity Today* 20 (10 October): 52–54. Available in the Shepherding-Discipleship file, Holy Spirit Research Center, Oral Roberts University, Tulsa, Okla.

Poloma, Margaret. 1989. *The Assemblies of God at the Crossroads: Charisma and Institutional Dilemmas.* Knoxville, Tenn.: University of Tennessee Press.

Prince, Derek. 1974. "The Church of the Seventies." *New Covenant* 4, no. 2 (August): 10–11.

———. 1976. *Discipleship, Shepherding, Commitment.* Fort Lauderdale, Fla.: Derek Prince Publications.

Quebedeaux, Richard. 1976. *The New Charismatics.* Garden City, N.J.: Doubleday.

———. 1983. *The New Charismatics II.* San Francisco: Harper and Row.

Rahner, Karl, S.J. 1967. *The Christian of the Future.* Trans. W. J. O'Hara. New York: Herder and Herder.

Ranaghan, Kevin. 1972a. "A Catholic Perspective." *New Covenant* 1, no. 11 (May): 17–19.

———. 1972b. "The Lord, the Spirit, and the Church." *New Covenant* 2, no. 2 (August): 1–5.

———. 1972c. "On Listening to the Spirit." *New Covenant* 1, no. 10 (April): 16–17.

———. 1976. "Catholic Charismatic Renewal: Giving Vigorous Response to God's Word." *New Covenant* 6, no. 6 (December): 22–23.

———. 1978. "How Should We Respond?" Interview with John Blattner. *New Covenant* 7, no. 8 (February):10–13.

———. 1982. *Renew the Face of the Earth*. South Bend, Ind.: Greenlawn Press.

———. 1987. "Statement of Policy Provides a Pattern for Working Together." *AD 2000* 1, no. 1 (February): 3.

Ranaghan, Kevin, and Dorothy Ranaghan. 1969. *Catholic Pentecostals*. New York: Paulist Press.

———. 1980a. "God's Warning, God's Remedy." *New Covenant* 9, no. 11 (May): 13–16.

———. 1980b. "The Revolving Door Syndrome." *New Covenant* 9, no. 12 (June): 20–21.

———. 1983. "Charismatics and Charismaniacs." *New Heaven, New Earth* 1, no. 8 (August–September): 2

Ratzinger, Joseph Cardinal. 1988. *Church, Ecumenism, and Politics*. New York: Crossroads Publishing.

Reed, David. 1978. "Origins and Development of the Theology of Oneness Pentecostalism." Ph.D. diss., Boston University.

"Reflections: Larry Christenson and Rodman Williams." 1972. *New Covenant* 1, no. 8 (February): 5.

Reimers, Adrian. 1983. "In Jesus' Name." *New Covenant* 12, no. 7 (February): 27–28.

A Report on the 1976 Charismatic Leaders Conference. Available in the Shepherding-Discipleship vertical file, Holy Spirit Research Center, Oral Roberts University, Tulsa, Okla.

Rifkin, Jeremy, and Ted Howard. 1979. *The Emerging Order: God in the Age of Scarcity*. New York: G. P. Putnam's Sons.

Riggs, Ralph M. 1949. *The Spirit Himself.* Springfield, Mo.: Gospel Publishing.

Riss, Richard. 1979. "The Latter Rain Movement of 1948 and the Mid-Twentieth Century Evangelical Awakening." M.A. thesis, Regent College, Vancouver, British Columbia.

———. 1988. "Latter Rain Movement." In *Dictionary of Pentecostal and Charismatic Movements,* ed. Stanley Burgess and Garry McGee, 532–34. Grand Rapids, Mich.: Zondervan Books.

Robeck, Cecil, Jr. 1987. "Pentecostals and the Apostolic Faith." *One in Christ* 23, no. 1–2: 110–30.

———. 1988. "National Association of Evangelicals." In *Dictionary of Pentecostal and Charismatic Movements,* ed. Stanley Burgess and Garry McGee, 634–36. Grand Rapids, Mich.: Zondervan Books.

Robertson, Pat. 1975 memo on Shepherding. Available in Shepherding-Discipleship file, Holy Spirit Research Center, Oral Roberts University, Tulsa, Okla.

Robins, Roger. 1984. "A Chronology of Peace: Attitudes towards War and Peace, 1914–1918." *Pneuma* 6, no. 1 (Spring): 3–24.

Robinson, Martin. 1987. "To the Ends of the Earth: The Pilgrimage of an Ecumenical Pentecostal, David J. du Plessis, 1905–1987." Ph.D. diss., University of Birmingham, England.

Rogge, Louis P. 1984. "The Relationship Between the Sacrament of Anointing of the Sick and the Charism of Healing within the Catholic Charismatic Renewal." Th.D. diss., Union Theological Seminary, New York.

Roman Catholic Church and Faith and Order Commission of the World Council of Churches. 1984. *The Apostolic Faith in the Scriptures and in the Early Church (Rome Report 1983).* Reprinted in *Ecumenical Review* 36, no. 3 (July): 329–36.

Rusch, Wiliam G. 1985. *Ecumenism: A Movement Towards Church Unity.* Philadelphia: Fortress Press.

Rushdoony, R. J. 1973. *The Institutes of Biblical Law.* Nutley, N.J.: Craig Press.

Ruthven, Jon. 1989. "On the Cessation of the Charismata: The Protestant Polemic of Benjamin B. Warfield." Ph.D. diss., Marquette University, Milwaukee.

Sandeen, Ernest R. 1970. *The Roots of Fundamentalism: British and American Millenarianism, 1800–1930.* Chicago: University of Chicago Press.

Sandidge, Jerry L. 1987a. "Documentation." *Ecumenical Trends* 16, no. 2 (February): 30–32.

———. 1987b. *Roman Catholic/Pentecostal Dialogue [1977–1982]: A Study in Developing Ecumenism.* 2 vol. Frankfurt am Main: Verlag Peter Lang.

Scanlan, Michael, O.S.F. 1976. "Preparing for Difficult Times." *New Covenant* 6, no. 3 (September): 4–7.

———. 1986. *Let the Fire Fall.* Ann Arbor, Mich.: Servant Publications.

———. 1988. "Dear Brothers and Sisters." *Firewatch* 6, no. 5 (July): 1.

Schlesinger, Arthur M. 1932. "A Critical Period in American Religion, 1875–1908." *Massachusetts Historical Society Proceedings* 64: 532–47.

Schoonenberg, Piet, S.J. 1974. "Baptism with the Holy Spirit." In *Experience of the Spirit,* ed. Georges Combet and Laureat Fabre, 20–37. New York: Seabury Press.

Schreck, Alan. 1983. "Are Catholics Saved?" *New Covenant* 12, no. 7 (February): 8–11.

———. 1984. *Catholic and Christian: An Explanation of Commonly Misunderstood Catholic Beliefs.* Ann Arbor, Mich.: Servant Publications.

Shaw, S. B. 1905. *The Great Revival in Wales.* Toronto: A. Sims.

Sherrill, John. 1965. *They Speak with Other Tongues.* New York: Pyramid Books.

———. 1982. "What Prayer Groups Need Now." *New Covenant* 12, no. 2 (September): 12–16.

———. 1986. "The FIRE is burning BRIGHT." *New Covenant* 15, no. 7 (February): 28–30.

Shields, Ann. 1982. "What Prayer Groups Need Now." *New Covenant* 12, no. 2 (September): 12–16.

Slasser, Robert. 1977. *A Man Called Mister Pentecost.* South Plainfield, N.J.: Bridge Publications.

Smith, Harold B. 1987. "America's Pentecostals: Where They Are Going." *Christianity Today* 31, no. 15 (16 October): 27–30.

Smith, Mike. 1967. "Spiritualists Claim 'Gift of Tongues' at Exorcism Rites." *Notre Dame Observer* (13 April): 1–2.

Smith, Robert Pearsall. 1870. *Holiness through Faith: Light on the Way to Holiness*. Boston: Willard Street Tract Repository.

Smith, Timothy L. 1962. *Called unto Holiness*. Kansas City, Mo.: Nazarene Publishing House.

———. 1983. "An Historical Perspective on Evangelicals and Ecumenism." *Midstream* 22, no. 3–4 (July–August): 308–25.

Spittler, Russell, ed. 1976. *Perspectives on the New Pentecostalism*. Grand Rapids, Mich.: Baker Book House.

———. 1978. "Agorafitti: Marketplace Scribblings." *Agora* 1, no. 4: 13–14.

Stead, W. T. 1905. *The Revival in the West: A Narrative of Facts*. London: The Review of Reviews Publications Office.

Storey, William. 1972. "Interview on the Charismatic Renewal." Interview by John Reedy, C.S.C. *A.D. Correspondence* 2, no. 3 (14 September): n.p.

———. 1975. "Reform or Supression: Alternatives Seen for Charismatic Renewal." Interview by John Reedy, C.S.C. *A.D. Correspondence* 4, no. 11 (24 May): n.p.

Stott, John R. W. 1964. *The Baptism and the Fullness of the Holy Spirit*. Downers Grove, Ill.: Inter-Varsity Press.

Strader, Karl. 1975. "Charismatics Criticized." *Pentecostal Evangel* 62 (4 May): 13.

Stransky, Thomas, ed. 1965. *The Decree on Ecumenism*. Paramus, N.J.: Paulist Press.

Stronstad, Roger. 1984. *The Charismatic Theology of Luke*. Peabody, Mass.: Hendrickson Publishers.

Suenens, Leon Cardinal. 1974. *A New Pentecost?* Trans. Francis Martin. New York: Seabury Press.

Sullivan, Francis A., S.J. 1974. "'Baptism in the Holy Spirit': A Catholic Interpretation of the Pentecostal Experience." *Gregorianum* 55, no. 1: 49–68.

———. 1975. "The Ecclesiological Context of the Charismatic Renewal." In *The Holy Spirit and Power: The Catholic Charismatic Renewal*, ed. Kilian McDonnell. New York: Doubleday.

———. 1978. "The Role of Tradition." In *Theological Reflections on the Charismatic Renewal: Proceedings of the Chicago Conference, October 1–2, 1976*, ed. Charles Haughey, S.J., 88–103. Ann Arbor, Mich.: Servant Publications.

———. 1982. *Charisms and Charismatic Renewal: A Biblical and Theological Study*. Ann Arbor, Mich.: Servant Publications.

———. 1986. "Subsistit In," *One in Christ* 22, no. 2: 115–23.

———. 1988. "Catholic Charismatic Renewal." In *Dictionary of Pentecostal and Charismatic Movements,* ed. Stanley Burgess and Garry McGee, 110–26. Grand Rapids, Mich.: Zondervan Books.

Sweet, W. W. 1944. *Revivalism in America*. New York: Abingdon Press.

Synan, Vinson. 1971. *The Holiness-Pentecostal Movement in the United States*. Grand Rapids, Mich.: William D. Eerdmans Books.

———. 1973. "Charismatic Walls." *New Covenant* 2, no. 10 (April): 1–2.

———. 1984. *In the Latter Days*. Ann Arbor, Mich.: Servant Books.

———. 1987a. "Joint Witness Leads to World Evangelization." *AD 2000* 1, no. 1 (February): n.p.

———. 1987b. *The Twentieth Century Pentecostal Explosion*. Altamonte Springs, Fla.: Creation House.

Szasz, Ferenc Morton. 1982. *The Divided Mind of Protestant America, 1880–1930*. Tuscaloosa, Ala.: The University of Alabama Press.

Tavard, George. 1962. *Two Centuries of Ecumenism*. New York: Mentor-Omega Books.

———. 1989. "Ecumenical Theology and the Catholic Church." *One in Christ* 25, no. 2: 103–13.

Taylor, George Floyd. 1907. *The Spirit and the Bride*. Dunn, N.C.: Privately published.

———. 1921. "Our Church History." *Pentecostal Holiness Advocate* (3 February): 3–11.

Thiselton, Anthony C. 1980. *The Two Horizons: New Testament Hermeneutics and Philosophical Description with Special Ref-*

erence to Heidegger, Bultmann, Gadamer, and Wittgenstein. Grand Rapids, Mich.: William B. Eerdmans Publishing.

Thomas Aquinas. 1969. *Summa Theologiae.* Blackfriars English translation, ed. Thomas Gilby, O.P., and T. C. O'Brien, O.P., gen. eds. *Summa Theologiae.* Blackfriars English trans. Garden City, N.J.: Image Books.

Thompson, A. W. N.d. *A. B. Simpson: His Life and Work.* Tulsa, Okla.: Christian Publishing Services.

Thorp, David. 1984. "A Plan for Prayer Groups." *New Covenant* 13, no. 6 (January): 5–7.

Tifft, Susan. 1988. "Balancing Minds and Souls." *Time* 132 (17 October): 62.

Torrey, Reuben A. 1895. *The Baptism with the Holy Spirit.* New York: Fleming H. Revel Company.

———. 1898. *What the Bible Teaches: A Thorough and Comprehensive Study of What the Bible Has to Say concerning the Great Doctrines of Which It Treats.* London: James Nisbet.

Tozer, A. W. 1943. *Wingspread: A Study in Spiritual Altitude.* Harrisburg, Pa.: Christian Publications.

Trepanier, James R., C.S.C. 1968. "The Cursillo Movement in the Light of Vatican Council II's Decree 'On the Apostolate of the Laity.'" M.A. thesis, Catholic University of America, Washington, D.C.

Tugwell, Simon, O.P. 1971. "He Will Baptize You With the Holy Spirit." *New Blackfriars* 52, no. 613 (May): 268–73.

———. 1972. "Reflection on the Pentecostal Doctrine on Baptism in the Holy Spirit." *Heythrop Journal* 13, no. 3 (July): 268–81.

Tugwell, Simon, O.P., and Peter Hocken, eds. 1976. *New Heavens? New Earth?* Springfield, Ill.: Templegate Publishers.

United States Catholic Bishops Conference. 1984. *A Pastoral Statement on the Catholic Charismatic Renewal.* Washington, D.C.: United States Catholic Conference.

"Vatican Enters Dialogue on Pentecostalism." 1972. *New Covenant* 1, no. 7 (January): 6–7.

Verhalen, Philip. 1976. "Faith in a Secularized World." *Catholic Charismatic* 1, no. 2 (May/June): 4–7.

Wacker, Grant. 1984. "The Functions of Faith in Primitive Pentecostalism." *Harvard Theological Review* 77 (July/October): 1353–75.

————. 1985. "Marching to Zion." *Church History* 54 (December): 496–511.

Wadworth, E. M. 1952. "Miracle without Money." *Pentecostal Evangel* 39 (20 April): 4.

Wagner, Peter C. 1987. *Strategies for Church Growth: Tools for Planning Evangelism and Missions.* Ventura, California: Regal Publishers.

————. 1988. *The Third Wave of the Holy Spirit.* Ann Arbor, Mich.: Servant Publications.

Warnock, George. N.d. *The Feast of Tabernacles.* Privately published.   Available at Holy Spirit Research Center, Oral Roberts University, Tulsa, Okla.

Weber, Timothy P. 1983. *Living in the Shadow of the Second Coming.* Grand Rapids, Mich.: Academic Books.

Wessels, Roland H. 1966. "The Doctrine of the Baptism in the Holy Spirit Among the Assemblies of God." Th.D. diss., Pacific School of Religion, Berkeley, Calif.

Wheelock, Donald Ray. 1983. "Spirit Baptism in American Pentecostal Thought." Ph.D. diss., Emory University, Atlanta.

White, Alma. 1949. *Demons and Tongues.* 4th ed. Zeraphath, N.J.: The Pillar of Fire Press.

Wild, Robert. 1975. *Enthusiasm in the Spirit.* Notre Dame, Ind.: Ave Maria Press.

Wilkerson, David. 1964. *The Cross and the Switchblade.* Old Tappan, N.J.: F. H. Revell.

————. 1973. *The Vision.* Old Tappan, N.J.: Jove Publications.

Willebrands, Johannes Cardinal. 1985. "On Reception." *Ecumenical Trends* 14, no. 3 (March): 38–47.

————. 1987. "Vatican II's Ecclesiology of Communion." *One in Christ* 23, no. 3: 179–91.

Williams, Ernest S. 1949a. "Are We Pentecostal?" *Pentecostal Evangel* 36 (9 April): 2–3.

————. 1949b. "Spiritual Gifts." *Pentecostal Evangel* 36 (16 April): 3–4.

————. 1953. *Systematic Theology.* 3 vols. Springfield, Mo.: Gospel Publishing.

Wimber, John, and Kevin Springer. 1986. *Power Evangelism*. San Francisco: Harper and Row.

Winehouse, Irwin. 1959. *Early History of the Assemblies of God*. Springfield, Mo.: Gospel Publishing.

Wood, Laurence W. 1980. *Pentecostal Grace*. Wilmore, Ky.: Francis Asbury Publishing.

Word of God community. 1969. Transcript of discussion on pentecostalism. Available in the Charismatic Renewal, vertical file, Word of God Community Archives, Word of God Headquarters, Ann Arbor, Mich.

World Council of Churches. 1971. *Common Witness and Proselytism: A Study Document*. Reprinted in *Ecumenical Review* 23, no. 1 (January): 9–43.

Yocum, Bruce. 1976. *Prophecy: Exercising the Prophetic Gifts of the Holy Spirit in the Church Today*. Ann Arbor, Mich.: Servant Books.

———. 1978. "He Has Not Spoken in Secret." *New Covenant* 7, no. 8 (February): 4–9.

Zablocki, Benjamin. 1971. *The Joyful Community*. Baltimore: Penguin Books.

Ziegler, James. 1988. "North American Congresses on the Holy Spirit and Evangelization." In *Dictionary of Pentecostal and Charismatic Movements,* ed. Stanley Burgess and Garry McGee, 641. Grand Rapids, Mich.: Zondervan Books.

Index